PREDESTINATION AND FREE WILL

PREDESTINATION AND FREE WILL

PREDESTINATION AND FREE WILL

A Comparative Theological Study

Ömer Atilla Ergi

BLUE DOME

*"Adherence to causality is a requirement of
respect to their Creator."*

Fethullah Gülen

Published by Blue Dome Press
335 Clifton Ave.
Clifton, NJ, 07011, USA
www.bluedomepress.com

ISBN: 978-1-68206-033-9
E-book: 978-1-68206-540-2

Library of Congress Cataloging-in-Publication Data

Names: Ergi, Ömer A., author.
Title: Predestination and free will : a comparative theological study /
   Omer Atilla Ergi.
Description: Clifton : Blue Dome Press, 2023. | Includes bibliographical
   references and index.
Identifiers: LCCN 2023011972 (print) | LCCN 2023011973 (ebook) | ISBN
   9781682060339 (paperback) | ISBN 9781682065402 (ebook)
Subjects: LCSH: Predestination (Islam) | Predestination. | Free will and
   determinism--Religious aspects--Islam. | Free will and determinism. |
   Gülen, Fethullah--Teachings.
Classification: LCC BP166.3 .E74 2023 (print) | LCC BP166.3 (ebook) | DDC
   297.2/27--dc23/eng/20230501
LC record available at https://lccn.loc.gov/2023011972
LC ebook record available at https://lccn.loc.gov/2023011973
Printed in India

CONTENTS

Preface 9

Glossary of Terms 11

Contents

Preface

The concepts of predestination and free will have been and continue to be two of the most difficult problems of classical and contemporary theology and philosophy. The debate on the perplexing coexistence of predestination and free will has been the focal point of discourse among theologians and philosophers since antiquity. The deliberations on determinism also played an important role in the formation of Islamic theology, as the creedal statements of Islamic doctrines define belief in predestination as one of the essential articles of creed while asserting that human agents possess some form of will defined as *irāda al juz'iyya*, 'the minor will' in the Arabic lexicon.

Evidently, the creed of mainstream Islam necessitates that the two concepts are reconciled or at least a conceivable argument is provided to support the notion that predestination could indeed coexist with free will. Arguments for coexistence constructed on scriptural revelation and Prophetic tradition were proposed by various Muslim theologians from the formative period to contemporary times, during which several theological schools emerged due to a number of significant differences in views. This book is primarily based on an examination and analysis of the theological arguments proposed by mainstream Islamic theologians and Fethullah Gülen, a contemporary Muslim scholar, and his theoretical framework on the reconciliation of predestination and free will. The methodology of this project includes comparative and detailed analysis of arguments put forward by formative, classical and contemporary Islamic scholars and examination of arguments proposed by Western theologians and philosophers with an objective to establish the similarities and differences in the theoretical frameworks of scholars from different schools, traditions, and faiths.

The main argument of this book is based on the theological premises proposed by Fethullah Gülen and mainstream Sunni theologians that support the coexistence of predestination and free will.

Acknowledgements

Although this project is based on comparative analysis of theological and philosophical arguments proposed by many scholars and academics from different faith traditions, cultures, and schools of thought, Gülen's literature was the primary focus of this project. For this reason, first and foremost, I would like to thank the distinguished sholar, Fethullah Gülen who was my primary inspiration in writing this book.

A special thanks to my editor Vicki Snowdon for her great work, flexibility and assistance in nurturing this project.

I would also like to take the opportunity to acknowledge the invaluable support provided by Professor Salih Yucel and Professor Mehmet Ozalp who have shown great encourement and reassurance all the way until the completion of the book.

And how could I forget the continuous support and contributions of a few cherished advisors, Professor Ismail Albayrak, Dr. Recep Dogan, Dr. Derya Iner, Dr. Suleyman Sertkaya, Dr. Hakan Coruh and Associate Professor Zuleyha Keskin for providing instrumental assistance to this project.

And of course, many thanks to my beloved wife Tulin who has shown great patience and support during my long hours in front of the computer, especially on weekends. And, to my dear friends who for the last three years persistently asked me when the book will be ready for publishing.

Finally, I would like to thank the Almighty Lord for blessing me with such a wonderful family, friends, colleagues and giving me the opportunity to complete and publish this book.

Glossary of Terms

Ahl al Sunnah wa'l jamā'ah
Refers to mainstream Islam adherents to Prophet Muhammad's tradition

Ahkām
Ruling or judgment

'Amal
Deeds – a term generally used for all human deeds, good or evil.

'Aqīda
The creed of Islam containing the six essential articles of belief. A Muslim is obligated to have belief in all six articles.

'Aql
Literally intellect: however, in Islamic theology it is used in the context of 'reasoning.'

'Aradth
Accident; something that occurs due to randomness or chance.

Asbab
Plural of *sabab*. Means cause or, in the context of theology, causality.

Baqa
Eternity; everlasting; the attribute of endlessness.

Dharra
Atom; the smallest particle of matter.

Biqadarin
A due amount or a measure amount.

'Ilm
Divine Omniscience. Refers to the infinite knowledge of God. It is one of the affirmative attributes of God in Islamic theology.

Imamun mubin
Defined as Manifest Record by Gülen (2009) and refers to the all-encompassing or infinite knowledge of God, ie His omniscient attribute. Described as knowledge beyond which nothing can escape or exist; *imamun mubin* refers to Divine Knowledge.

Istita'a
Defined as the ability to perform an act. In the Arabic lexicon, the term is described as 'power' or 'ability' (Nasafi, 1993, p. 226). According to Nasafi (1993), there are two types of *istita'a*: one related to causes where the conditions must be right for it to apply; for example, a Muslim is required to fast during the month of Ramadan providing their health permits. The other is the power or ability that exists in living beings at the time of an act. This is the concept that concerns the debate about free will. According to Nasafi, *istita'a* is the ability that materialises at the time of an act; therefore, it is a vital

component of an act. Māturīdītes describe it as the power that brings about the act (p. 227).

Juz'-ī irāda

Refers to human free will. The exact translation of the term is 'minor or limited will.' When Islamic scholars refer to human will, they use the adjective 'minor or limited' as Islamic theological doctrines assert that 'absolute will' belongs only to God. As opposed to *kulli*, the term *juz'-i* means minor or limited.

Khaliq

The creator or originator.

Khalq

To create; the act of creation.

Kasb

Defined as 'acquisition,' it is an ability given to human free will for the purpose of petitioning for the creation of an action. It is a key concept for moral responsibility and accountability. It includes human intentions and inclinations towards an act. It is a faculty of free will that requests a human act to be created by God. The concept of *kasb* is crucial in the debate on free will as it is the source of moral responsibility and liability for all human acts.

Kitābun mubin

Defined as the Manifest Book by Gülen (2009), it is a title given to

Divine will or decree. The term also refers to God's creational and operational laws in the universe. It is delineated as the creation of objects or events that have prior existence in Divine knowledge. It also means God's timely creation of what is already been recorded in the Divine Register, *lawh al mahfuz*.

Kullī irāda

Refers only to the absolute will of God. In Islamic creed, no other being possesses absolute will. In Islamic theology, *kulli irada* is an attribute of God where *kulli* means total or absolute and *irada* means will. Classical scholars describe it as a 'will' that cannot be limited or restricted by anything.

Lawh al mahfūz

Mentioned in the Qur'an nine times either directly or indirectly. The term translates as 'the Preserved Tablet,' which is defined by Islamic scholars as the Divine Register where all things and events in the past, present and future are recorded. Islamic scholars refer to it as a register that contains all phenomena preordained or predestined by Divine will.

Lawh al mawh isbat

A register that contains amendable destiny. Some scholars refer to this as the probable destiny.

Ilmi muhīt
All-encompassing knowledge

Makhluq
Creation: what is created; an entity or living being that was created.

Mukhalafatun lil hawadith
An attribute of God meaning un-like the creation.

Mukallaf
Defined as a responsible agent or a person who has responsibility. In Islamic law, a person who has reached the age of adolescence be-comes religiously responsible.

Muktasib
Acquirer: the one who requests or desires for something to occur.

Musabbib al Asbab
The cause of causes, in reference to God.

Naql
What is transmitted; revelation; tradition.

Qiyam bī nafsī
An attribute of God meaning self-subsisting.

Qadar
'To measure' or 'to determine,' but in its derivations it means 'determination,' 'destiny,' 'giving a certain measure and shape,' 'dividing' and 'judging' in classical Arabic literature. Islamic theolo-gians, however, define the term as 'Divine measure,' 'Divine destiny,' 'Divine determinism' and 'Divine judgment in the creation of things.' In Islamic contexts, the theological discussions on determinism and free will in this study, the term *qadar* will generally carry the mean-ing 'Divine destiny, determination or will.'

Qada
Refers to the concepts of the cre-ation of what is recorded in the Di-vine Register when it materialises.

Qudrah
Power; an attribute of God.

Tadbir
Order and harmony based on nat-ural laws that indicate governance.

Tanasüb'ü illiyet
A term from the Ottoman lan-guage meaning the connection be-tween cause and effect.

Taqdir
Will of God; something that is willed by God.

Taqwin
An attribute of God meaning an ability to create, originate or bring into existence.

Taslim
Literally means surrendering. In Sufi teaching, it refers to unconditionally submitting to the will of God.

Tawḥīd
Meaning Divine Unity, it is the
most important article of the Islamic Creed.

Tawakkul
Reliance on God.

Wujud
Existence; an attribute of God
meaning the necessarily existent.

CHAPTER ONE

THEOLOGICAL DISCOURSE ON PREDESTINATION

Throughout known history, concepts of predestination, preordainment, determinism, compulsionism, indeterminism, free will and free action have been the focal point of discussions for many renowned theologians and philosophers, including a significant number of Muslim scholars. These profound topics maintain their popularity in contemporary philosophy and theology. There is a considerable amount of literature that predominantly focuses on the nature of human will and determinism; however, most of these scholarly works do not agree on a universally accepted argument for the reconciliation of determinism and free will where the philosophical premises are based on empirical evidence that substantiates the coexistence of the two concepts. Many contemporary philosophers and theologians continue to propose arguments for either determinism or free action. This is chiefly because of an apparent philosophical inconsistency and scientific incongruity that challenge the coexistence of determinism and free will. Evidently, these presumed inconsistencies and incompatibilities form a great hurdle for theologians and philosophers who wish to formulate a theory based on the coexistence of determinism and free will. The main argument of this book is based on the concept that determinism and free will can theologically be reconciled.

For Muslim theologians, establishing a philosophical argument that supports the coexistence of predestination and free will is quite significant because belief in destiny is one of the essential tenets of the Islamic creed, *'aqīda*. The literal meaning of *'aqīda* in the Arabic dictionary is "to tie a knot" or "to attach to something wholeheartedly"[1]. Theologically, it refers to a list of essential articles of faith that each Muslim within the tradition of *ahl al sunnah wa'l jamā'ah* is required to believe. Since the creed is the most important component of the Islamic faith, as much as it is in every faith tradition, research in the field of theology is imperative in contemporary times when there seems to be less focus on this in the Islamic literature that chiefly addresses social, political, practical, and cultural matters of the religion. Within the discipline of theology, concepts of predestination and free will occupy significant space. Although formative and classical scholars have established theo-

---

1   Wehr, H. (1976). *A dictionary of modern written Arabic* (J. M. Cowan, Ed.) (3rd ed). New York: Spoken Language Service, Inc.

logical methodologies to solve the problem of coexistence from creedal and philosophical perspectives, the development of modern science has seen the emergence of gaps that need to be filled.

The establishment of belief in Divine Destiny originates from several verses of the Qur'an and an authentic prophetic report referred to as the "Gabriel hadith" where Archangel Gabriel asked Prophet Muhammad (pbuh) to define faith. The Prophet then lists the six essential articles of faith, where one of them was "belief in destiny"[2]. The angel then confirmed the Prophet's definition. Based on this Prophetic report, all mainstream Islamic scholars agree that belief in Divine Destiny is an integral part of the Islamic faith. According to Muhammad al-Tahir ibn Ashur, the Arabic term *qadar* – along with its common meaning "due measure," also carries the meaning "knowing the actual reality of something or some event." Thus, apart from having meanings like "to create with due measure," "predestination" and "preordainment," *qadar* also refers to the precise knowledge of God[3].

While belief in *qadar* has become an essential article of the creed of Islamic theology, its doctrines also assert that human beings possess some form of free will, as human life on earth is considered as a period of testing during which all humans have moral responsibilities and therefore a liability towards their Creator[4]. The Qur'an refers to this responsibility with the following verse: "[He] who created death and life to test you [as to] which of you is best in deed..."[5] Accordingly, majority of Islamic theologians agree that such responsibility requires the existence of some sort of free will[6].

This, in turn, necessitates the formulation of an argument that verifies the philosophical premise that the two concepts are acquiescent. For this reason, Islamic scholars in general have shown great interest for the topics of determinism and free will. However, instead of using terms such as determinism, causal determinism or compulsionism, main-

2   Bukhari, n.d. 2:43.

3   Ibn Ashur, n.d. pg. 362.

4   Al-Tahāwī, A. J. A. M. (2011). *Al-Aqīdah al-Tahāwiyyah* [The creed of al Tahāwiyyah] (M. F. Hoosen, Trans.) n.p: Dar al-Hikmah.

5   Qur'an, 67:2.

6   Al-Tahāwī, A. J. A. M. (2011).

stream Islamic theologians use the terms 'destiny' or 'predestination,' for according to Islamic creed, there is an important distinction between compulsionism and Divine Destiny. While compulsionism suggests absolute determinism or fatalism, which gives no freedom of choice to human beings, the concept of Divine Destiny allows for the existence of free will.

The theological discourse on free will and Divine Destiny in Islam dates back to the time of Prophet Muhammad (pbuh). It is reported by Ali, the Prophet's son-in-law, that one day Prophet Muhammad said, "... There is not one amongst you who has not been allotted his seat in Paradise or Hell." Those present asked: "then, why should we perform good deeds, why not depend upon our destiny?" Thereupon he said: "No, do perform good deeds, for everyone is facilitated in that for which he has been created"[7]. In this report, although Prophet Muhammad asserts that the fate of all humans has already been decided, he also encourages his followers to uphold the principles of morality and human values. This indicates that humans should possess some form of free will that enables them to decide on a path to follow. For this reason, mainstream Islamic theologians have agreed that free will and predestination coexist[8]. However, reports like these and some pertinent verses from the Qur'an were interpreted differently by theologians of the formative period as some scholars withdrew from mainstream Islamic theology, *Ahl al Sunnah wa'l jamāah*, to form schools like the Jabrīyyah, a fatalist or compulsionist school, and Mu'tazila, the school of reason or rationalism[9].

The school of Jabrīyyah

The name Jabrīyyah derives from the Arabic root word *jabr* or *jabran*, which means "to force," "forcibly" or "compulsorily". The school's theological discourse claims destiny is something that is experienced compulsorily by human beings; therefore, human will is only an illusion. The term *jabr* or *jabran* does not appear in the Qur'an, but *Jabbar*,

---

7   Muslim, n.d. 33:6400

8   Maghnīsāwī, A. M. (2007). *Imam Abu Hanifa's al-Fiqh al-akbar explained* (A-R. ibn Y. Mangera, Trans.). London: White Thread Press.

9   Robinson, N. (1998). Ash'arī and Mu'tazila. *Muslim Philosophy.*

which etymologically comes from the same root word as *jabr*, is mentioned once, referring to an attribute of God as being the One who can do whatever He wills by force and on nine occasions for people who dominate or oppress others.[10] Based on this etymological definition, the school of Jabrīyyah maintains that God has predetermined the lives of all human beings; therefore, there is no room for free will in such divine scenario[11].

The Jabrīyyah view is important for critical analysis purposes as it rejects the mainstream view that the two concepts can coexist. The fatalistic or compulsionistic view of Jabrīyyah on Divine Destiny is also based on the verse: "And you do not will except that Allah [God] wills. Indeed, Allah [God] is ever knowing and wise."[12] The derived conclusion is that since nothing or no one can supersede the will of God, human beings cannot possess free will in the true sense. This argument is interesting as mainstream Islamic scholars do not dispute the inference that all phenomena, events and actions, including human actions, materialize through the absolute will of God[13]. The mainstream scholars argue that human free will is a requirement of moral responsibility. Therefore, an annulment of free will is also an annulment of moral responsibility.

The Qur'an supports the existence of human free will with the verse: "Allah [God] does not charge a soul except [with that within] its capacity. It will have [the consequence of] what [good] it has gained, and it will bear [the consequence of] what [evil] it has earned."[14] The verse indicates that humans have the capacity to act; therefore, they will face the consequences of their actions.[15] For this reason, mainstream scholars believe the verses indicating predestination and free will do not contradict; on the contrary, they support each other. For the mainstream scholars,

10   Abdulbaqi, M. F. (n.d.). *Jabr* [Title translation]. Location: Al Mu'jam.

11   Al-Shahrastānī, M. A. K., Öz, M., & Dalkılıç, M. (2008). *El Milel ve-l Nihal: Dinler, mezhepler ve felsefi sistemler tarihi* [History of religions, sects and philosophical systems]. Istanbul: Litera Yayıncılık.

12   Qur'an 76:30.

13   Maghnīsāwī, A. M. (2007). *Imam Abu Hanifa's al-Fiqh al-akbar explained* (A-R. ibn Y. Mangera, Trans.). London: White Thread Press.

14   Qur'an 2:286.

15   Al-Razī, F. (n.d). *Al Tafsir* [The exegesis].

this view is further strengthened with the verse: "And whatever strikes you of disaster – it is for what your hands have earned..."[16].

The school of Mu'tazila

The rationalist school of Mu'tazila, on the other hand, interprets these verses as, not only do human beings possess total freedom to act, but they also possess the power to create their own actions.[17] The Mu'tazilites did not reject predestination altogether, as Hisham ibn 'Amr, a renowned Mu'tazila scholar, stated that "God is the All-Knowing and All-Powerful since eternity in the past, but I cannot say He knows the states of matter in the future."[18] The intention was to protect *tawḥīd*, Divine Unity, one of the five principles of the Mu'tazila theology, where they believed that prior knowledge of future states of matter would give matter an eternal existence, even if it was in the form of knowledge. For this reason, they claimed that human agents are the originators of their actions.

They arrived at this conclusion by claiming the etymology of the term *qadar* (destiny or due measure) is derived from the term *qada*, which means "to compare" or "to provide an example." Thus, for the Mu'tazilites, the exegesis of the verse "God creates human actions" is "God provides an example about the creation of human actions."[19] So, according to some Mu'tazila scholars, this verse affirms that God has knowledge of human actions prior to their creation, but He does not create them. For the Mu'tazilites, *qadar* does not carry the meaning "forcing someone into doing something;" rather, it indicates God's commandment and judgment. All Mu'tazila scholars concur on the notion that God does not create evil, unlawful acts and the acts of others, except His own.[20]

---

16 Qur'an, 42:30

17 Al-Tahāwī, A. J. A. M. (2011). *Al-Aqīdah al-Tahāwiyyah* [The creed of al-Tahāwiyyah] (M. F. Hoosen, Trans.) n.p: Dar al-Hikmah.

18 Al-Ashari, n.d. pg. 130.

19 Sinanoğlu, A. (2006). Fate comprehension of Mu'tazila, the first partisan of freedom school in Islam. pg. 74. n.p.: *KSÜ İlahiyat Fakültesi Dergisi*.

20 Ibid.

For this reason, Muʻtazila theologians reject the opinion that God creates human acts and argue that *qadar* refers to God's pronouncement of an incident or event. They further claim, in the following verse about Lot: "So We saved him and his family, except for his wife; We destined her to be of those who remained behind"[21] – the term "destined" should be interpreted as "discretion" as it indicates that God is enunciating the inevitable demise of Lot's wife, which came about through her own doing, rather than preordaining it.

These evident differences in view originate primarily from the hermeneutics of the scripture where the term *qadar* is related to several root words, such as *qudrah*, meaning power, and *ahkām*, which refers to judgment. For the Muʻtazilites, the term *qudrah* refers to the power of God, as it comes from the same root word *qadir,* the powerful, or *al Qadir*, one of the names of God in Islamic theology meaning the All-Powerful. For this reason, the Muʻtazilites believe that *qadar* refers to acts of God. They separate human acts from the concept, claiming they are caused by humans through a power instilled in them by God. However, contrary to wide belief that the Muʻtazila reject Divine Destiny altogether, their teachings suggest the rejected component of predestination is "God's predestination and creation of human acts".

Ahl al Sunnah wa'l Jamā'ah (the schools of the mainstream)

Mainstream Islamic theology repudiates the Muʻtazila claims and argues that God alone is the creator of all acts in existence, including human actions. They conclude that human actions transpire through the will and power of God. They support this argument with verses like: "Say, I possess not for myself any harm or benefit except what Allah wills"[22]. Furthermore, they argue that Divine Destiny is also evident in the Qur'an, where a significant number of verses indicate preordainment. For example, in reference to human provisions, the Qur'an states: "But He sends [provisions] down in an amount which He wills"[23]. The Arabic term *biqadarin* is used here as "in an amount," which also means

---

21   Qur'an 27:57.

22   Qur'an 10:49.

23   Qur'an 42:27.

in a "predestined amount or measure." For the mainstream scholars, the preordainment of God is unquestionable as it is affirmed by text and tradition. According to al-Razī, the verse means: "God has preordained the provisions of human beings with wisdom and according to their needs"[24].

The Gabriel hadith mentioned previously is supported by another hadith narrated by Abu Hurairah who said: "Prophet Muhammad (pbuh) defines *iman*, belief, as: "it is to believe in God, His angels, Divine Books, Prophets, the Hereafter and Divine Destiny."[25] Prophet Muhammad's inclusion of "belief in Divine Destiny" in the list of faith essentials encouraged the mainstream scholars to formulate theological arguments based on premises that define preordainment and free will as coexisting realities.

Muʻtazilites, on the other hand, do not deny Divine Destiny but argue that humans possess the will, power, and ability to change the state of matter. The evident distinction between the Muʻtazila and concurring positions of the mainstream theologians is, although the Ashʻarites and Māturīdīs agree on the abilities of human agents as acquisitors or doers of their acts, they reject the Muʻtazila claim that the power to change the state of matter originates from humans. They assert the act is created by God based on *kasb*, acquisition that involves a proclivity by human agents to act. For this reason, the mainstream scholars approach predestination from the perspective of Divine Knowledge and argue that whatever the human agent will decide to do, it is already known by God. This argument finds support from a Prophetic tradition where a man came to Prophet Muhammad and asked: "does using medicine for prevention and treatment alter Divine Destiny?" He replied: "Whatever changes is Divine Destiny as well"[26]. The implication is that changes that occur due to human intervention are also defined as Divine Destiny, as no event or action can escape the infinite knowledge of God. Therefore, although human agents have multiple paths to choose from, the path they ultimately choose has pre-existence in Divine Knowledge, which is referred to as Divine Destiny. Accordingly, God's prior knowledge of human choices and actions does not nullify their free will.

---

24   Al-Razī, F. (1981). *Mafatih al-Ghayb*. Beirut: Dar al-Fikr.

25   Bukhari, n.d. 50:4777.

26   Ibn Majah, n.d. 31:2.

This methodology of reconciliation is quite important in mainsream theology as Fethullah Gülen also builds his arguments on the views of formative, classical and pre-contemporary Islamic theologians, such as Abu Hanīfa, al-Tahāwī, Abu Hasan al-Ash'arī, Abu Mansur Al-Māturīdī, Abu Mu'in al-Nasafi, Muhammad al-Al-Shahrastānī and Said Nursi.

Al-Nasafi, one of the most notable theologians of the Māturīdīyah school, contributes to the methodology of reconciliation by arguing that human acts are the product of *irāda al juz'īyya* (minor will), *kasb* (acquisition), *irāda kullīyyah* (absolute will) and *qudrah* (Divine power), indicating they materialise from the coherent function of the minor free will, acquisition, absolute will and power. While minor will and acquisition belong to human agents, absolute will and power to create belongs to God. According to al-Nasafi[27], creation of human acts can only be attributed to God as this theological principle is established through *naql* (revelation) and *'aql* (reasoning).

Mu'tazilites, on the other hand, claimed that if God was the creator of human actions, He would be responsible of all rebellious and evil acts humans perform and this concept would be theologically inconsistent with the commandments that recurrently encourage humans to perform good deeds. Furthermore, God's promise of reward and punishment would be illogical if good and evil acts were created by Him[28].

Al-Nasafi repudiates this claim by arguing, although verses like "do as you will"[29], "do good deeds"[30] and "they will be rewarded for what they used to do"[31] indicate that humans possess the freedom to act in certain ways, verses like "God is the creator of all" and "He creates you and what you do" indicates that human acts are created by God. Al-Nasafi, however, adds that these are words of glorification and do not mean

---

27   Al-Nasafi, M. I.-M. (1993). *Tebsiratu'l edille fi usûli'd-dîn.* pg. 174. Ankara: Diyanet İşleri Başkanlığı Yayınları.

28   Qadī, A. (2013). *Sharhu'l Usuli'l Hamsa* (I. Çelebi. Trans. Istanbul: Pasifik Ofset

29   Qur'an 41:40.

30   Qur'an 22:77.

31   Qur'an 56:24.

that humans play no role in the causation of their actions.[32] Al-Nasafi argues that there is a difference between performing and creating an act. He responds to the Mu'tazilites who claim that the term "He creates what you do" refers only to idols made by human hands, by asserting the term refers to 'amal, deeds or acts performed by human agents. Therefore, according to al-Nasafi, attributing the act of creating to any agent other than God would make it impossible for theologians to prove the unity and oneness of God[33]. Al-Nasafi's concern can be understood as tawḥīd, which is the concept of Divine Unity in Islam, is the primary article of the creed of Islamic theology.

This is particularly significant for the mainstream theologians as tawḥīd not only means God has no partners in Divinity, but also He has no partners in His transcendent and affirmative attributes, such as wajib al wujud (necessary existence), baqa (endlessness), qidam (beginningless), qiyam bī nafsīh (self-subsistence), mukhalafatun lil hawadith (other than His creation), quḍrah (omnipotence) and takwin (creating or bringing into existence). According to the mainstream theologians, assigning any of these Divine attributes to anyone other than God would be considered a violation of tawḥīd.

However, the philosophical dispute between the Mu'tazilites and mainstream theologians does not focus on God's creative abilities; rather, it is on the concept of istita'a (an ability to act). The Mu'tazilites claim that human agents always possess a God-given ability to act, but Maghnīsāwī argues this ability to act "coincides with the action, not before it or after it"[34]. According to Imam Azam Abu Hanifa, if humans always possessed this ability to act, there would be no need for God at the time of the action. In saying that he also acknowledges the existence of this ability, as the Qur'an states "Allah does not charge a soul except [with that within] its capacity"[35], indicating that human beings possess an ability to act. While al-Qari argues that people who do not possess this abili-

---

32   Al-Nasafi, M. I.-M. (1993). Tebsiratu'l edille fi usûli'd-dîn. pg. 174. Ankara: Diyanet İşleri Başkanlığı Yayınları.

33   Ibid.

34   Maghnīsāwī, A. M. (2007). Imam Abu Hanifa's al-Fiqh al-akbar explained (A-R. ibn Y. Mangera, Trans.) pg. 123. London: White Thread Press.

35   Qur'an 2:286.

ty are not morally responsible just as "mentally incompetent are not held accountable for belief and that a mute person is not required to articulate his [her] belief with his [her] tongue…"[36]

For that reason, mainstream Islamic theologians concur on the concept that *istita'a* (ability to act) is a quality that God creates upon human acquisition of an action providing the necessary causation created by God is in place. To cite an analogy, when a specific living species wishes to jump, God will create the act of jumping, providing the species is able to jump. This ability defined as *istita'a* is also given by God. For example, an elephant will not be able to jump even it wished as it is not biologically structured to jump. So, will, acquisition, ability, causality, and creation of the act by God are the necessary components for an act to occur.

Evidently, the disagreement between the Mu'tazila and *Ahl al Sunnah wa'l Jamā'ah* schools intensifies predominantly on the creation of human actions rather than free will as both schools agree on the concept that humans possess some form of free will. Excluding the fatalistic or compulsionistic perspectives of the Jabrīyyah, most Islamic schools of theology agree on the existence of human will; however, the mainstream scholars further argue that free will and Divine Destiny are compatible and can be reconciled. I believe that for a more comprehensive understanding and for comparative purposes, it is also important to briefly explore the views of Western theologians and philosophers.

Western philosophy and theology on determinism and free will

Evidently, the problem of free will has also been one of the main topics of theological and philosophical discourse in the West. There is some evidence that Aristotle initiated the discourse about determinism and indeterminism; however, historical records suggest Epicurus was one of the first to propose the argument 'occurrence of natural events can be classified into two groups: deterministic and indetermin-

---

36　Maghnīsāwī, A. M. (2007). *Imam Abu Hanīfa's al-Fiqh al-akbar explained* (A-R. ibn Y. Mangera, Trans.) pg. 125. London: White Thread Press.

istic.'[37] The concepts of determinism and free choice were one of the focal points of philosophical discourse for the thinkers of antiquity as prominent philosophers like Aristotle, Epicurus, Zeno of Citium, Plato, Chrysippus, Socrates and others have talked about causal determinism, fate, theological determinism, determinism in general physics and free action.

In the West, discussions on determinism and free action continued with the involvement of Neoplatonists and Christian theologians. Many theories were produced, most of them based on amendments to Stoic determinism, which eventually became a mere mention in discourse on causal determinism. Interestingly, as is discussed in contemporary philosophy and physics, Stoic determinism was based primarily on cosmology that focused on teleology, the purpose argument that states natural phenomena occur with purpose.[38] Stoic determinism was further elucidated by Chrysippus with an analysis of the principles of causality.

However, Stoic determinism also contains the element of ontology, as, according to Bobzien, the Stoic theory on causality involves interactions between corporeal and incorporeal elements, which suggest that motion of matter is reliant on a metaphysical element. Consequently, Stoic teachings conclude that there is a power that causes the causation, and this power is not contingent on causality as it is responsible for all phenomena in nature.[39]

The idea that all causes are caused by one ultimate power, "the One" was later emphasised by the Neoplatonist movement that emerged around the third century[40]. The teachings of this movement influenced many thinkers, including Christian theologian Thomas Aquinas and Muslim theologians like al-Farabī and Ibn Sina (Avicenna). The reason that some of the Neoplatonist arguments were welcomed by Jewish, Christian, and Muslim theologians was that they were founded on the premise of an 'uncaused cause' – the 'first cause' or 'unmoved mover' – a

---

37   Epictetus. (1990). *Letter*. Raleigh, N.C: Alex Catalogue.

38   Bobzien, S. (1998). *Determinism and freedom in stoic philosophy*. Oxford: Clarendon Press.

39   Ibid.

40   Remes, P. (2008). *Neoplatonism*. n.p.: Acumen publishing.

concept that was compatible to their creeds, which basically stated God is the cause of all causes.

Although the argument of 'uncaused cause' solved the creedal issues regarding the origin of all phenomena, there still was a need for an explanation regarding moral responsibility. Basically, if human actions were caused by an uncaused cause, how could the agent be morally responsible? The theological principle that claimed all events are caused by God needed to be reconciled with human free will, as religious doctrines and universal values demanded moral responsibility for human agents.

In response to this problem, Thomas Aquinas argued in his *Summa Theologiae* that man has free will as "he acts from free judgment and retains the power of being inclined to various things."[41] Furthermore, in responding to the claim that humans have no free will because it is written, "For the good which I will, I do not, but the evil which I will not, that I do"[42], Aquinas argued, if humans had no free will, commandments, prohibitions, reward and punishment would have no meaning.[43] Aquinas further argued that human decisions are not like a stone moving downwards [due to the gravitational pull of the earth]; they result from free action. Consequently, it can be said the arguments provided by Aquinas conclude that Divine Destiny and free will coexist; however, a philosophical methodology on how they could coexist is not clearly defined in his arguments.

In contemporary times, this concept of coexistence is still not defined, as according to Sean Carroll: "asking whether free will exists is a lot like asking whether time really exists."[44] The relevance is, although one experiences the flow of time throughout one's natural life, scientifically one cannot prove its existence since time is not a physical property. Interestingly, Carroll believes: "it is possible to deny the existence of something while using it all the time."[45] He argues that some scientists do

---

41   Aquinas, T., & Morris, S. (1991). *Summa Theologiae*. n.p.

42   Romans, 7:19.

43   Aquinas, T., & Morris, S. (1991). *Summa Theologiae*. n.p.

44   Carroll, S. (2011). On determinism. *Discover*. Retrieved from http://blogs.discover.

45   ibid.

not believe that time is real, yet they are quite capable of showing up to a meeting on time. Here, he is implying "when people make use of a concept and simultaneously deny its existence, they are in fact claiming that the concept in question is nowhere to be found in some fundamental description of reality."[46] Regarding this paradox, he states "the discussions about the existence of free will often centre on whether we really need to include such freedom as an irreducible component of reality, without which our understanding would be fundamentally incomplete."[47] On the other hand, there are those who believe free will is a fundamental component of reality although its existence cannot be proven through the laws of nature. This view is based purely on human experience and philosophy of ethics and morals rather than scientific data.

The argument about the existence of free will is important to ethics, morality and, of course, criminal law, for without it, the justice system cannot find any person guilty or innocent of a crime. According to common law, the test of accountability in acts of crime is defined with the Latin term *actus reus non facit reum nisi mens sit rea* – "the act is not culpable unless the mind is guilty"[48] – concluding that a person can only be found guilty of a crime if they have a 'guilty mind,' meaning the mental capacity to distinguish right from wrong. This suggests that to have the mental capacity to distinguish the right from wrong, humans need free will and an ability to act freely. Muslim theologians also argue that the existence of free will is imperative as the creedal doctrines of Islam assert that humans will be held accountable for their actions on earth. The Qur'an establishes this with the verse: "This is what you are promised for the Day of Account."[49] Libertarians in the West also agree with the necessity of free will, not for ontological reasons but for its necessity for moral responsibility.

According to Robert Kane, free will is the capability of agents to be the generators and controllers of their own ends and purposes.[50] He ar-

---

46   Ibid.

47   Ibid.

48   Lanius, D. (2019). *Strategic indeterminacy in the law.* Pg. 113. Oxford: Oxford University Press.

49   Qur'an 38:53.

50   Kane, R. (1996). *The significance of free will.* New York: Oxford University Press.

gues that acting freely means to be unconstrained in the pursuit of your purposes. However, Kane also argues, if free will is caused by something else and the explanatory chain of causes can be traced to God or destiny, then the ultimacy would not lie with the agents but with something else. The confusion over whether a simple act of a person pointing their index finger at an object is the consequence of free will or predestination is evident in the statements made by Kane. It seems even the most prominent philosophers and scientists have not come to consensus on the debate whether free will truly exists or not. Kane argues that what is often called the free will problem is really a cluster of questions revolving around the conception of human freedom, which is the power of creating one's own purpose.[51]

The topic of free will is important in theology and philosophy because it involves other significant matters, such as morality, dignity, responsibility, rationality, creativity, autonomy, and others. So, the fundamental debate is between scientists is who argue that nature is governed by classical mechanics—which suggests the fate of everything in the physical world is predetermined—and those who argue that free will, to some degree, is a necessary component of reality; this debate continues to be the focus of attention in the discipline of philosophy. Of course, when the topic is determinism and free will, one cannot ignore the strong presence of ontology.

In contemporary Christian theology, free will is defined as the ability to make choices without external coercion.[52] Since the term 'free will' does not appear in the Bible, Christian theologians have debated as to what extent this free will is to be understood. There are two main positions: compatibilism and libertarianism. While the compatibilist view is that one's freedom is restricted by one's nature, therefore one can only choose what one's nature allows them to choose, the libertarian view suggests one's free will is not restricted to one's nature.[53] A subdivision of the libertarian view, on the other hand, claims a person's choices are not knowable by God until they occur, but Slick argues that the Biblical

---

51   Ibid.

52   Slick M. (2017) *What is libertarian free will and is it biblical?* Christian Apologetics & Research Ministry.

53   Ibid.

position on free will is compatibilism, which claims a person is only allowed to do what their nature permits them to do. To some extent, this view agrees with the views of the mainstream Muslim theologians as it can be argued that compatibilism is the closest viewpoint to Islamic view on destiny and free will.

Gülen's perspective on Divine Destiny and free will

In relation to contemporary arguments around Divine Destiny and free will, one of the noteworthy analyses within the theoretical framework of mainstream Islamic theology comes from Fethullah Gülen, who offers several premises to demonstrate that both concepts are real and predestination and free will can truly coexist. Gülen contributes to discussions on the topic from theological and philosophical perspectives. Primarily, Gülen's arguments are based on the creed of mainstream Islamic theology. He constructs his position on the teachings of renowned scholars, such as Abu Hanīfa, Abu Mansur al-Māturīdī, Said Nursi and several other mainstream scholars, and then strengthens them through philosophical allegories emblematic to his personal theological methodology, which will be explained below.

According to Gülen, the providence of humans and the entire universe is already known by God, but this Divine knowledge, which originates from the omniscient attribute of God, does not divest humans off free will.[54] Based on the famous Nursi argument, Gülen asserts that knowledge depends on the actual, but the actual does not depend on knowledge.[55] In other words, empirical data, which can be defined as knowledge, depends on the reality of events or what occurs in nature; however, the actual phenomenon that eventuates in nature does not depend on empirical data gathered by scientists. For example, an alteration in the data or information known through knowledge will not change the phenomenon, which eventuates in nature.

Accordingly, God's knowledge of human destiny does not eliminate moral responsibility because an individual behaves in a certain way regardless of God having prior knowledge on how they would behave.

---

54   Gülen, F. (2009). *Essentials of the Islamic faith*. NJ: Tughra Books.
55   Ibid.

For Gülen, free will does not contradict Divine Decree and determination; on the contrary, it verifies it. Gülen argues, in connection to human free will, Divine Decree originating from the omniscient attribute of God acts on prior knowledge, which also encompasses an act that a human intends to perform. Therefore, human agents, using their free will, intend to perform an act that then is created by God.[56] The argument suggests that Divine Decree and Destiny confirm the existence of free will. So, according to Gülen, human agents do not act in a certain way because God has predestined it; rather, God knows how they will act, and their acts confirm God's omniscience.

Through this methodology, Gülen argues that although human beings possess free will, they cannot bring anything into existence unless God wills it.[57] Gülen further claims that the existence of free will does not challenge Divine Destiny; on the contrary, they go hand in hand. He indicates that humans possess a power that either takes them to eternal bliss or punishment; this is free will. He further argues that the existence of free will does not form an obstacle for Divine Decree and Predestination, as Divine Decree acts on prior knowledge of how humans intend to use their free will and wills the creation of that human act.[58] According to Gülen, this is a confirmation of free will.[59] Gülen also acknowledges the significance of causality in the eventuation of events by concluding that God is the cause of all causes. Being a contemporary scholar of the mainstream Islamic theology, he provides substantial literature supporting the argument that Divine Destiny and free will coexist.

---

56   Ibid.

57   Gülen, F. (2000). *Essentials of the Islamic faith*. Fairfax, Va: The Fountain.

58   Gülen, F. (2000). *Essentials of the Islamic faith*. Fairfax, Va: The Fountain.

59   ibid.

CHAPTER TWO

HISTORICAL DEVELOPMENT OF DISCOURSE ON DESTINY AND FREE WILL IN ISLAMIC THEOLOGY

This chapter will focus on the philosophical problem of free will and Divine Destiny as these concepts have been one of the major areas of theological discourse for scholars throughout Islamic history. Available literature suggests that different schools of theology have formulated contrasting views with an objective to solve these philosophically paradoxical concepts. Although the mainstream theologians have established several arguments based on reason, text and tradition, the debate continued among Islamic theologians throughout the formative, classical and modern periods. It seems that certain philosophical aspects of the problem remain unsolved, as Muslim theologians from different schools of thought have not reached a consensus in several theoretical aspects on the pertinent concepts.

Historical evidence suggests the development of discourse on determinism and free will in Islamic theology is delineated by three distinctive periods during which several different schools of theology have emerged:

The formative period (632–944): According to Montgomery Watt, the formative period of Islamic theology begins in 632 and ends in 950.[1] I am of the opinion that the formative era concluded with the death of al-Māturīdī on 944. Historical data suggests that early Muslims focused on creedal matters of Islam and controversial theological debates were avoided. The second period of the formative era witnessed the emergence of different theological views and the establishment of some theological schools. The systemization of the mainstream Islamic theology occurred in the third period of the formative era with the establishment of the Ash ʿariyyah and Māturīdīyyah schools of theology.

The classical period (944–1800): Theological discourse intensified primarily on the names and attributes of God, epistemology, and evidence for the existence of God. The concepts of Divine Destiny and free will were profoundly debated. The classical period includes the introduction of philosophical debates and the discipline of logic in *kalam* into Islamic theology. This period continues to the modern era. Some scholars argue that all matters of theology and religion were discussed during this period.

---

1   Watt, W. M. (2009). *The Formative Period of Islamic Thought*. Oxford: Oneworld.

The modern period (1800–current): There is a popular view among contemporary scholars that the modern period commenced with Abdul Aziz al-Dehlawī. Al-Dehlawī was a hadith scholar and theologian who published several works on hadith and theology. After al-Dehlawī, Muhammad Abduh, Muhammad Iqbal and Said Nursi proposed some new theological perspectives that mark the beginning of a new era in Islamic theology. This period chiefly focuses on analytical study of the creed, reason, logic, Qur'anic exegesis, and hermeneutics being integrated into theological arguments. This period also includes responses to contemporary issues that arise from scientific or philosophical challenges.

Any academic discussion on the problem of free will requires exploration of these significant periods in Islamic scholarship. All schools of Islamic theology concur on the existence of Divine Destiny as it is a creedal article of Islam; however, the differences in opinion arise from the delineation and definition of its quintessence in relation to human will and actions. The primary objective here is to conduct a detailed examination of these challenging concepts by focusing specifically on the views of the four major schools of the formative period and their successors in the classical and modern periods, scholars who made significant contributions to the topics of destiny and free will. It is essential to note that the majority of the Muslim population in the contemporary world continues to follow two of the four theological schools of thought formed in the formative period.

The formative period (632–944)

The formative period commences with the death of Prophet Muhammad and continues until the establishment of the mainstream Islamic schools of theology. This period is so significant in the development of Islamic thought that it needs to be examined within three different phases. The first period is the era of the *Ḥulafa-i Rashidun*, the caliphate of the four companions of Prophet Muhammad (pbuh). This is followed by the Ṭabiūn period in which the first theological schools began to emerge, then the two major schools of mainstream Islam, Ashʿariyyah and Māturīdīyyah were established during the third period, thus Islamic theology was systemised as a discipline.

In the formative period, the development of discourse on destiny and free will is connected to ambiguity around the meaning of some key concepts of creed. The different interpretations of these theological concepts led to the formation of various theologies. Some of the key concepts that led to segregation and formation of opposing theologies were the definitions of Divine Destiny, Attributes of God, theodicy, free will and creation of human actions. It can be argued that all these concepts revolve around the notion of predestination and free will.

The early period of the formative era

The Qur'an is the primary source of information for all Muslims; therefore, any study concerning a theological concept of Islam needs to commence with the Qur'an. For this reason, in the discipline of Islamic theology, the incongruent perspectives of various schools on destiny and free will originate from different theological interpretations derived from the creed of Islam and hermeneutical study of certain verses from the Qur'an, such as: "It is God Who has created you and all that you do."[2]

According to classical exegesis scholars, al-Mahallī and al-Suyutī, this verse should be understood in the light of the following verse: "When God created you and whatever you make, [whether it be] your act of carving and that which you have carved."[3] Such verses ostensibly indicate compulsionism or determinism, as they establish that occurrences and their products, including human actions, are predetermined, and imposed by God. Moreover, creedal statements assert that belief in destiny is a mandatory component of faith; therefore, the belief system of Islam obligates its followers to have faith in predestination. This denotes that God predetermines and creates all events in the universe, including events that transpire throughout human life.

The idea receives further support from the Qur'an, which also states: "...God guides whomever He wills" (Qur'an 28:56) stipulating

---

2   Qur'an 37:96.

3   Al-Mahallī, J.-D. M. A., Suyutī, J., & Mu'assasat Āl al-Bayt lil-Fikr al-Islāmī. (2008). *Tafsir al-Jalalayn* [Exegesis of the two Jalaluddins] (F. Hamza, Trans.) pg. 518. Louisville, Ky: Fons Vitae.

that one cannot be guided unless God wills it. According to al-Ṭabarī this verse specifically refers to Abu Talib, Prophet Muhammad's uncle who died as a disbeliever, by addressing the Prophet with the declaration "you cannot guide whom you like, to be guided, but [it is] God [who] guides whomever He wills, and He knows best those who will be guided."[4]

The hermeneutical analyses of this verse also seem to point out the invalidity or at the very least the insignificance of free will. Yet, on the other hand, the Qur'an also states: "And every soul will be compensated in full for whatever [good or evil] it has done [in the world]; and indeed He [God] knows best all that they do"[5] and "And that human has only that for which he labours."[6] Al-Mahallī and al-Suyuṭī understood this verse as, "man shall have only what he [himself] strives for..."[7] On the other hand, Fakhr al-Dīn al-Razī, a renowned exegete and theologian, interpreted the verse as "surely every responsible person, *mukallaf*, will receive the consequences of his labour."[8] While, al-Nasafi, a Māturīdī theologian, concluded that the meaning of the verse indicates that everyone will harvest the fruits of their labour in full and without a necessity for witnesses or recorded evidence.[9] Therefore, in contrast to the previous verse, this verse points to human responsibility as the Qur'an emphasises that human agents are morally responsible and will be held accountable for their actions, which in turn requires the existence of free will and free action.

Consequently, the theological confusion and perplexity originates from Qur'anic verses where it is stated that everything, including human actions, are predestined and originate from God, while there is also a

---

4   At-Tabari, n.d. 1:449.

5   Qur'an 39:70.

6   Qur'an 53:39.

7   Al-Maḥallī, J.-D. M. A., & al-Suyūṭī, J. (2007). *Tafsir al-Jalalayn* [Exegesis of the two Jalaluddins] (F. Hamza, Trans.). Amman: Royal Aal al-Bayt Institute for Islamic Thought.

8   Al-Razī, F. (n.d). *Al Tafsir* [The exegesis].

9   Al-Nasafî, M. M. (2003) *Tebsiratu'l-Edille*. Ankara: Hüseyin Atay, Şaban Ali Düzgün.

requirement for moral responsibility, which suggests humans possess some form of freedom to act, which evidently makes them liable agents. For this reason, Islamic theologians were compelled to address this philosophical problem, thus their attempts led to disagreements between major schools of theology throughout history. One of the main reasons for the rigorous disputes was the deterministic implications of the scripture that also assigned accountability to human agents.

Belief in predestination, or as it is more commonly phrased in Islamic theological discourse 'Divine Destiny', is one of the six essential articles of the creed of Islam. The notion of predestination originates from the sacred text of Islam as the Qur'an states: "Indeed, all things, We have created with predestination."[10] Al-Mahallī and al-Suyutī (2008) explained this verse as:

Truly everything (*inna kulla shay'in* is in the accusative as a dependent clause because of a verb governing it) **have We created in a measure, by ordainment** (*bi-qadarin*, 'in a measure', is a circumstantial qualifier referring to *kulla*, 'every', in other words, 'already predetermined'...[11]

While al-Ṭabarī interpreted the verse as truly everything was preordained and created by God in wisdom. He added that this verse was revealed after idol worshippers challenged Prophet Muhammad firmly on the topic of predestination. Therefore, for Muslims, then necessity of belief in predestination, or more commonly known as Divine Destiny, is primarily derived from the Qur'an.[12] The requirement for belief in predestination finds further support from a few prophetic narrations reported in the famous authentic hadith collections, such as Bukhari and Muslim. To cite an example, according to a report by Abu Huraira, Prophet Muhammad mentions a discussion between Adam and Moses where Adam explains his expulsion from paradise was preordained

---

10   Qur'an 54:49

11   Al-Mahallī, J.-D. M. A., & al-Suyūṭī, J. (2007). *Tafsir al-Jalalayn* [Exegesis of the two Jalaluddins] pg. 634. (F. Hamza, Trans.). Amman: Royal Aal al-Bayt Institute for Islamic Thought.

12   Ṭabarī, & Yaghmaʾī, Ḥ. (1961). *Tarjumah-'i tafsir-i Tabari* [Translation of Tabari exegesis].

long before he was created.[13] In another authentic narration reported by
Abu al-Aswad, two men from the clan of Muzaīna asked Prophet Muhammad if the deeds people do are decreed for them and if their fate in
the hereafter is predetermined by their decisions to act upon prophetic teachings. Prophet Muhammad (pbuh) explained that everything is
decreed by destiny and preordained for them.[14] Consequently, belief in
predestination has become an essential article of the Islamic creed as the
two fundamental sources of Islam – the Qur'an and Prophetic tradition –
support this theological principle. Consequently, the analysis of certain
verses from the Qur'an and Prophetic tradition indicates the presence of
determinism in natural phenomena.

Conversely, the Qur'an also affirms the existence of free will with
such verses: "there is nothing for man except for which he strives"[15],
"[He] Who created death and life to test you [as to] see which of you
best in deed..."[16] and "He [God] is not questioned about what He does,
but they [humans] will be questioned".[17] Al-Razī summarises this with
the statement: "All human deeds are recorded, and everyone shall see the
results of their acts, good and evil in the hereafter".[18] The Arabic term
sawfa used in the verse means that reward and punishment are delayed
to a future time in this life or the hereafter. Such verses indicate that
human agents have moral responsibility and some form of ability to act
freely, which makes them accountable for their actions. In view of that,
the concepts of moral responsibility, free will and predestination have
compelled the mainstream Islamic theologians to formulate theories
supporting the coexistence of free will and predestination.

From a historical perspective, the theological discourse regarding
free will and predestination goes back to the time of the companions of
Prophet Muhammad (pbuh), defined as the early period of the formative
era. One of the earliest and most illustrious discussions about predestination took place between 'Umar ibn al-Khattab, the second Khalifa after

---

13   Muslim, n.d. 46:6409.

14   Muslim, n.d. 46:6406.

15   Qur'an 53:39.

16   Qur'an 67:2.

17   Qur'an 21:23.

18   Al-Razī, F. (n.d). *Al Tafsir* [The exegesis].

Prophet Muhammad's death, and Abu Ubayda when, during a journey to Damascus, they received news of a plague outbreak at their intended destination. Upon hearing the news, 'Umar ibn al Khattab decided to return to Medina and Abu Ubayda asked: "Are you running from the destiny of God?" To which 'Umar ibn al-Khattab replied: "I wish I did not hear this from you. Yes, I am running from the destiny of God, to the destiny of God," as he pointed his finger towards Medina.[19]

The discussion between 'Umar ibn al Khattab and Abu Ubayda indicates that while Abu Ubayda approached the concept of predestination from a compulsionistic perspective, 'Umar ibn al Khattab attempted to reconcile the two concepts by claiming, no matter what the human agent intends to do through their free will, the ultimate result will be their destiny. It can be argued that, according to 'Umar ibn al Khattab, although human destiny is preordained, the decision to choose a particular path originates from free will. The debate between 'Umar ibn al Khattab and Abu Ubayda indicates the theological discourse about predestination and the differences in opinion had commenced in the early periods of Islamic history, although hadith scholars and historians do not report many other significant discussions during the rule of the four caliphs.

There is, however, one other incident reported by Abdullah ibn 'Umar, son of Caliph 'Umar. They asked ibn 'Umar about people who commit various sins and claimed it was all within the knowledge of God, "so what could they have done to change it"? He replied, indeed what they did was within the knowledge of God, but the knowledge of God does not compel anyone to commit sins.[20] In relation to reconciliation of predeterminism and free will, Abdullah ibn 'Umar's statement could be regarded as the foundation of mainstream Islamic theology. It seems that the literature provided by mainstream scholars of the classical period indicate that Abdullah ibn 'Umar's elucidation was assumed as a general theological guideline in the later periods, which led to the formulation of the argument that the infinite knowledge of God does not nullify free will.

19   Ibn Hajar. (n.d.). *al-İsaba fi tamyizi'z-sahaba*. V. II. Mısır: Maktabatu't-Dirasa-ti'l-İslami. pg. 242.

20   Ibn Murtada, A. Y., & Diwald-Wilzer, S. (1961). *Kitāb ṭabaqāt al-Mu'tazilah* [Biography of Mu'tazila scholars]. Beirut: Mu'assasah al-Rayyan.

The emergence of theological schools

According to al-Murtada, the debates on the essence of free will escalated significantly following the formation of the rationalist school of Mu'tazila during the second stage of the formative period after the conclusion of the period of the four caliphs.[21] The school known for its nonconformist views on free will and human actions claims the creation of human actions needs to be apportioned to humans. This initiated a debate on the origination of human acts as the claim infers that as free and responsible agents, humans must be the originators of their own actions.

The Mu'tazila School was formed in the eighth century following a theological debate that took place in the study circle of Hasan al-Basrī, who was one of the towering scholars of Tabiun (generation that followed the companions of Prophet Muhammad). Historical records suggest Wasil ibn Ata challenged al-Basrī during a theological debate about the situation of a grave sinner. Ibn Ata maintained that human actions are a minor component of belief, thus a grave sinner can neither be a believer nor a disbeliever.[22] Ibn Ata further argued that a person in this situation would remain between the two states until they repent or die as a disbeliever. He explained this position with a theological term *al-manzila bayn al-manzilatayn* – a state between the two stations.[23]

The disagreement led to the formation of the school of Mu'tazila. As they formulated various theological perspectives on many important topics, their views on free will and Divine Destiny became controversial in Islamic theology. The Mu'tazila School of theology claims that humans possess the ability to originate their own actions; consequently, the assertion led to the denial of Divine Destiny in connection to human actions, along with several other theological positions that seem to con-

---

21   Al-Murtada, A.-M. L. A. Y., & Arnold, T. W. (1902). *Al-Mutazilah: Being an extract from Kitābu'l Milal wa-n Nihal*. Leipzig, Germany: Harrassowitz.

22   Al-Shahrastānī, M. A. K., Öz, M., & Dalkılıç, M. (2008). El Milel ve-l Nihal: Dinler, mezhepler ve felsefi sistemler tarihi [History of religions, sects and philosophical systems]. Istanbul: Litera Yayıncılık.

23   Al-Baġdādī, A.-Q. I.-T. (1928). *Kitāb uṣūl ad-dīn* [The book of systematic theology] pg. 71. Istanbul: Matbạ'at ad-Daula.

tradict the fundamental beliefs of the Islamic creed. Consequently, this claim led to their segregation from mainstream Islamic theology.

According to Alamīrī, the Muʿtazilites are renowned for their defence of Divine Unity and Justice.[24] For the Muʿtazilites, since God is absolute in His justice and will not treat anyone unjustly, for humans to be held accountable they need to possess the ability to generate their own actions. Alamīrī argues that Bishr al-Muʾtamir was the first Muʿtazila to propose the concept of humans generating their own acts.[25] This concept was the basis of the dispute between the Muʿtazilites and mainstream scholars as it was taken to suggest that agents other than God have the capability to generate acts and events. This violated the creedal principle 'God is the only agent who can create.' The Muʿtazila argument has another implication that questions God's omniscience as it claims God's knowledge of future events would terminate human capacity to act freely. The Muʿtazila's philosophical questioning of Divine attributes such as *ʿilm* (omniscience), *takwin* (the attribute as being the only originator) and other theological matters caused their separation from mainstream Islam.

The name 'Muʿtazila' comes from the root word *iʿtizal*, which means 'to withdraw'. The term is a plural noun form of the verb 'to withdraw', translated into English as 'the withdrawers'. This name was given to them because of their unorthodox views on many theological matters on which mainstream scholars concurred.

As mentioned above, one of these disputed matters was the concept of human freedom in action. The Muʿtazila scholars argued that human agents had unconditional freedom and control over their acts, maintaining that the notion of causation originates from human free will; therefore, humans have the freedom to create their own actions. This perspective also suggests that human agents possess an inherent power to act. This is a power that is independent of God's will.

While the argument challenged the views of mainstream Islamic theology, in many ways, it was analogous to libertarianism, which would become an established philosophical view in the West during the 17th

---

24   Alamiri, Z. (2021). Some critical reflections on Al Jahiz's notions of tab and tiba (innate dispositions). *Australian Journal of Islamic Studies*, 6(1), 32-46.

25   ibid

century with the writings of John Locke, who was later known as the father of liberalism.[26] Like the Muʿtazilites, modern libertarians also reject determinism altogether, regardless of the argument whether it is controlled by God or laws of physics.

One of the main reasons that compelled the Mutʾazilites to argue that human agents are the originators of their actions was theodicy, the discipline dealing with the problem of evil. They concluded that God does not will or create evil; therefore, its initiation should be assigned to humans. The views of the Muʿtazila were considered as innovations by the rest of Islamic scholarship, who produced a considerable amount of literature refuting the Muʿtazila claims. This reactionary process also led to the formation of other polarised schools holding a position completely opposite to that of the Muʿtazila perspective. The school of Jabrīyyah was one of the most noted of these schools, which based its arguments on determinism or compulsionism.

Jahm ibn Safwan, founder of the school of Jabrīyyah, championed the notion of compulsionism or absolute determinism, as he argued against free action by claiming humans were like leaves dragged by the wind, thus the direction of their journey was determined by the wind.[27] For the Jabrīyyah, just as a stone tossed into the air falls downward, so too are human acts that could not befall any other way expect as they were predetermined. The school of Jabrīyyah supported their views by referring to the previously mentioned verses such as: "It is God, who creates you and your actions"[28] and "God guides whom He wills [to the straight path]".[29] Although, in a literal sense, these two verses support the Jabrīyyah view, as they signify that human acts could not materialise in the absence of God's will and power, the Muʿtazila's hermeneutical conception of the verses was that human agents originate their own actions through the power God has granted them. They acknowledged that God is the origin of this power by claiming that God could remove this power any time He wished.[30] While a faction of Jabrīyyah called Mutawassita

26   Boaz, D. (2007). A note on labels: Why libertarian? Cato Institute.

27   Al-Shahrastānī, M. (1975). *Al-Milal Waʾn Nihal*. Beirut: n.p

28   Qurʾan 37:96.

29   Qurʾan 24:46.

30   Martin, M. (2013). *Use of Reason in Early Islamic Theology* (Kindle ed.). n.p.: Am-

argues that human agents possess some form of power, this power has no effect on human acts.

The Mu'tazilites, on the other hand, further argued that humans are liable agents due to their ability to make moral choices; for this reason, they possess a God-given power to cause their own actions. Many theologians believe that the concept of theodicy played a decisive role on the Mu'tazila perspective as they claimed the creation of evil contradicts the attributes of an All-Good and All-Just God; thus, evil must originate from man. The concept of theodicy was a serious problem in Christian theology as well, as Augustine of Hippo also argued that evil cannot originate from God; thus, it must be attributed to human free will.[31] Consequently, the problem of evil compelled the Mu'tazilites and some Christian scholars to formulate an argument that attributes the origin of evil to human agents.

While the principal objective of the Mu'tazila position was to exalt God from being assumed as the originator of evil, Jabrīyyah's aim was to defend God's *thubutī sifat* of *takwin* (creating, originating), one of the eight affirmative attributes of God, by arguing that all phenomena, physical and metaphysical, are preordained and designed by God.

Theologically, it seems that the perplexity and disagreement originate from the Qur'anic term *qadar*, translated as predestination or Divine Destiny, but which also carries the literal meaning of 'due measure': "Surely, We created everything with due measure (*qadar*)"[32]. Exegetes generally interpret the term 'due measure' as "[already] predetermined" as well. The Mu'tazilites, however, interpreted the term as God creates the human capacity in certain measure but allows them to make their own choices and initiate their own actions. This means a human agent shapes their own destiny through their free will; therefore, evil originates from human will. Accordingly, the Mu'tazila School claimed that God would not create evil because God neither wills nor commands immoral human behaviour. Moreover, the Mu'tazila scholars argued that predes-

---

azon Digital Services Inc.

31   Russell, R. P. (Trans.). (2004). *The Fathers of the Church: St Augustine the Teacher, the Free Choice of the Will, Grace and Free Will*. Washington, D.C: Catholic University of America Press.

32   Qur'an 54:49.

tination would nullify free action; therefore, human agents could not be held responsible for their actions in a predetermined world. However, this view creates two major theological problems for mainstream creed scholars; one is the denial of predestination, and the other is the creative powers are not assigned to God only.

In mainstream Islamic theology, the ability to create belongs only to God. The term *khalq* (creation) in an Islamic context means bringing something into existence from a non-existent state or originating, shaping, and giving measure to a property or event that was already created and, for this reason, the Qur'an states: "God is the creator of all things..."[33] and He has the power of "disposing them as He wills". Therefore, the common theological response to the Mu'tazila argument is: Is it possible to attribute creative powers to human agents in light of the above verse?

For this reason, the school of Jabrīyyah proposed an uncompromising argument against the Mu'tazila claim. According to Jahm ibn Safwan, since all phenomena are created by God and He is the All-Knowing, humans could not possess the power to create or any form of free will in a real sense.[34] Therefore, in total contrast to the Mu'tazila view, the school of Jabrīyyah believes that God predetermines and originates everything in nature – including the materialisation of human acts. Accordingly, for them, the human free will is nothing but an illusion.

The school of Jabrīyyah established a similarity between the fate of human agents and natural laws as their 'humans are like stones falling towards the earth' analogy indicates the law of gravity, which is constant and cannot be defied. This is because the Jabrīyyah view supports absolute compulsionism as according to etymology, the term Jabrīyyah comes from the root word *jabr*, which means 'to impose by force'.[35] Abu Ishaq al-Isfarayīnī believes that the school of Jabrīyyah constructed their arguments on the following notion: since no one but God has the au-

---

33   Qur'an 39:62.

34   Ibn Asakir, A.-H. (1928). *Tabyīn kadhib al-muftarī*. Dimashq: Matba'at al-Tawfiq.

35   Isfarāyinī, A. -M. T. M., Kawtharī, M. Z.-H., & Ḥusaynī, I. -A. (1940). *al-Tabṣīr fī al-dīn wa-tamyīz al-firqah al-nājiyah 'an al- firaq al-hāliki*. Cairo: Maṭba'at al-Anwār.

thority to decide what comes into being, He predestines and creates everything in existence, which includes human decisions and acts.

The Jabrīyyah scholars support this view with the Islamic theological concept of *lawh al mahfūz*, the Preserved Tablet, in which all phenomena within the space-time continuum are registered: "No disaster strikes upon the earth or among yourselves except that it is in a register before We bring it into being".[36] According to mainstream scholars, this verse enunciates that God has pre-recorded every event in the universe long before He created them. Consequently, this and similar verses that contain deterministic implications seem to support the Jabrīyyah view.

Moreover, the conversation between Adam and Moses also supports the Jabrīyyah view, as according to Prophet Muhammad, Moses blamed Adam for causing humanity to be expelled from paradise, to which Adam responded by saying "how can you blame me for an act which God preordained forty years before my creation".[37] The narration implies that Adam's was preordained and recorded long before his creation. Based on this Prophetic narration, the school of Jabrīyyah argues that there was no other path available for Adam, and since Adam represents the entire humanity, everything is preordained for humanity as well; therefore, there is only one path that human beings could take and that is the path predestined for them. This is called *taqdir*, Divine Decree, and all Islamic theologians agree that nothing can occur or eventuate in the universe without *taqdir*.[38]

Al-Shahrastānī explains that the Jabrīyyah embraced absolute compulsionism because every event God creates and/or will create is already recorded in a Divine Register; for this reason, they argued, if it is already known and predestined, then humans cannot be free in their decisions or acts.[39] The Jabrīyyah School further strengthened its argument with the following verse: "…God sends astray whom He wills and guides

---

36   Qur'an 57:22.

37   Muslim, n.d. 33:6409.

38   TDV. (2020). Takdir. Islam Ansiklopedisi.

39   Al-Shahrastānī, M. (1975). *Al-Milal Wa'n Nihal*. Beirut: n.p

whom He wills…"[40] arguing that all causes originate from the cause of all causes; therefore, causation originates from God.

From a theological perspective, the Jabrīyyah argument has some valid premises. However, it fails to address some important issues of Islamic theology, such as moral obligation and answerability. Mainstream Islamic theologians, in contrast, argue for moral responsibility as the Qur'an also states: "So by your Lord, We will surely question them all; about what they used to do"[41] and "So whoever does an atom's weight of good will see it; And whoever does an atom's weight of evil will see it".[42] Moreover, the Qur'an empowers humans with verses like: "God does not burden any soul with more than it can bear: each gain whatever good it has done and suffers its bad".[43] According to al-Razī, al-Mahallī and al-Suyutī, this verse means no soul will be requited for the sins of another or rewarded for what they have not earned. The verse indicates human agents will be held accountable for their behaviour and face the consequences of their actions; accordingly, they need to be free agents as this scenario requires the reconciliation of Divine Decree and human will.

For this reason, mainstream theologians label the Mu'tazila and Jabrīyyah schools as two extremities. It is interesting that, fundamentally, the positions of these two schools seem to have distinctive similarities to the two contrasting views of modern philosophy: libertarianism and incompatibilism, where the former argues for total freedom in human actions and the latter for determinism or compulsionism. However, there is an evident distinction between the views of Western philosophers and Muslim theologians, as most philosophers do not invoke the supernatural into their arguments, whereas Islamic theology is based on the notion that God is the ultimate cause of all phenomena. Although there is consensus on this among all Islamic schools of theology, mainstream Islamic theologians reject the views of Mut'azila and Jabrīyyah as the former attributes creative abilities to human agents and the latter rejects freedom in action and discards moral accountability altogether. Interestingly, the polarised standpoint of the Mu'tazila and Jabrīyyah eventually led to the

---

40   Qur'an 14:4.

41   Qur'an 15:92-93.

42   Qur'an 99:7-8.

43   Qur'an 2:286.

systemisation of the mainstream Islamic theology as a discipline called *Usul al Dīn*, the methodology of religion that focuses on the principles of belief. The discipline includes extensive literature on predestination.

The establishment and systemization of mainstream Islamic theology

Mainstream Islamic theology was established as a systemised discipline with the formation of the Ash'ariyyah and Māturīdīyyah schools. As with many other theological problems, these two schools adopted a view that follows the middle path in the free will problem, arguing that while all events and acts are caused by God, human agents possess a nominal free will, meaning insignificant when compared to God's absolute will, but enough to make them morally responsible for their actions. For mainstream scholars, belief in Divine Destiny is an integral part of faith. They conclude that Divine Destiny is made up of two components, *qadar* and *qaḍa*. The followers of the Hanafī school of thought, particularly the Māturīdī theologians, agree that *qadar*, generally defined as destiny, is the infinite knowledge of God and *qaḍa* refers to the materialisation of this knowledge at the predetermined time. According to al-Māturīdī view, *qaḍa* is the creation of an event by God's will when it is time for it to occur.[44]

The Ash'arī scholars propose a similar premise but give diametrically opposite meanings to *qadar* and *qaḍa*; that is, the former refers to the materialisation of what is known, and the latter is knowledge of God. For the Māturīdīs, however, *qadar* is the prior knowledge of God about everything that has and will occur within the spectrum of eternity in the past and future, and this knowledge includes the specifics of all entities in existence, such as their shapes, qualities, measurements, time of materialisation and demise. For this reason, Māturīdī scholars agree on the notion that *qadar* originates from God's affirmative attributes of *irāda* (Divine Will) and *'ilm* (Divine Knowledge). They further argue, since *qadar* refers to bringing something into existence, then it

---

44   Al-Māturīdī, M. M., & Topaloğlu, B. (2005). *Kitâbu't-Tevhîd Tercümesi* [Translation of Kitāb al Tawḥīd]. Ankara: İSAM.

originates from God's affirmative attribute of *takwin*, which is the Divine ability to create.

While the Māturīdīs assert that Divine Destiny is real and human actions are created by God, they also assign moral responsibility to humans. Māturīdīs believe that human qualities, such as self-awareness, cognitive skills, being aware of events taking place in the external world, ability to solve problems, accumulate knowledge and plan, accordingly, are some of the essential elements that distinguish humans from the rest of creation.[45] These qualities give humans the ability of analysis, evaluation, judgment, and decision-making. So, for the Māturīdīs, having an ability to make decisions means one has the freedom to act in a certain way. This indicates the existence of will and moral responsibility.

For the Māturīdīs, since the Qur'an and hadith frequently caution people about the consequences of their actions, it is evident that humans were given some form of will and freedom of action. The Arabic term for free will is *irāda*, which comes from the root word *warada*, a verb meaning 'to want' or 'to desire'[46] and, according to Māturīdīs, absolute will belongs to God and is a necessary, affirmative attribute of God. Māturīdīs believe, since God commands humans to acknowledge and worship Him, it is evident that acknowledging and worshipping Him can only be realised through the usage of intellect and free will. For this reason, al-Māturīdī concluded that an act is an occurrence, something that originates or, in the case of humans, a behaviour.[47]

Al-Māturīdī further argued that human agents do not possess a metaphorical ability to act but a real capability to act. This means they are the owners of their acts as they are the doers. However, to avoid the presumption that the Māturīdī view is the same as the Muʿtazila based on the verse: "Allah is the creator of all things"[48], renowned Māturīdī scholar, Abu al-Yusr al-Pazdawī clarified the concept by defining the term act or action as a 'thing' and argued that it is 'something' that God

---

45   Ozakpınar, Y. (2002). *İnsan Düşüncesinin Boyutları* [Dimension of human thought]. Istanbul: Ötüken Yay.

46   Ibn Manzur. (1968). *Lisanü'l-Arab* [Language of the Arab]. Beirut: Daru Sadr.

47   Al-Māturīdī, E. M. (2005). *Te'vilatu'l - Kur'an* [Interpretation of the Qur'an]. Istanbul: Mizan Yayınevi.

48   Qur'an, 6:102.

creates.[49] He implies that, although the ability to act is given to human agents, God, in an actual sense, brings the act into existence.

Nur al-Dīn al-Sabunī, another prominent Māturīdī scholar, argued that an 'act' or 'action' is the materialisation of something that has probable or contingent existence.[50] Here, al-Sabunī points out that all acts are contingent; therefore, they necessitate origination. By using the term 'contingent,' he is indicating they are only possibilities and everything that has possible existence must depend on a necessarily existent Being. Since mainstream theology asserts that creating or originating belongs only to a Being whose existence is a necessity, human acts are created by God.

At the same time, Māturīdīs also believe humans, through the concept of *kasb* (acquisition), play a significant role in the causation of their acts; therefore, they are considered the doers of their acts. By the term 'act,' al-Māturīdī is referring to acts performed through free will. The reason why al-Māturīdī pointed this out is that he believes acts are of two kinds:

- Acts performed without the involvement of free will.
- Acts performed through free will.[51]

For al-Māturīdī, acts performed without the involvement of free will are things like blood circulation, hair growth, heartbeat, shivering and so on. This means human agents have no control over these acts. On the other hand, acts performed through free will are defined as acts that necessitate reward or punishment, as they are acts that humans perform freely and are not compelled to do so. Since these types of acts are acquired with intent and commonly performed with purpose, human agents become morally accountable for their consequences. It is evident within mainstream Islamic theology the Māturīdī methodology exhibits a slight inclination towards the Muʿtazila perspective with the signifi-

---

49   Pezdevi, Y. (1989). *Ehl-i Sünnet Akaidi* [Creed of *ahl al Sunnah*] (Ş. Gölcük, Trans.). Istanbul: Kayıhan Publishing.

50   Şabuni, A. M., & Topaloğlu, B. (1979). *Māturīdiyye akaidi: Al-Bidāyah fī uşūl al-dīn* [The creed of Maturīdī] pg. 136. Ankara: Diyanet İşleri Başkanlığı.

51   Al-Māturīdī, E. M. (2005). *Te'vilatü'l - Kur'an* [Interpretation of the Qur'an]. Pg. 229. Istanbul: Mizan Yayınevi.

cant difference that maintains the theological principle: 'humans are not the originators of their acts.'

Māturīdīs also repudiate the claims made by the Jabriyyah by arguing, since humans possess intellect, the capability to distinguish between right and wrong, and an ability to make a choice between them; these competencies make them morally responsible agents and indicate that free will is not an illusion. For the Māturīdīs, this is indisputable as the Qur'an frequently mentions liabilities and prohibitions directed at humans. Being the addressee of such responsibilities and prohibitions requires the existence of free action. Due to this responsibility, the Qur'an categorises humans as believers, disbelievers, polytheists, hypocrites, transgressors, and sinners. According to al-Māturīdī, there would be no point in this categorisation unless humans were given the freedom to choose between good and evil.[52] Al-Māturīdī establishes a balance between the creation of acts by God and the performance of acts by humans with the argument: "human acts belong to God in the first degree and to humans in the second degree".[53] This means, while God is the originator of the act, the human agent is the causer and doer of the act.

Ash'arītes, the other major school of the mainstream Islamic theology, also takes the intermediary position between the compulsionist and rationalist schools. They argue that acquisition and creation of an act are different things that require some form of power. Like the Māturīdīs, the Ash'arītes also believe, while human agents acquire the acts, God originates them. Therefore, by intending and inclining towards a certain act, human agents become the acquirers (*muktasib*), and by originating the act, God becomes the creator (*khaliq*). This means the power possessed by human agents is acquired and the power possessed by God is absolute; therefore, God's power is not contingent. Accordingly, the Ash'arītes believe acquisition entails a power to perform an action and this power is created in humans by God through their petition to do an act.[54] So, for the Ash'arītes, human free will is not enough to cause an action to transpire; however, it plays a role in the process of materialisation of the

---

52   Ibid.

53   Ibid.

54   Sharif, M. M. (1963). *A history of Muslim philosophy: With short accounts of other disciplines and the modern renaissance in Muslim lands.* Wiesbaden: Harrassowitz.

act, where through power, will and causality, God creates the occurrence of the action.

In comparison to the Māturīdī view, the Ash'arī perspective seems to display a slight proclivity towards the Jabriyyah. For this reason, the Ash'arītes introduced the notion of *kasb*, human acquisition, as *kasb* allocates some form of moral responsibility to humans. Many scholars believe there is a semantic difference between the Ash'arī and Māturīdī positions on the quintessence of free will. While both schools attempt to resolve the opposing views of the Jabriyya and Mu'tazila by proposing the scenario of acquisition, which accommodates the coexistence of Divine Destiny and moral responsibility, it is also important to note the freedom given to human agents by the Ash'arītes is more limited than that of the Māturīdīs as the Ash'arī theology does not examine the essence of free will in detail.

Ash'arītes' deliberate avoidance of a detailed analysis of free will can be based on the reason that they have focused chiefly on responding to the claims of the Mu'tazila, who concluded that human actions are not predetermined. As mentioned earlier, one of the primary reasons for the Mu'tazila's rejection of determinism was to absolve God of creation of evil. They argue that evil originates from human will and materialises through human actions. To substantiate the Mu'tazila argument, Mu'ammar al-Sulamī claims that matter, made up of *darrah* (atoms), was created by God but *aradth* (accidents) originate from the motions of matter. This is interesting as modern studies in the field of quantum physics indicate indeterminism at subatomic levels, a study that will be briefly examined in the upcoming chapters.

Al-Sulamī, parallel to the view of indeterminism at atomic levels, assigns the responsibility of creating accidents to human agents whose actions have a real effect on physical substances.[55] For the Mu'tazilites, this gives humans a potential power to act. This is like inertia, a law of physics that states matter will continue in its existent state of rest or uniform motion until an external force changes this state. Therefore, the Mu'tazila argument infers that human agents possess this required force

---

55   De Cillis, M. (2014). *Free will and predestination in Islamic thought: Theoretical compromises in the works of Avicenna, Ghāzālī and Ibn 'Arabī*. Abingdon, Oxon: Routledge.

to change the state of matter. Ash'arītes, on the other hand, reject the Mu'tazila perspective that is believed to be influenced by the Aristotelian view, which argues that matter is dominated by a causal process where atoms that make up matter are infinite in numbers. The Ash'arītes challenge this with a counterargument, claiming that matter is perishable; therefore, the ultimate creator of matter and its smallest components is God. This, in turn, makes God, not only the creator of matter, but also the 'mover' and originator of all events, which include human actions.

The Mu'tazila, on the other hand, was still concerned with the notion 'God creates human acts,' by arguing the concept would render God as the doer of the malevolent acts committed by human agents.[56] Consequently, it seems like the main theological dispute between the Mu'tazilites and *Ahl al Sunnah wa'l Jamāʿah* arose from the concept of theodicy. The Mu'tazila believed that creating human actions would also mean predetermining them, which would compel human agents to perform the acts that include evil. According to this argument, since human agents play no role in decision-making and the creation of the act, God would be considered the creator of evil. Mu'tazilites believe this is not possible for God; therefore, the only other plausible alternative is that humans create their own actions.

Abu Hanīfa repudiated the Mu'tazila claim of humans originating their actions by arguing that "all actions of servants [humans] pertaining to their motion and stillness are in reality their acquisition, while Allah Most High is their Creator".[57] For Abu Hanīfa, although acts of disobedience and evil are also created by God, they are neither commanded nor approved by Him. According to Maghnīsāwī, several factors are involved in the materialisation of human acts:

Kasb (acquisition) – Humans acquire the action.

Maksub (acquired) – In accordance with the principles of causality, this acquisition connects them to their will and power to act.

Makhluq (created) – Divine Will and Power creates the action as a result of the connection between human will and Divine Will.[58]

---

56 Işık, K. (1967). *Mutezile'nin doğuşu ve kelâmî görüşleri* [The birth of Mu'tazila and its theological views]. Ankara: Ankara Üniversitesi Basımevi.

57 Imam Azam, E. H. (1982). *Fıqh al Akbar*.

58 Maghnīsāwī, A. M. (2014). *Imam Abu Hanīfa's al-Fiqh al-akbar explained* (A-R.

Al-Qarī also comments on Abu Hanīfa's views by arguing "the difference between acquisition (*kasb*) and creation (*khalq*) is that in acquisition, the acquirer (*kasīb*) is not totally independent, while in creation (*khalq*), the creator is totally independent".[59] Like al-Māturīdī, al-Qarī clarifies this by arguing that human will and acquisition play no part in the materialisation of involuntary human acts, such as shivers, spasms or convulsions, while they play a significant role in the eventuation of voluntary acts. This makes humans morally accountable.

This theological position of the mainstream schools during what is known as the formative period in Islamic history became a guideline for the majority of their successors. Although the views of the two major schools in mainstream theology are analogous, there are some slight variations in their theoretical frameworks. These slight differences in the views of Ash'arītes and Māturīdīs are considered semantic variants by many. Perhaps formation of these schools, which led to the systemisation of mainstream theology, will shed some light on the emergence of these semantic variations.

Mainstream school: The school of Ashariyyah

Mainstream theological schools were formed primarily in response to the rationalist school of Mu'tazila during the formative period. Abu al-Hasan al-Ash'arī is the founder of one of the two mainstream Islamic schools of theology. Initially he studied under 'Ali al-Jubba'ī, who was a celebrated Mu'tazila scholar. According to a report, al-Ash'arī left al-Jubba'ī's circle following a theological debate on free action.[60] Al-Ash'arī asked al-Jubba'ī a hypothetical question about the fate of three brothers where one died as a believer, the other as a disbeliever and the third as a child. Al-Jubba'ī indicated the first would enter paradise and the second will end up in hellfire. For al-Jubba'ī, God had taken the third brother as

---

ibn Y. Mangera, Trans.). (2. ed.). London: White Thread Press

59   Ibid. pg. 122.

60   Al-Ash'arī, A. I., & McCarthy, R. J. (1953). *The theology of al-Ash'ari: The Arabic texts of al-Ash'ari's Kitāb al-Luma and Risalat Istihsan al-khawd fi'ilm al-kalam, with briefly annotated translations, and appendices containing material pertinent to the study of al-Ash'arī.* Beirut: Imprimerie Catholique.

a child, so he does not grow up to become a disbeliever and consequently face eternal punishment. Al-Ash'arī then asked why God had not taken the second brother as a child to protect him from punishment in hell as well. Al-Jubbā'ī failed to respond to the question with a logical argument. The debate resulted in al-Ash'arī leaving the circle of al-Jubbā'ī.[61] Ash'arī's withdrawal eventually led to the formation of the theological school of Ash'ariyyah.

It can be argued the school of Ash'ariyyah was formed in reaction to the school of Mu'tazila. The Mu'tazilites argued that good and evil are objective values that can be determined by human intellect and God is All-Just; therefore, His justice compels Him to act in accordance with moral values. Ash'arītes, on the other hand, held the position that God's justice is a matter for belief; therefore, human agents cannot distinguish between good and evil using their reason alone (in the absence of revelation).[62] The Ash'arī view became quite popular, mainly in the Arab world, as the majority of Muslims were discontented with the Mu'tazila position. Consequently, the Ash'arī views were considered mainstream theology by many scholars. Accordingly, their views on Divine Destiny and free will also became a benchmark mainly in the Arab world and neighbouring provinces.

For the Ash'arītes, free will and predestination are based on conditional coexistence where predestination (the will of God) has a real existence and human free will a nominal one, meaning it has an intangible existence. Ash'arītes argue that humans have nominal or theoretical control over their inclinations; thus, free will is limited to an inclination or preference made from the many possibilities presented by God. The Ash'arītes believe a perfect, efficient cause would annul free will; thus, human free will can only have a nominal or relative existence, which would not require a perfect cause.

According to Ash'arītes, absolute will belongs to God and hence every event in the universe occurs through this Divine Will and this includes human acts as well. This means human agents act through a provisional power created by God and this is enough for them to be accountable for their actions. For the Ash'arītes, if human agents had the

---

61   Ibid.

62   Robinson, N. (1998). *Ash'arī and Mu'tazila*. Muslim Philosophy.

ability to create their own actions, they would also possess the power to design the flawlessness of their results as well. However, it is evident that not all human acts yield perfect results. This means they do not possess the power to create the projected results. Therefore, the school of Ash'ariyyah believes God creates the act and the result or, in other terms, the cause and effect. They reach this conclusion through the notion that nothing is obligatory on God; thus, He creates what He wills.[63]

Accordingly, the materialisation of all human actions is also contingent on God's will. This means humans are not the originators of events, which includes the cause and effect. Ash'arītes assert that human acts depend on the existence of an intangible free will, which petitions the Divine Will for the creation of the requested action. Consequently, they conclude, in order to have moral responsibility, humans need to have some form of free will, even if it is some kind of nominal inclinations. This means, although human will is insignificant in its quintessence, it possesses the capability to make a choice from the possible paths presented to it.

In a broad sense, the proposed arguments indicate that the Ash'ariyyah perspective tends to lean towards Divine determinism in human acts, with the exception that it allows the existence of a theoretical free will. Perhaps this ostensive inclination is due to their strong opposition to the Mu'tazila perspective, which persuaded the Ash'ariyyah scholars to formulate inflexible arguments to refute the claim that humans are the originators of their own actions. Essentially, the Ash'arītes construct their theological approach on the creedal principle of God's omnipotence as they consider God to be the creator of good and evil acts. For this reason, Ash'arītes argue that God does not need a reason to create an act or entity, nor does He have any obligation towards humans or anyone for that matter.

Despite their slightly deterministic approach, the Ash'arītes have also incorporated moral accountability in their philosophical equation by proposing the concept of acquisition (*kasb*), which refers to a power to acquire an act that is created by God. Al-Ash'arī defines this power

---

63   Abdulhamid, I. (1995). Ebü'l-Hasen Alî b. İsmâîl b. Ebî Bişr İshâk b. Salim el-Eş'arî el-Basrî. In Abdulhamid I. (Ed.) *Islam Ansiklopedisi* (v. 11, p. 445). Ankara: Turkiye Diyanet Vakfi.

as *istita'a*, an ability created by God through the commandment '*kun*' – 'be' – at the instant of the action and vanishes after completion of the action.[64] This view is derived from the verse, "…When He decrees a matter, He only says to it: 'Be' and it is".[65] Al-Qushayrī asserts that when God decides on an affair, nothing can oppose or be exempt from it.[66] Accordingly, for the Ash'arītes, humans' power to act is created by God through the command "be."

Therefore, the Ash'arītes believe humans are liable for their acts by means of acquiring the act, *kasb*, through a power, *istita'a*, which is created by God, at the moment of the act. Consequently, even though the human is the agent who causes the act, the act of creating the cause and effect belongs to God. Accordingly, for the Ash'arītes, an act that is predestined and created by God does not nullify moral responsibility.

Ash'arītes further argue the entire process of predestination consists of two theological components: preordainment and the creation of what is already known. This view attributes all creative powers to God; in other words, everything comes into existence through the Will and Power of God and ceases to exist through His command. Ash'arītes believe *qaḍa* (preordainment) refers to the 'blueprint' of all phenomena in existence and *qadar* (execution) refers to the creation of all properties, events and acts that were already predetermined by God.

The Ash'arītes base their intransigent position on the following verse: "God created you and what you do".[67] Moreover, al-Ash'arī argued "that no evil or good on earth exists without the will of God. All beings [all phenomena] come into existence through His will".[68] For this reason, most Ash'arī scholars refrain from discussing human free will in detail. Perhaps this is the reason as to why some scholars deduced they

---

64   Ibn Furak, & Gimarat, D. (1987). *Mujarrad maqālāt al-Shaykh Abī al-Ḥasan al-Ash'arī: Min imlā' al-Shaykh al-Imām Abī Bakr Muḥammad ibn al-Ḥasan ibn Fūrak* (t. 406/1015). Beirut: n.p.

65   Qur'an, 2:117.

66   Qushayri, A. (2015). *Laṭā'if al-Isharat bi-Tafsīr al-Qur'ān*. Beirut: Dār al-Kutub al-'Ilmīyah.

67   Qur'an, 37:96.

68   Al-Ash'ari, A. I., & Ritter, H. (1929). *Kitāb maqālāt al-Islāmiyyīn wa-iktilāf al-muṣallīn*. pg. 289. Istanbul: Maṭbaʿat al-dawla

are more aligned with the incompatibilist views of the Jabrīyyah than the libertarianist views of the Muʿtazila.

Mainstream school: The school of Māturīdiyyah

The theological school of Māturīdiyyah has been named after Abu Mansur Al-Māturīdī. Although the school is not well known in the West due to its Samarkand, Uzbekistan origins, which is outside the Arab world, and to the fact some of its literature is difficult to understand, it is one of the two major schools of theology in mainstream Islam. It has strong ties with the Hanafi school of Islamic jurisprudence as adherents of this school follow al-Māturīdī in matters of ʿaqaīd (creed). Māturīdī theology repudiates the Muʿtazila and Jabriyya views and holds that free will and predestination coexist and that the existence of one does not invalidate the other.

One profound difference from the school of Ashʿariyyah is, Māturīdīs argue that human free will is based on inclinations. Since inclinations are abstract, which means they do not have real or substantial existence, their origin can be attributed to humans. This implies that human free will is so inconsequential that it only has a theoretical existence; thus, its inclinations do not need to be 'created.' For the Māturīdīs, free will is an extraordinary quality given to humans by God so they can be morally responsible for their actions. For this reason, some scholars believe the difference between Ash'ari and Māturīdī perspectives is in minute details yet the distinction in reference to the nature of free will is significant because, unlike the Ash'arites, Māturīdīs did not refrain from talking about the human free will in detail, presenting it as a God-given ability to make free choices.

The school of Māturīdiyyah has apportioned more freedom to human will, arguing that free will can logically coexist with the will and preordainment of God. Al-Māturīdī acknowledges the significance of human free will with a condition that it is an abstract entity, meaning it does not possess any creative powers.[69] Therefore, unlike the Muʿta-

---

69   Al-Māturīdī, M. M., & Topaloğlu, B. (2005). *Kitâbu't-Tevhîd tercümesi* [Translation of Kitāb al Tawḥīd]. Ankara: İSAM, Türkiye Diyanet Vakfı İslam Araştırmaları Merkezi

zilites who claim human agents originate their acts, al-Māturīdī argues that humans do not possess the ability to create physical actions. According to al-Māturīdī, embracing the Mu'tazila argument would mean "not all things are created by God".[70] For this reason, just like the Ash'arītes, Māturīdīs repudiate the Mu'tazila claim by asserting that God creates human acts based on a petition from free will.

Technically, the Māturīdī School precedes the Ash'arī school as al-Ash'arī was still a member of the Mu'tazila School when al-Māturīdī commenced his teachings in accordance with the mainstream Islamic theology. Following the formation of both schools, while the adherents of the Shafī and Malikī schools of Islamic jurisprudence followed the Ash'ariyyah creed ('aqīda), the Hanafites adopted the views of the school of Māturīdīyyah. Although Abu Hanīfa did not address the topic of free will in an all-inclusive way, he established certain creedal principles for Hanafi theologians to follow. Given this, a brief analysis of Abu Hanīfa's perspective will be beneficial in understanding the Māturīdī view.

As cited by Maghnīsawī, Abu Hanīfa explains that God knew in pre-eternity all things prior to their being, and hence apportioned and ordained them all.[71] According to Abu Hanīfa there can be no alteration in the knowledge of God; hence, all that would occur in the future already pre-existed in God's knowledge. Abu Hanīfa further argues that God has pre-recorded in the *lahw al mahfūz*, the Preserved Tablet, all things tangible or abstract.[72] Therefore, Abu Hanīfa also repudiates the Jabrīyyah's claim of absolute determinism with the exposition: what is written in the Preserved Tablet is not written without description or an antecedent cause. This is important as the Māturīdīyyah theology is based on this philosophical premise. It means predestination or Divine Destiny includes cause and effect. So, for example, the Preserved Tablet does not record someone's destiny as "[such and such person] will be a disbeliever" in a commandment or mandated fashion; rather, it is registered as "[such and such person] will choose to become a disbeliev-

---

70   Al-Māturīdī, M. M., Topaloğlu, B., & Aruçi, M. (2003). *Kitāb al-Tawḥīd* [Book of unity] pg. 207. Ankara: Waqf Diyānat Turkiyā, Markaz al-Buḥuīh al-Islāmīyah

71   Maghnīsawī, A. M. (2007). *Imam Abu Hanīfa's al-Fiqh al-akbar explained* pg. 106. (A-R. ibn Y. Mangera, Trans.). London: White Thread Press

72   Imam Azam, E. H. (1982). *Fiqh al Akbar.*

er".[73] The argument specifies the effect is mentioned with the antecedent cause, which includes the individual's decision made freely; therefore, the Hanafī understanding of predestination is not based on compulsionism or absolute determinism, but on prior knowledge of God. This argument is significant as, while the Muʿtazilites base their arguments on causes alone and the Jabriyah on effects, the Hanafites took both the cause and effect into account.

Abu Hanīfa also expounded on the concept of *istitaʾa* by describing it as a "God-given power that enables human actions".[74] This implies an ability to act entails accountability. According to Hanafis, God creates this power and ability so human agents can acquire their actions as free agents. The combination of acquisition and creation enables the coexistence of God's absolute Will and human will.

Abu Hanīfa's brief but concerted definition of free will and predestination includes refutations to the Muʿtazila and Jabrīyyah schools through acknowledgement of the coexistence of preordainment and moral responsibility, although he refrains from deep theological discussions on the issue. Abu Hanīfa's sensitivity towards the issue is based on the creedal principle: "Ordaining, decreeing and willing are His [God's] attributes in pre-eternity without description".[75] On this basis, he refrains from further analysis.

On the other hand, as the Muʿtazila teachings became the dominant theology during the Abbasid era in the 8th century, mainstream scholars felt duty-bound to respond to their arguments through more detailed analytical examinations. Al-Māturīdī produced several works refuting the Muʿtazila claim; one of the main areas of focus in his theological repudiation of the Muʿtazila view was the topic of predestination and free will.

---

73   Maghnīsāwī, A. M. (2007). *Imam Abu Hanīfa's al-Fiqh al-akbar explained* pg. 108. (A-R. ibn Y. Mangera, Trans.). London: White Thread Press.

74   Abū Hanafi, & Oʿz, M. (1981). *İmâm-ı Âʾzamın beş eseri: El-Âlim veʾl-müteʾallim, el-fıkh el-ebsât, el-fıkh el-ekber, Risâletü Ebî Hanîfe, el-Vasiyye* [The five books of Imam Azam] pg. 75. Istanbul: Kalem Yayıncılık.

75   Maghnīsāwī, A. M. (2007). *Imam Abu Hanīfa's al-Fiqh al-akbar explained* pg. 108. (A-R. ibn Y. Mangera, Trans.). London: White Thread Press.

In the Islamic tradition of theological methodology, the school of Muʿtazila is known as the school of "justice," the Ashʿarītes is "will and power" and the Māturīdītes as the school of "wisdom". For this reason, the Māturīdiyyah perspective appears to be the "centre of mass" between rationalism and traditionalism as many scholars believe al-Māturīdī has formulated a theology based on a synthesis of rationalism and traditionalism. This is the reason that Māturīdīs believe God acts with wisdom in all acts, and in the context of the creation of humans Divine Wisdom requires them to be responsible agents for assessment purposes.

Responsibility necessitates freedom to act, and for this reason, al-Māturīdī argued that acquisition (*kasb*) through 'minor will' (*juzʾ-ī irāda*) belongs to human agents while the causation of the act belongs to God.[76] Accordingly, the human act is not coercive, it is voluntary; therefore, although God brings the act into existence, He is not considered to be the doer.

According to al-Māturīdī, ordaining, fashioning and shaping are creative acts beyond human capability. Such acts require creative powers; therefore, human agents receive this power through acquisition (*kasb*) at the instant of the act. Al-Māturīdī further argued that an agent without power or ability to act cannot be held accountable because it would be irrational to hold someone responsible for an act they are incapable of doing.[77] This view finds substantial support from the verse, "God does not charge a soul except [with that within] its capacity.[78] Ibn Kathir explains this verse as "God does not ask a soul what is beyond its ability"[79], meaning an agent will be held accountable only for actions he/she is capable of doing.

For this reason, Māturīdīs believe in defining free will as a minor cause (inclination) for the materialisation of human actions. However, just like the Ashʿarītes, they stress that God causes all actions intended by

---

76   Al-Māturīdī, M. M., & Topaloğlu, B. (2005). *Kitâbüʾt-Tevhîd tercümesi* [Translation of Kitāb al Tawḥīd]. Ankara: İSAM, Türkiye Diyanet Vakfı İslam Araştırmaları Merkezi

77   Ibid.

78   Qurʾan, 2:286.

79   Ibn Kathir, I. U. (2000). *Tafsir ibn Kathir* [Exgesis of Ibn Kathir] (abridged) pg. 49. Riyadh: Darussalam.

human agents to materialise. Therefore, according to Māturīdīs, human liability originates from the ability of acquisition (*kasb*). For Māturīdīs, this requires an inner struggle, which either results in making a negative or positive decision. This indicates an ability to make decisions and act freely. Māturīdīs believe, since humans have the potential to be educated and rehabilitated, they can make important decisions to change their ways and act upon them. Furthermore, significant changes can occur through strong will and this is the reason that humans are subjected to a test in their earthly lives. For this reason, Māturīdīs divided human acts into two categories:

- Acts realised through free will, which indicates acts that are intended, decided, and then executed through a God-given ability to act.

- Acts realised in the absence of free will, which indicates involuntary actions such as the automated functions of human organs.

For the Māturīdītes the former requires precondition, which is to do with an objective of achieving a specific result. This indicates the existence of free will, which denotes an ability to act freely. According to Māturīdīs, if a person is doing something without any comprehension or understanding of the purpose of the act, this would mean an external agent has a role in their actions. Since humans are agents that possess cognitive skills and an ability to choose between right and wrong, good, and evil, using their intellect and judgment, they must have free will.

For this reason, al-Māturīdī asserts that, through experience, every human feels free to act on their decisions. Consequently, he defines free will as an incorporeal quality given to humans by God. For the Māturīdītes, there is no conflict between human free will and God's creation of acts, as the act is initiated by a metaphysical entity (human free will), which has an intangible existence brought into existence by Divine Will and Decree.[80] Al-Māturīdī's view also challenges the view that human actions are regulated by causal determinism or antecedent events, for al-Māturīdī identifies God as the ultimate cause of causality. So, although the Māturīdītes acknowledge the necessity of causality, they assert that God is *musabbib al asbab*, the cause of all causes.

---

80   Al-Māturīdī, M. M., & Topaloğlu, B. (2005). *Kitâbu't-Tevhîd tercümesi* [Translation of Kitāb al Tawḥīd]. Ankara: İSAM, Türkiye Diyanet Vakfı İslam Araştırmaları Merkezi

Al-Māturīdī's views on predestination, free will and many other concepts of theology were gradually systemised into a discipline with the formation of the school of Māturīdīyyah. Historical data suggests the segregation of theological schools, which began in the first period of the formative era, concluded with the establishment of the two major schools of mainstream Islamic theology, which evidently marked the end of the formative era.

The classical period (944–1800)

The classical period of Islamic theology begins with the death of al-Māturīdī. This period sees the intensification of theological discourse on epistemology, evidence for the existence of God, attributes of God and the origin of causality regarding human actions. Predestination and free action are profoundly debated in this period where philosophical debates and logic are introduced into the discipline of *kalam*. According to scholars, all matters of theology and religion were discussed in this period and the views of al-Ashari and al-Māturīdī were further developed by their successors.

The arguments on destiny and free will also intensified with the standpoint of the school of Ash'ariyyah being further explicated during the classical period in the comprehensive works of al-Ghazali, one of its most renowned scholars. Al-Ghazali focuses primarily on causality and the origin of events and acts. According to al-Ghazali, the fundamental principle of the Ash'ariyyah view on causality is that all phenomena originate through Divine Omnipotence, including human actions.[81]

Al-Ghazali expounds this view by arguing that causes are inert properties, which cannot produce effects on their own; therefore, the will and power of God is the only cause that creates all effects in the universe, which includes human acts. Al-Ghazali's argument on the nature of causality is based on the concept that what is believed to be a necessary connection between 'cause and effect' is in fact not necessary; al-Ghazali asserts the connection is based on the prior power of God to

---

81   Al-Ghazali, M. (1993). *Tahafut al-Falasifa* [The incoherence of the philosophers] (J. Jihami, Ed.). Beirut: Dar Fikr al-Lubnani.

create cause and effect in sequential order.[82] This means, according to al-Ghazalī the connection is not necessary, as the cause and effect need to be created by the power of God. Consequently, al-Ghazalī does not reject causality altogether but maintains that natural laws are subject to the will and creation of God; therefore, they will be necessary for as long as God wills them to be. For this reason, the Ash'arītes believe that even free will and human inclination to perform an action ultimately originate from the will of God.

Regarding human will and inclination, al-Ghazalī believed that their origins cannot be attributed to humans either, simply because they also have a tangible and substantial existence. Therefore, for the school of Ash'ariyyah, God also creates human inclinations in connection to a petition from free will. As mentioned previously, the Ash'ariyyah view seems to display a propensity towards compulsionism since al-Ghazalī argues that "the cause-and-effect relation between events are not mandatory"[83] and cause and effect occur due to God's will; however, he also confers on the petition from human free will, acknowledging the role played by human will however insignificant it may be. Consequently, for the Ash'arītes, this petition, which entails acquisition for the creation of an act, is enough to hold humans responsible for their actions. However, the argument also incorporates the concept that the request for the creation of a specific human act and the final product pre-exists in God's infinite knowledge even before the individual acquires it. Therefore, the decision made by a human agent to perform an act was already predestined regardless of the many options ostensibly available to them.

Al-Ghazalī believes that *kasb*, meaning acquisition of an action, is not the same as the act itself; hence, *istita'a*, the ability to acquire, does not mean power to act. Therefore, even the ability to acquire is created by God so human agents can be empowered to act. He further clarifies his position on the matter by stating: "God is the only One to invent human acts. He does not exclude them to be objects of human acqui-

---

82   Ibid.

83   Yavuz, Y. S. (1995). *Ebü'l-Hasan el-Eşarî (ö. 324/935-36) tarafından kurulan kelâm mektebi* [The school of theology established by Abu'l Hasan al-Ash'arī] pg. 450. In Islam Ansiklopedisi. Ankara: Turkiye Diyanet Vakfi

sition..."[84] There is a subtle nuance between the views of al-Ash'arī and al-Ghazalī as the latter appears to display somewhat more deterministic view than the former. However, al-Ghazalī does not neglect human free will altogether as he argues that God creates human acts through His omniscience and omnipotence which also encompass what humans will acquire in the future.

Al-Shahrastānī, another prominent Ash'arīte scholar, supports this view by arguing that God's knowledge does not alter; the knowledge He has prior to creating the existence is not different from the knowledge He has post-creation.[85] This means, since the knowledge of God is all-inclusive, He creates what He already knows. As a result, it can be said the Ash'arī argument is more analogous to compulsionism than libertarianism. From the mainstream theological perspective, the Ash'arī view authenticates the notion of predestination, which has entered the list of essential articles of the Islamic creed.

Abu Muin al-Nasafī, one of the most prominent scholars of the Māturīdīyyah School, on the other hand, argues that God creates human acts, but humans are responsible for acquiring them through their ability to choose. Just like al-Māturīdī, al-Nasafī maintains that human agents acquire their acts through their free will but play no part in their creation. So, moral responsibility for the Māturīdītes originates from an ability to act freely. Evidently, by creating the acts petitioned by the minor will (*juz'-i irāda*), God becomes their creator and, by acquiring and performing these acts, humans come to be called their doers.[86]

In principle, al-Nasafī's views on free will are closer to that of the Mu'tazila perspective with two major differences in opinion:

First, al-Nasafī rejects the Mu'tazila claim that humans are the originators of their own actions by emphasising God is the only agent who has the ability to bring all natural phenomena in the universe into existence – this includes human acts.

---

84   Al-Ghazalī, M. (2014). *Ihya' Ulumuddin* [The revival of the religious sciences]. Kuala Lumpur: Pustaka Al Shafa. p. 101

85   Al-Shahrastānī, M. (1975). *Al-Milal Wa'n Nihal*. Beirut: n.p.

86   Al-Nasafī, M. I.-M. (1993). *Tebsiratü'l edille fi usûli'd-dîn*. Ankara: Diyanet İşleri Başkanlığı Yayınları.

Second, he repudiates the Mu'tazila claim that the power to act is present in human agents prior to the act, by arguing the power to act is present only at the time of the act.[87]

This theological argument is important because, according to al-Nasafī, if the power of *istita'a*, ability to act, existed prior to an act, then humans would not need God for the creation of their actions, which means with such ability humans can create their own actions without dependency on God's power and will. Moreover, having the power to create would mean all human acts would be perfect in result, meaning they would all turn out just the way they were planned by the human mind. However, quite often, premeditated human acts do not produce the planned results. The Māturīdī theologians' view is that human agents may intend to do an act, but God may or may not permit this act to materialise in the intended or planned way.

Al-Nasafī's assiduousness on the topic originates from the consensus of *Ahl al Sunnah wa'l Jamā'ah* scholars who assert the act of bringing into existence cannot be consigned to anyone or anything other than God. For al-Nasafī, the views of the Mu'tazila and Jabrīyyah schools are opposite extremes that only coincide on the theological argument of 'an act cannot be controlled by two agents.' This implies this argument will result in a paradox where, for example, one agent may decide the subject to turn right and the other to the left. If the subject does not move at all, the power of both agents would be annulled. In a situation where the subject turns left, the power of the former is annulled; accordingly, turning right would nullify the power of the latter.

This means human acts are either created by human agents or God. The Mu'tazila and Jabrīyyah agree on the concept that two agents cannot have authority over the same act. For this reason, while the Mu'tazilites argue that human agents must originate and control their acts, the school of Jabrīyyah maintains that God originates and executes all human acts. With their polarised perspectives, while the former negates the existence of Divine Destiny in relation to human acts, the latter rejects the existence of free will. These two polarised theological positions have some similarities to the Western philosophical views of libertarianism and incompatibilism with the important distinction that modern philos-

---

87   Al-Nasafī, M. M. (1987). *Kitâbu't-Temhîd li-Kavâidi't-Tevhîd.* Cairo: n.p

ophy does not allow much room for Divine Determination. The Western perspective of libertarianism argues for absolute freedom in human acts, while incompatibilism uses classical mechanics to make a case for absolute determinism.

In contrast, al-Nasafī argues for coexistence by introducing the notion of 'inclination,' "the essence of the power of choice [*istita'a*], as a theoretical or relative matter that may be attributed to God's servants [human beings]".[88] Although the Ash'ariyyah view is analogous to this, they believe this power or ability of inclination has a form of existence in a corporeal sense. For the Ash'arītes, having a corporeal existence means it needs to be created. For this reason, they refrained from attributing it to human agents. Consequently, the methodological difference of opinion between the Ash'arites and Māturīdīs originates from the argument of whether the human ability of preference is a created entity.

According to al-Nasafī the answer to this question is no, because *juz'-i irāda*, the minor human will, is nominal, theoretical, or metaphysical; therefore, freedom of choice or action can be accredited to humans. For the Māturīdītes, God has blessed humans with the ability of inclination or preference; it is an innate quality of being human and they have a limited or restricted dominance over it. For this reason, al-Nasafī argued: "The acts performed by human beings belong to human beings in regard to *kasb*, acquisition, but belong to God in regard to their materialisation".[89] According to al-Nasafī, God originates human acts, and He is the one who creates the cause and final product as well. Since humans do not possess the power of creation, their share in their actions is nothing but an acquisition. Due to this ability of acquisition, Māturīdītes believe humans become accountable for their actions.

The Mu'tazilites, on the other hand, argue against the concept that God creates human actions by claiming, if He created them, then He would be responsible for them, as the argument suggests that God commits good and evil deeds; therefore, this would be incongruous.[90] Al-Nasafī repudiates this claim by arguing that verses such as: "Do whatever

---

88   Ibid. p. 482.

89   Ibid. pg. 223.

90   Ibid. pg. 128.

you will"[91] and "...do good"[92] clearly indicate that humans can acquire the act while God gives quantifiable existence to that act. So, while humans do not have the power to bring their actions into existence, they possess the ability to acquire them, so they are liable for their behaviours. So, for the mainstream scholars, the following verse also supports this claim: "So, whoever does an atom's weight of good will see it. And whoever does an atom's weight of evil will see it"[93].

Ali Ünal (2013) interprets the verse as:

> Whatever a person does is not unnoticed by God, and He records whatever people do. Both in this world and in the Hereafter, everyone will see and receive the consequences of their deeds [acts]. This is the basic principle of belief in God's justice and the Hereafter.[94]

This means that Divine justice requires that human agents are responsible for their own acts whether they are good or evil. Al-Nasafî further argues that it is not possible for God to command or prohibit an act in the absence of human free will. Therefore, while the school of Māturīdiyyah asserts that humans have free will and through this 'will' they have the ability to acquire an act, they also conclude that God preordains human acts, as the Qur'an states: "He creates you and what you do".[95] According to al-Nasafî, it would be impossible to prove God's unity or oneness in a theoretical scenario where the ability of creation is attributed to any agent other than God. Moreover, al-Nasafî puts a condition on the creation of an act by claiming, in order to create an act, an agent needs to have prior knowledge about the *minutiae* of the act. Therefore, for the Māturīdīs, if humans have the power to create an act, as argued by the Mu'tazilites, they would be equipped with the knowledge of bringing something into existence from a non-existent state, which includes knowledge of its quintessence, attributes, states and mo-

---

91   Qur'an, 41:40

92   Qur'an, 22:77

93   Qur'an, 99:7-8

94   Unal, A. (2013). *The Qur'ān with annotated interpretation in modern English.* pg. 1190.

95   Qur'an, 32:17

tions. For this reason, al-Nasafi claims, since humans have no knowledge of these essentials, they are not the originators of their own actions.

Fahkr al-Din al-Razī, one of the most renowned Ash'arī scholar also shares al-Nasafi's views on this concept. He believes that humans do not possess detailed knowledge about their own acts, so they cannot be the originators of those acts and this is evidence that God creates human acts. According to al-Razī's argument, God gives a body to an act petitioned through human free will in accordance with His customary laws in nature.

To cite an example, when humans use a language to speak, meaningful words flow out of their mouths due to two imperative biological phenomena: vocal cords produce audible pressure variations in the air, then the sound travels out of the mouth but transforms into meaningful words through the motion and shape of the tongue and mouth. Although all humans who have the ability of speech use this biological process, no one is aware of the exact motion and shape that the mouth and tongue take in producing different words, unless one is specialised in this field. From the mainstream perspective, this indicates human agents are not the designers of the process or result; however, they are the initiators and acquirers of the act. This necessitates the existence of free action. In this sense, the theological school of Māturīdīyyah acknowledges that human agents possess the freedom to act. However, this freedom is defined as a limited tendency or proclivity to perform an act.

Based on the views of prominent Muslim philosopher Ibn Rushd, known in the West as Averroes, Abdülgaffar Arslan believes that freedom in action is a problem that cannot be solved from ontological or epistemological perspectives.[96] According to Ibn Rushd the relation between destiny and free will is one of the most complex problems of theology and religious philosophy.[97] In his book, *Al-Kashf an Menahij al-Adillah*, which carries the meaning "Exposition of the Methods of Proof", Ibn Rushd lists some of the Qur'anic verses that appear to be paradoxical

---

96   Arslan, A. A. (1980). *İslam İnançları ve Felsefesi* [Islamic beliefs and philosophy]. Istanbul: Çağrı Yayınları.

97   Ibn Rushd, & Kasim, M. (1964). *Manajihu'l Adilla fi Aqaidi'l Milla* [The Exposition of the Methods of Proof Concerning the Beliefs of the Community]. Cairo: n.p.

from a philosophical perspective, and then attempts to solve the issue through 'aql (reason).[98] To cite some examples: "No disaster strikes upon earth or among yourselves except that it is in a register before we bring it into being – indeed that, for God, is easy"[99] indicates absolute determinism. On the other hand: "that is for what your hands have put forth and because God is not ever unjust to [His] servants"[100] suggests human agents are morally responsible for their acts. According to Ibn Rushd the first verse asserts that all phenomena in nature are preordained, yet, according to the second verse, although human acts are not necessary, they are probable and humans play a role in the procurement of their acts.[101]

Ibn Rushd then analyses the Muʿtazila position, which claims that God has no intervention in human acts and compares this to the Jabriyyah view, which argues that humans play no role in the causation of their acts. Ibn Rushd then points out that Ash'arites took a middle path between these two views by introducing the concept of *kasb*, acquisition, with an objective to solve the issue of cause and effect. Bearing in mind that inanimate objects do not possess this ability, he further argued, to solve the problem of ability to act, Ash'arites also introduce the concept of *istitaʾa*, power to act. On the other hand, al-Juwaynī, an Ash'arī successor, clarifies the concept by indicating that humans have this ability of acquisition and the power to perform a particular act only at the time of the action, not prior to or after the action.

For the Ash'arites, this argument was an attempt to establish a causal connection between the absolute will of God and the limited will of humans. While the argument concedes that all acts occur through the will of God, it also establishes that human agents are 'beings' that possess some form of will. For Ibn Rushd, on the other hand, the role that humans play in their actions is closely related to concepts like good and evil, right and wrong, lawful or unlawful, authentic or false, and so

---

98   Ibid.

99   Qur'an, 57:22

100   Qur'an, 3:182

101   Ibn Rushd, & Kasim, M. (1964). *Manajihu'l Adilla fi Aqaidi'l Milla* [The Exposition of the Methods of Proof Concerning the Beliefs of the Community]. Cairo: n.p.

on. He believes, if human agents play no role in the origination of their actions, there would be no difference between good and evil, right and wrong; therefore, humans would not need to make an effort to refrain from what is unlawful and seek what is lawful. According to Ibn Rushd, whether it is physiological, psychological, or experimental, everything in nature has a cause. This view suggests the connection between cause and effect should be acknowledged and accepted as natural phenomena. This will allow a settlement between the absolute will and power of God and human freedom in action.

It is evident that Ibn Rushd's approach to the problem is philosophical rather than theological. Ibn Rushd's arguments also indicate that he places a significant emphasis on causal determinism as he argues: "one cannot deny the significance of cause-effect relation in the process where the intellect reaches a level of understanding about how nature works".[102]

So, it can be said that Ibn Rushd's argument is an attempted repudiation of al-Ghazali's theology, which asserts the connection between cause and effect is unnecessary as both are created by God. Moreover, since human actions are delimited by physical laws, Ibn Rushd defines Divine Destination as boundaries and limitations established by God to causality and human involvement in the process of causality; therefore, *lawh al mahfūz*, the Preserved Tablet, which contains all future knowledge, should also be understood through this concept. This attempt to provide a philosophical reasoning to the coexistence of Divine Destiny and free will has some significant inconsistencies with the views of the majority of mainstream theologians as, according to the mainstream view, God's knowledge is all-encompassing and future events registered in *lawh al mahfūz* do not depend solely on causality.

The concept of divine register removes the possibility of causal determinism where the occurrence of events is determined solely by natural causes. This is supported with the verse: "all things [events] We have kept in a clear register".[103] This means an event that is already known and registered prior to its occurrence cannot be determined

---

102   Arslan, A. A. (1980). *İslam İnançları ve Felsefesi* [Islamic beliefs and philosophy] pg. 491. Istanbul: Çağrı Yayınları

103   Qur'an, 36:12.

by causality. Accordingly, Ibn Rushd's argument contradicts the mainstream view, which concludes that, since God has the attribute '*ilm*, knowledge, from which nothing can escape, all human acts have prior existence in Divine Knowledge; therefore, they were all recorded in what is known as the Preserved Tablet. According to the mainstream view, this repudiates the argument that Divine Destiny refers to causality or causal determinism.

In relation to causality, Muslim theologians also debate pedantically on the theological discourse, which focuses on the origin of acts and human responsibility as the consequences of these acts. They divide 'acts' into two categories; an act done through free will and the result it produces. For example, throwing a stone with the intention to break a window is considered an act acquired through free will, while the actual breaking of the window is an act that is produced as a result. Mu'tazilites argue that humans are the originators of the initial act realised through free will and the final result. Al-Nasafi, on the other hand, rejects this claim by arguing that human involvement in throwing the stone is limited to acquisition, while the act of throwing and the result – the actual breaking of the window – are created by God. However, the responsibility for the result or consequences of the act belong to the human agent as they intended to break the window and acquired this specific act.

It is evident the principal argument between the Mu'tazila and the mainstream Islamic theology focuses on whether human acts and their final products are created by God. Ash'arītes conclude that all stages of an act originate with God. They base their argument on three essential premises:

- God's creation of human ability of acquisition (*kasb*)
- God's creation of the power to act (*istita'a*)
- God's creation of human ability to perform the act (*iktīsab*).[104]

Ash'arītes define this process as a God-created power that manifests in human agents during the act. It is also referred to as 'the power to act' created by God but acquired by human agents. For the Ash'arītes, this definition allows human agents to possess freedom over their actions through the deployment of their free will. It can be argued the

---

104   Schwarz, M. (1972). *Acquisition (Kasb) in Early Kalam*, Islamic Philosophy and The Classical Tradition. Oxford: n.p.

Ash'arī view concludes that human will is governed by the absolute Will of God. Because of this, some define the Ash'arī view as a modified and improved version of the Jabrīyyah view. The Māturīdītes, on the other hand, approach the issue of free will from the human experience perspective as they argue humans believe and submit to God using their free will and intellect. Māturīdīs argue that human agents can change their behaviour through education and training, which indicates that free will plays an important role in their actions. Therefore, a righteous act performed through free will occurs through the agent's wish and desire to do good and this sometimes may require a human agent to go against their impulses.

A comparative study of the arguments put forward by classical scholars like al-Nasafī and al-Bāqillānī indicates agreement between the Māturīdī and Ash'arī schools in reference to the God-given power or ability to act at the time of the action This view finds support in the Qur'an as some verses mention this God-given power: "Indeed, we have given him a power on earth and showed him the ways"[105] and "He said, that in which my Lord has established me is better but assist me with power [your strength] ..."[106] Therefore, mainstream *kalam* scholars argue it is evident an ability to act is given to humans during an act; however, the theological conundrum of 'an act cannot have two originators' has to be solved as well. In an attempt to solve this problem, al-Bāqillānī argues that human acts originate through the effect of two powers.[107] While Divine Power originates the quiddity of the act, human agents produce the quality of the act. This formula asserts that, since the effect on the created act originates from human will and power, human agents become answerable for the consequences of the act, whether it is good or evil.[108]

Al-Bāqillānī constructs his argument on the Ash'arī view where God creates in human agents, *istita'a*, to act at the time of acquisition. Based on these arguments, it can be said the mainstream Islamic the-

---

105   Qur'an, 18:84.

106   Qur'an, 18:95.

107   Bāqillānī, M. I.-T., & MacCarthy, R. J. (1957). *Kitāb at-tamhīd* [The book of prefix]. Beyrouth: Librairie orientale.

108   Ibid.

ology clearly argues for the coexistence of Divine Destiny and free will. Accordingly, they strongly oppose the unconditional libertarianism of the Muʿtazila and the absolute compulsionism of the Jabrīyyah. In light of the evidence at hand, it can be argued the main difference in the views of the mainstream scholars and Mu'tazilties is the human power to act: while the Muʿtazila claim that human agents possess this power at all times, mainstream scholars argue it is a power given to humans at the time of the acquisition of the act. The disagreement with the school of Jabrīyyah, on the other hand, originates from moral responsibility, where mainstream scholars argue that human agents cannot be held responsible in a compulsionistic scenario where free will is utterly negated.

Al-Sabunī, another prominent scholar of the classical period, further elaborates on the concept of origination of acts, arguing that human acts have contingent existence; therefore, they are only possibilities.[109] This indicates that they require origination, which means, although human agents possess *istita'a*, a power to act, this power is contingent; therefore, it needs to be provided by an agent whose existence is necessary – namely, God.[110] Here, al-Sabunī establishes a theological principle upon which all mainstream scholars agree by arguing, since all phenomena and events in the universe, including human acts, are contingent in relation to God, human agents cannot be the originators of their acts. This view is supported by another renowned scholar of the classical period, al-Sharif al-Jurjānī, who argues that *qaḍa* (materialisation of destiny) is the will of God having an effect on matter at specific times and for specific reasons.[111] Therefore, al-Jurjānī also agrees with al-Sabunī on the concept that contingent events require a necessary agent for their formation.

Historical data from the classical period indicates the mainstream scholars of the era have also focused on responding to the Muʿtazila and Jabrīyyah claims by following a middle path to establish that Divine Destiny can coexist with free will. As can be seen from the evidence above,

---

109 Şabuni, A. M., & Topaloğlu, B. (1979). *Mātūrīdiyye akaidi: Al-Bidāyah fī uṣūl al-dīn* [The creed of Maturīdī] p. 136. Ankara: Diyanet İşleri Başkanlığı

110 Ibid.

111 Al-Jurjānī, A. M., & Abū A. M. A. (2017). *al-Taʿrīfāt* [Definitions of Islamic terminologies]. Location: Publisher.

customarily, unlike most scholars of philosophy, all *kalam* scholars construct their arguments on the foundations of revelation, tradition, and reason. Predominantly, mainstream theologians, such as al-Ghazalī, al-Nasafī, al-Shahrīstanī, al-Bāqillānī, al-Razī, al-Sabunī and al-Jurjānī have interpreted *naql* (transmission or tradition) through *'aql* (intellect or reasoning) in their methodologies of building a theological argument. These scholars have resorted to using the power of reasoning to interpret the revelation where the meaning of the scripture is ambiguous or unclear. Further, these theologians are authorities in their disciplines, who have conducted meticulous studies of the text and tradition. They are considered scholars from the camp of *ahl al ray*, 'people of reason', who adopted the 'reason-based-on-revelation' approach to interpret sacred text and tradition where the meaning of the verses or prophetic tradition were allegorical. The application of the methodology of the people of reason continues in the modern period as it has found significant support from contemporary mainstream scholars.

The modern period (1800–current)

Although there are different views on when the modern period in Islamic theology begins, several scholars have the opinion that the modern period begins with Abdul Aziz al-Dehlawī. Al-Dehlawī has written over fifty books on various matters of Islam. He is regarded as a hadith scholar and an exegete. Although al-Dehlawī is considered to be the first scholar of the modern period, he does not have much literature on theological matters. In this book we will focus on four key figures from the modern period, Muhammad Abduh, Muhammad Iqbal, Said Nursi and Fethullah Gülen.

Muhammad Abduh

Abduh, a scholar renowned for his reformist views, is regarded as a main figure of Islamic modernism and reviver of Mu'tazilism although his stance on predestination is more aligned with the mainstream perspective.[112] In his work, Abduh addresses the topic of Divine Destiny and free will by arguing that Divine Destiny consists of all events in na-

---

112   Al-Rahim, A. H. (2006). Islam and Liberty. Journal of Democracy, 17(1), 166-169

ture, with their doers, conditions and causes, and God's knowledge of all these. Therefore, according to Abduh, God's knowledge of future events is specific, not what can possibly occur.[113] Abduh further argued that human will entail acts that are brought into existence by God when their causes necessitate their occurrence. So, for Abduh, unlike the common Muʿtazila view, free will is not negated by Divine knowledge. He believes, while predestination is a general rule that governs human behaviour in relation to their cultures, tradition and customs, there is no *jabr*, compulsion, that impacts the freedom of individual human agents.[114] He comes to this conclusion through analysis of sixty-four verses from the Qur'an, which indicates *irāda*, free will, and *kasb*, acquisition. Although Abduh's views resemble the general understanding of mainstream scholars, his emphasis on human freedom seems to be more than that of any mainstream scholar before him as he unreservedly asserts that determinism would negate human responsibility altogether, yet humans are morally responsible beings; therefore, they possess motive and tendency to do good or evil. This means that motivation enables human agents to do whatever they will.

It can be argued that Abduh's perspective inclines towards the Muʿtazila view as he claims that although the supporters of compulsionism use the verse: "He creates you and what you do [with your own hands]"[115] as evidence for determinism, they neglect the part "what you do with your own hands". So, for Abduh, this power to act was given to humans by God and it is a power that God can remove if He wills. The relevance in Abduh's view is the argument seems to indicate this given power is always present, which evidently parallels the Muʿtazila view.

Like the scholars of the formative period, Abduh does not favour theological discussions on predestination. He addresses the topic of *kasb*, acquisition of human acts, in a way analogous to libertarianism, arguing that in all situations human acts are realised through their will and acquisition. He argues that God's prior knowledge of human acts

---

113   Abduh, M., & Imārah, M. (1972). *Al-Aʿmāl al-kāmilah* [the perfect deed]. Beirut: n.p

114   Abduh, M., Masaʾad, I., & Cragg, K. (2004). *The theology of unity: Risālat al-tauḥīd.* London: Allen and Unwin

115   Qur'an, 37:96

does not form a barrier to human will or acquisition.[116] Abduh's views on human freedom to act is much broader than that of the classical Ash'arī view on acquisition. Although many regard him as the reviver of Mu'tazilism, his views on free will seem to incline towards the Māturīdiyyah understanding.

Muhammad Iqbal

Another important scholar of the modern period is Iqbal. Iqbal argues, while the Ash'arītes focus on defending Islamic beliefs the Mu'tazilites reduce religion to logical concepts.[117] Conversely, Iqbal focuses on freedom in action and, with some resemblance to Abduh's view, he also argues for absolute freedom in action and responsibility, claiming: "the future exists as an open possibility, not as a fixed order of events..."[118] Interestingly, Iqbal also concludes there could be no doubt about God's foreknowledge of future events, but this foreknowledge does not negate human free will. For Iqbal, Divine knowledge regarding the future is not same as predestination; it exists in God's mind as an open possibility. This suggests that Divine knowledge includes human actions as possibilities but not with specific details of the acts that have not been performed yet. Such argument puts limitations to Divine knowledge and has some parallels to the Mu'tazilites and libertarians; therefore, the argument would be rejected by most mainstream scholars. In saying that, there are claims that Iqbal was influenced by Western libertarian philosophy in his younger days when he travelled to England and Germany for higher education where he eventually completed his doctorate in philosophy.

Conversely, it would be a great injustice to limit Iqbal's views to two statements. Eight years before his death he published a book titled *Reconstruction of Religious Thought*, a volume in which he addresses the topic of Divine knowledge in detail. In this book, Iqbal argues that Divine knowledge cannot be justified through the concept of passive omni-

---

116   Abduh, M. (1986). *Tevhid Risalesi: Risaletü't – tevhid* [The book of divine unity]. Ankara: Fecr Yayınları

117   Iqbal, S. M. (1971). *The reconstruction of religious thought in Islam*. Lahore: Sh. Muhammad Ashraf

118   Ibid. p. 79.

science as this would limit God's freedom.[119] So, for Iqbal, claiming that God knows everything that exists would imply that existence is independent of God and He only has knowledge of it. This argument implies that knowledge of finite and temporal things limits God's knowledge as it assumes what is known has independent existence. According to Iqbal, God's knowledge is all-inclusive regarding possibilities and is not limited to what exists in space-time continuum.

Iqbal believes that Divine knowledge about the past, present and future of the universe is also passive omniscience as this argument would limit God's act of creation to space-time continuum. Iqbal's solution to this is: the future exists as an open possibility, not as predetermined order of events with fixed results.[120] It can be argued that Iqbal proposes this argument with the intention of establishing that the creativity of God is ongoing, not limited to a model that presumes the space-time continuum is an order of events that have already been created. However, this argument negates God's foreknowledge of specifics and renders it equivalent to knowledge contingent to conditions of causality; therefore, it does not involve preordainment.[121] For this reason, Maruf contends that the Iqbal argument rejects God's knowledge of the future with an objective to preserve God's freedom in action and originality in creation.[122]

I would argue that from a mainstream perspective there is a theological problem with Iqbal's argument about Divine knowledge as it portrays God as an agent who 'waits' for future events to unfold because His knowledge of future events is limited to possibilities. This argument assigns contingency to God by claiming that He is bound by the space-time continuum. This view also contradicts several prophetic narrations that assert, on the night of *miraj*, ascension, Prophet Muhammad (pbuh) was shown the inhabitants of Paradise and Hell, which clearly refers to events that would eventuate in the future. The narrations about Prophet Muhammad's ascension indicate that he was taken out of the space-time

---

119   Iqbal, S. M. (1971). *The reconstruction of religious thought in Islam*. Lahore: Sh. Muhammad Ashraf

120   Maruf, M. (2003). *Iqbal's philosophy of religion: A study in the cognitive value of religious experience*. Lahore: Iqbal Academy Pakistan.

121   Ibid.

122   Ibid.

continuum to a point between contingent and necessary existence. This gave him a brief opportunity to glimpse into the past, present and future. For this reason, mainstream scholars have consensus on the view that 'God is not bound by space-time.' Accordingly, human freedom to choose from the paths available to them does not negate the concept that God has specific knowledge about the future.

Said Nursi

One of the most prominent theologians of the modern period, Said Nursi, offers an interesting argument on using reason in explaining the problem of free will:

Of necessity everyone perceives in himself a will and choice; he knows it through his conscience. To know the nature of beings is one thing; to know they exist is something different. There are many things which although their existence is self-evident, we do not know their true nature... The power of choice may be included among these. Everything is not restricted to what we know; our not knowing them does not prove the things we do not know do not exist.[123]

Here, Nursi implies the existence of free will is self-evident, but also stipulates its true essence is not known to man. Nursi supports the al-Ash'arī and al-Māturīdī views on free will by arguing that humans cannot be the originators of their actions for, if this was to be true, it would totally annul their free will. He elaborates on this by arguing that confirmed rules of philosophy state: "If a thing is not necessary, it may not come into existence [of itself]." That is, "there has to be a cause for a thing to come into existence. The cause necessarily requires the effect. Then no power of choice would remain".[124] The argument here is that if an act can be explained through causality where a perfect cause has resulted in the effect (act), then there would be no need for free will.

This argument also challenges al-Ghazalī's argument, which maintains that the connection between cause and effect is not necessary. The Nursi argument asserts that "there has to be a real complete creative

123   Nursi, S. (1993). *The Words* (V. Şükran, Trans.). p. 480. Istanbul, Turkey: Sözler Publications.

124   Ibid. p. 482.

cause before something can exist, but a complete cause makes existence of something compulsory so there will be no room for choice".[125] So, according to Nursi, actions are the final products of a preference between alternatives presented to human free will; hence, human involvement in free action has a nominal role. Nursi responds to the question: "if God creates man's actions, then why is it that a man who commits murder is called a murderer when it was God who created the action?" – with the following statement:

According to Arabic grammar, the active participle functioning as the subject is derived from the infinitive, which denotes a relative affair or deed, not from another word derived from the infinitive which expresses an established act. Therefore, since it is man himself who does the deed denoted by the infinitive, he is the murderer. That is, man wills to do something and accordingly does it, so he is the doer or the agent of his acts… God creates man's acts and gives external existence to them; He does not perform those acts.[126]

For Nursi, the agent who wills and performs the act is responsible for the act, not the one who creates it. So, according to Nursi, liability lies with the agent who acquires the action rather than the one who creates it. Nursi's argument can be elucidated with an analogy where an individual jumps off a cliff and breaks their leg. It would be irrational for this person to blame gravity for their misfortune although the injury could not have occurred in the absence of gravity. According to mainstream Islamic theology, God creates the series of events during the jump and the force of gravity; however, the decision to jump originates from the individual's free will; therefore, they are to blame.

Although Nursi offers a profound look into the concepts of preordainment, Divine will, creation and free will, which may be analogous to Abu Hanifa's perspective, he also argues that predestination and free will point to the magnitude of one's belief and submission, so they are not concepts indicated by science or philosophy. Consequently, Nursi's perspective stipulates that science cannot formulate or test the principles of predestination or free will through empirical data. This means they are not concepts that can be quantified through experimentation. This

---

125   Nursi, S. (1997). *The Words*. p. 137. Izmir, Turkey: Kaynak Publishing.

126   Ibid. p. 138.

being said, Nursi attempts to formulate a theological argument to explicate the Islamic understanding of destiny and free will with an approach that aims to incorporate the 'justice' theme of the Muʿtazila, the 'will' and 'power' theme of the Ashʿariyyah and the 'wisdom' theme of the Māturīdīyah. His argument consists of an assertion that humans have free will, so they do not deny responsibility for their evil inclinations, and Divine Destiny exists so they do not ascribe good deeds to themselves.

Nursi's formula coerces human agents to moral responsibility while accrediting God for the origination of their actions. According to Nursi, evil in human acts resides in the human agent's free will and potential, not in the creation of the act. In a philosophical way, this also provides a solution to the Muʿtazila's concern about theodicy, which led them to argue that human agents are the generators of their actions. Nursi explains this with the following argument: Divine Will and predestination are free from evil and immorality in relation to the end result, and due to the element of causality, they are also exempt from injustice. He elaborates this with the argument: "Divine Destiny [predestination] always takes into consideration the primary cause, not the apparent secondary cause and [thus] always does justice".[127] So, unlike the Jabrīyyah that condemns humans to punishment although they had no choice in their actions, Nursi ascribes responsibility to human agents for being the primary causes of their actions.

It can be argued that Nursi's view on predestination and free will, although he is an Ashaʿrī scholar, seems to display propensity towards the 'wisdom' theme of the Māturīdītes as he argues that human justice is based on an apparent cause, but Divine Determination is based on real justice, which prevails through Divine wisdom. He makes his point with a hypothetical scenario where a court sentences a man to imprisonment for a crime he did not commit. Divine Destiny allows the sentence to be carried out because the man had committed a similar crime before but was not apprehended for it. So, for Nursi: "God is absolutely just in all His acts…"[128] According to Nursi's argument, God cannot be accused of injustice for creating evil, which evidently is acquired by human free will. Ultimately, Nursi's proposal is based on the consensus of mainstream

---

127   Ibid. p. 133.

128   Ibid.

classical Islamic scholars who believe the coexistence of predestination and free will is viable.

Nursi's methodology of reconciliation of predestination and free will is based on the creedal code that Divine knowledge entirely encompasses natural phenomena, including human acts. Therefore, while everything is predetermined and registered by God, which is also stipulated by the Jabriyyah school, humans are responsible for their actions, being the primary cause through their free will and acquisition, as argued by the Māturīdītes and Ash'arītes. Regarding events that occur beyond human will, Nursi refers to Divine justice, which acts through wisdom. Nursi argues that these are beyond human control and cautions people about questioning Divine Destiny as one cannot change the past. He concludes that "one who criticizes Divine Destiny, hits his head on a stone, while his skull may break, what was written will not change".[129]

Nursi believes one of the main reasons why Mu'tazilites and the Jabriyyah were deceived by the paradox of coexistence of predestination and free will is that they analysed cause and effect separately, whereas, according to Nursi, the two concepts are inseparable. This means in *lawh al mahfūz*, the Preserved Tablet, future events are recorded as a particular event destined to occur because such and such a cause will produce such a particular effect.

This argument finds strong support from the Qur'an where a verse refers to a group of polytheists who blamed predestination for their disbelief. The verse states: "those who associated [idols] with God, will say, 'If God had willed, we would not have associated [anything] and neither would our fathers, nor would we have prohibited anything'..."[130] This claim also resembles the views of the compulsionists who argue that humans play no role in their decisions or actions. For this reason, Nursi clarifies the concept of destiny by arguing what is written is based on cause and effect. This means, according to Nursi's argument, if a man throws a stone and breaks a window, it shall be written in the Preserved Tablet in a descriptive fashion, for example, 'such and such man will wilfully throw a stone and break the window,' not in a commanding or enforcing fashion as 'the window will be broken by such and such man.'

---

129   Nursi, S. (1988). *Mesnevi-i Nuriye*. p. 28. Istanbul: Sözler Yayınevi.

130   Qur'an, 6:148.

This suggests the cause and effect are recorded together in the Divine Registry.

However, although the human agent's act of breaking the window was already recorded in Divine Destiny long before they were created, they are still held accountable for being the primary cause of the act. Nursi's argument concludes that the actual act of casting the stone (cause) and breaking the window (effect) are created by God while the acquisition of the act is requested by the human agent. This view repudiates the Mu'tazila view, which argues that the window would not have been broken had the person not thrown the stone, and the Jabrīyyah view that would argue the window would have been broken even if the person had not thrown the stone. Nursi's view in this scenario is that destiny includes cause and effect; however, the consequences are unknown to humans until the actual event occurs.

So, for Nursi, although human free will is too inefficient to cause an effect, God made it a simple condition for His Divine Will to come into effect. For this reason, human free will acquires a specific act that is then created by God, but the effect is unknown to man until it takes place. Consequently, Nursi's answer to the question: "will the window break or not if the man does not throw the stone?" – would be: "we do not know the consequences of an act until the effect takes place".[131]

Nursi further argues: "He [God] guides man in whatever direction man wishes, by the use of his free will so that he remains responsible for the consequences of his choice".[132] Evidently, this methodology of reconciliation proposes the existence of predestination does not nullify the existence of freedom in action. As was affirmed by Māturīdīyyah, Ash'ariyyah and Jabrīyyah, Nursi also confirms that belief in predestination is an essential article of the Islamic creed and supports his view with the verse: "And no grain is there within the darkness of the earth and no moist or dry [thing] but that it is [written] in a clear record [Preserved Tablet]."[133]

For Nursi, Divine Destiny consists of two essential components: first is the Divine Knowledge that encompasses all phenomena past,

---

131   Ibid.

132   Ibid. 138.

133   Qur'an, 6:59.

present and future, and second is the Divine Will defined as: "the creational and operational laws of the universe."[134] Nursi also addresses the problem of evil by arguing that "predestination includes both causality and Divine Destiny."[135] In general, human agents assess incidents from the perspective of apparent causality and this sometimes results in misinterpretations. Divine Destiny, on the other hand, is just, meaning the result always serves justice. Nursi further asserts that Divine Knowledge and Divine Will indicate the Preserved Tablet in which all acts and events are pre-recorded. Nursi's in-depth analysis of the topic constitutes a combined perspective constructed on the views of Ashʿariyyah and Māturīdiyyah that acknowledges the coexistence of predestination and free will, thus offering a comprehensive understanding of the mainstream view on the topic.

A brief study of contemporary views indicates that the majority of modern scholars base their arguments on similar concepts; however, they do not delve into deep philosophical arguments, but use simple analogies to convince their audience. Zakir Naik, for example, responds to the question – where is the human free will when the Qur'an states that "not even a leaf falls without the will of God?" – by arguing that one cannot blame the power stations that supply electricity if a person puts their finger into the socket and gets a shock. With this analogy, he implies the power supply of all events and acts originates from God, but the decision to use it for good or evil is given to human beings. It can be argued, just like the classical scholars, the common view of contemporary mainstream scholars is that Divine Destiny is a type of knowledge that does not nullify free will.

In conclusion, it can be argued the problem of free will and predestination has been addressed by Islamic theologians throughout history, resulting in the formation of several schools of theology with some remaining within mainstream scholarship while others segregating from it by offering contrasting views to the mainstream understanding of the Islamic creed. Although several theological perspectives were formulated by the mainstream Islamic theologians, some aspects of the main concepts remain unclear as even mainstream theologians have not reached

---

134   Nursi, S. (1994). *The letters*. p. 140. London: Truestar.

135   Nursi, S. (2009). *Kastamonu lâhikası* [Kastomonu notes]. p. 169. Istanbul: Sözler.

consensus on some philosophical details of the concept that free will and predestination coexist.

Concisely, mainstream Islamic theologians agree on the notion that humans do not possess the power of creation; therefore, they are not the generators of their actions. Conversely, they also repudiate the concepts of absolute determinism or compulsionism as they contradict the creedal teachings of Islam, which confirm moral responsibility and assert that humans possess some form of limited minor will. This confirms the notion that mainstream Islamic theologians agree on the model that proposes the coexistence of predestination and free will. It is evident that there are some significant dissimilarities in the views of Muslim theologians who lived in different periods of Islamic history; however, there is a consensus among the majority that Divine Destiny and free will can theologically be reconciled.

In addition to examination of the historical development of the discourse in Islamic history, a brief study of philosophical arguments provided by Western scholars will offer further support to this comparative analysis.

CHAPTER THREE

A COMPARATIVE EXAMINATION OF WESTERN LITERATURE ON PREDESTINATION AND FREE WILL

T he main objective of this chapter is to briefly analyse Western literature on libertarianism, compatibilism and incompatibilism with an aim to compare the similarities and differences with Islamic theological perspectives. This is important for comparative analysis as some of the theological arguments of the school of Mu'tazila have been influenced by Western philosophy, specifically Aristotelian philosophy. The problem of free will was also addressed by Augustine of Hippo, who lived almost two centuries before the emergence of Islam. Kamal believes that Islamic theology may have also been influenced by his views.[1] Munk and Joel also claim that the views of the Mu'tazila and Ash'ariyyah are founded on premises put forward by Greek philosophers and Syrians who challenged their arguments.[2]

There are also valid grounds for philosophical and theological examination of the similarities and differences between the Western schools of libertarianism, compatibilism, incompatibilism and Islamic schools of Mu'tazila, Jabrīyyah and *Ahl al Sunnah wa'l Jamāah*.

It is evident that just as in Islamic theology the concepts of free will and determinism have been problematic subjects in Western philosophy and theology since antiquity. The philosophical discourse on the problem of free will was present throughout the Hellenistic era and continued into the early Christian period, pre-modern and modern periods. It remains one of the most enigmatic topics of contemporary philosophy and theology. Although several theories and philosophical arguments have been developed throughout Western history the topic remains to be one of the most perplexing problems of philosophy today. The apparent philosophical inconsistency regarding the coexistence of a deterministic universe and free will have caused a polarisation among philosophers of the West, in a similar way to the formation of different theological schools in the early periods of Islamic history.

The polarised views on this topic are an indication that philosophers and theologians have not concurred on a common philosophical solution. Evidently, Western philosophers, just like Islamic theologians of the formative period, have divided into three major camps that con-

---

1   Kamal, M. (2003). *Mu'tazilah: the rise of Islamic rationalism*. Australian Rationalist, 62 (Autumn), 27-34.

2   Munk, S. & Joel, I. (1930). *Daldldt al-Hd'irin*. Jerusalem, ed. 1. p. 71

sist of "predeterminism," "absolute freedom" and "possible coexistence of free will and determinism."

To support the arguments above, we will focus predominantly on these three major views – libertarianism, compatibilism and incompatibilism in Western philosophy – arguing that, while they have some significant similarities with the positions of the Islamic theological schools of Muʿtazila, Jabrīyyah and *Ahl al Sunnah waʾl Jamāʾah*, there are important distinctions in the quintessential premises. Finally, we will argue that the key distinction between the philosophical views of Western scholars and Islamic theologians is that concepts proposed by all Islamic theologians are based on God-centric arguments while the Western philosophical perspective, particularly in contemporary times, has drifted towards theories based on determinism and/or indeterminism in classical mechanics and quantum physics with the inclusion of some philosophical references to the existence of free will.

This brief analysis of the development of theological and philosophical concepts on determinism and free will in the Western context will be constructive in inaugurating Gülen's contribution to addressing the problem of free will and determinism. It is also important to establish whether Gülen was inspired by Western philosophy in any way. One of the objectives of this brief analysis is grounded in the supposition that it will contribute to the methodology of establishing the innovativeness of Gülen's argument and its contribution to modern philosophy and Islamic theology.

Development of Western philosophical discourse on free will

Historical literature on the development of philosophy in the West indicates that arguments about the concepts of free will and determinism are not limited to modern philosophers.[3] So, what is the origin of the problem of free will and determinism, and how did it develop into one of the most intricate problems of philosophy and theology in the West?

---

3   Russell, R. P. (Trans.). (2004). *The Fathers of the Church: St Augustine the teacher, the free choice of the will, grace and free will*. Washington, D.C: Catholic University of America Press.

The philosophical arguments about free will and determinism go back more than two thousand years. According to Frede and Long, the concept of free will is inherited from antiquity.[4] Historical records suggest, although Aristotle may have commenced discussions about the possible existence of indeterminism, it seems that Epicurus was the first Greek philosopher who formulated the positions of determinism and indeterminism by arguing that "some things happen out of necessity, others by chance and others by our own agents."[5] Perhaps the arguments put forward by Epicurus laid the foundations of modern libertarianism, which proposes that humans are morally responsible for their actions. In a nutshell, by claiming that some things occur through their own agents, Epicurus argues for the existence of free will. Interestingly, arguments put forward by the school of Muʿtazila may have traces of the theoretical framework proposed by Epicurus as some scholars believe they were influenced by Hellenistic philosophy to some extent; however, establishing this requires further research.

On the other hand, Zeno of Citium, who was the founder of Stoicism, claimed every event has a cause and that cause necessitates the event. Zeno of Citium believed, given identical circumstances, the same result will occur. According to this view, natural laws control everything, which includes the human mind. Fundamentally, Zeno of Citium's view on absolute determinism corresponds to arguments put forward by the school of Jabrīyyah with an important distinction that the former attributes determinism to natural causes and the latter to a supreme agent. Chrysippus, who also belonged to the school of Stoicism, was the first philosopher to attempt to reconcile responsibility and determinism, which could be considered the foundations of the modern compatibilist view. Chrysippus challenged the idea that logical truths necessitate physical events.[6] He claimed: "An event is only necessitated if the physical cause for that event exists in the present."[7]

---

4   Frede, M., & Long, A. A. (2011). *A free will: Origins of the notion in ancient thought.* Berkeley: University of California Press.

5   Epictetus. (1990). *Letter.* Raleigh, N.C: Alex Catalogue.

6   Sharples, R. W. (Trans.) (1983). *Alexander of Aphrodisias on fate: Text, translation, and commentary.* London: Duckworth.

7   Information Philosopher, n.d., para. 11.

The statement also argues indirectly for the existence of free will; hence the notion of moral responsibility had entered Greek philosophy. Alexander of Aphrodisias expanded the argument in favour of moral responsibility and what is defined as libertarianism today by claiming certain events in nature do not have a predetermined cause. He argues that human agents are responsible for self-caused decisions and rejects the Stoic view that argued for foreknowledge. Epicurus was thinking along the same lines when he argued that necessity abolishes moral responsibility and chances are unpredictable, whereas human actions are autonomous and this is what we praise and blame.[8]

It seems, following the introduction of the concept of moral responsibility into Stoicism, other schools of Greek philosophy began to embrace it and developed their own theories about human freedom to act. It is believed Plato is the first Western philosopher to talk about free will. Plato argued that human agents are free to form systems based on faith, which creates the causes necessary for affirming the will.[9] He believed that causes originate from human decisions; therefore, free will exists. According to Plato, humans possess the ability to change their decisions based on their beliefs and this clearly indicates free will. Waxman argues that "Plato utilizes the phrase 'law of destiny' to describe the 'right' outcome that infers predestination or fate."[10] This concept indicates that destiny is a righteous or pious path that indicates universal good. For Plato, the law of destiny is connected to metaphysics as he believes that changes in decisions originate from the human soul, which forms the causes that result in the eventuation of acts in the material world.[11]

Although Plato's arguments seem to have an element of the compatibilist view, the notion of free will is limited to a spiritual decision between good and evil. However, he may have been the first philoso-

---

8   Epicurus. (2004). *Letter to Menoeceus* (R. D. Hicks, Trans.). Adelaide: The University of Adelaide Library. 133.

9   Waxman, R. (2016). *Five philosophers on free will: Plato, Leibnitz, Hobbes, Hume, and Hegel.*

10   Ibid. para. 4.

11   Hamilton, E., & Huntington, C. (1999). *The collected dialogues of Plato.* Princeton, NJ: Princeton University Press.

pher of antiquity to formulate a concept that allows free will and predestination to coexist. It can be said that Greek philosophers laid the
foundations of Western philosophy on the free will debate. According
to Frede and Long, various versions of Greek philosophy were adopted
by mainstream Christian theology.[12] The development of various arguments in the West was later constructed on the views of some prominent
Christian scholars.

Christian theology on determinism and free will

For Christian scholars, one of the earliest arguments about free
will and determinism comes from Saint Augustine. Augustine's view on
free will has its roots in theodicy as he felt the need to address the problem of evil from a theological perspective. As one of the pivotal teachers
of Christian theology, Augustine approached the problem of evil from a
Neo-Platonist perspective by claiming evil is lack of goodness and cannot be attributed to God as it originates from human free will.[13] To work
around this complex problem, Augustine argues that evil is rooted in the
absence of good; therefore, it is connected to human free will, while he
also believed that God is the only source of salvation.

There are some important parallels in the views of Augustine and
mainstream Islamic theologians, as they also argue that God does not
will evil on His creation and whatever evil befalls humans is from themselves, however, unlike Augustine, mainstream Muslim scholars conclude that good and evil are created by God. The difference in the views
seems to be semantic because, just as Augustine who states that evil is
"the result of a wrong act of the will by a rational creature...",[14] mainstream Muslim scholars also affirmed that God does not will evil. The
only difference in the two positions is that mainstream Muslim scholars

12   Hamilton, E., & Huntington, C. (1999). *The collected dialogues of Plato.* Princeton,
      NJ: Princeton University Press.

13   Russell, R. P. (Trans.). (2004). T*he Fathers of the Church: St Augustine the teacher,
      the free choice of the will, grace and free will.* Washington, D.C: Catholic University
      of America Press.

14   Fitzgerald, A., & In Cavadini, J. C. (2009). *Augustine through the ages: An encyclo-
      pedia.* 342

indicate that although God does not will evil, He creates it upon a request by the human free will. Interestingly, Augustine also argues for some form of determinism at a later stage in his teachings and received some criticism from his opponents. Historical evidence suggests that in the last years of his life, Augustine argued that free will and predestination worked well together.

This is significant as it suggests Augustine was trying to construct a formula that would allow a medium where free will and predestination could coexist. Frede and Long believe that Augustine's view is prevalently Stoic but has its roots in a Platonist perception.[15] However, Frede and Long also conclude that Augustine's argument for free will is profoundly different from any argument found in Greek philosophy. This conclusion is important because it instantiates the historical period when the debate about determinism and free will was officially introduced into Christian theology. Augustine's contribution to the argument is significant as his philosophy laid the foundations for other Christian theologians who proposed their own views on the concept of free will and determinism.

Inspired by Augustine's theological arguments, Thomas Aquinas claimed that man is free yet there is also Divine necessity that God is omniscient.[16] Aquinas' argument also supports the coexistence of the two concepts without clarification of how omniscience does not nullify free will. He further argued that God acts through the laws of reason. This argument is partially embraced by mainstream Islamic theology as it claims God acts through wisdom but cannot be constrained by it. Shanab points out that Aquinas was influenced by the famous Islamic theologian al-Ghazalī, particularly on the topic of causation as his views on God being the originator of causation are similar to those of al-Ghazalī.[17] As mentioned previously, al-Ghazalī's perspective on causation is that all

---

15   Frede, M., & Long, A. A. (2011). *A free will: Origins of the notion in ancient thought.* Berkeley: University of California Press.

16   Daly, J. J. (1958). *The metaphysical foundations of free will as a transcendental aspect of the act of existence in the philosophy of St. Thomas Aquinas.* Washington: Catholic University of America Press.

17   Shanab, R. E. A. (1974). Ghazalī and Aquinas on causation. *The Monist*, 58(1), 140-150.

phenomena originate from God's will; therefore, causation alone is not the originator of events and acts. In fact, al-Ghazalī goes to the extent that the link between cause and effect is not necessary. This view, however, does not support absolute determinism as God being the originator of all causation does not nullify human free will altogether. In relation to human acts, God's will is manifested on a simple condition of human preference. Accordingly, Aquinas also argues for free will with the condition that God's omniscience is not neglected. Although Aquinas includes the necessity of God's omniscience in the equation, he does not propose a philosophical solution explaining how the two concepts coexist.

Duns Scotus, on the other hand, disagrees with Aquinas on the concept of reason by claiming God's actions cannot be constrained by reason.[18] To some degree this claim is also compatible with mainstream Islamic theology for its theologians argue, although God acts through wisdom, He is not constrained by any laws or reason because all laws and reason are created by God; hence, God cannot be a slave to the laws He created. Consequently, the arguments proposed by Aquinas and Scotus are somewhat pertinent to the views of mainstream Islamic theologians.

Jewish theology on determinism and freewill

Discourse on the problem of destiny and free will is also evident in Jewish theology, although Rabbinic literature does not provide a comprehensive philosophical methodology of reconciliation other than the well-known comments of Rabbi Akiva who argued that "everything is foreseen [by God], yet man has the capacity to choose freely".[19] Just like Aquinas and several Muslim philosophers, Akiva believes that the two concepts coexist without providing an argument that is philosophically verifiable. Analysing Akiva's perspective, Rudman indicates the necessity of reconciliation as he points out the theological incongruity of absolute determinism by arguing, "a deterministic philosophy would imply that God Himself is ultimately responsible for the performance not only of

---

18   Duns, S. J., & Vos, A. (2003). *Duns Scotus on divine love: Texts and commentary on goodness and freedom, God and humans*. Aldershot, England: Ashgate.

19   Pirkei Avot 3:19.

the good actions of human beings but also the bad."[20] Rudman also concedes the presence of determinism in the Jewish and Christian Bibles poses philosophical problems for theologians of both faith traditions. For Rudman: "if human action and thought is controlled by a force external to the individual, then no law, whether it be man-made or Divine, can ever be just."[21] This necessitates the existence of free will, simply because the scriptures of Judaism, Christianity and Islam also point out that humans are morally responsible agents. Consequently, the need for a philosophical argument that reconciles the two concepts is not limited to philosophy alone, but is also applicable for theologians of three Abrahamic faith traditions.

Free will debate during the Renaissance and Enlightenment centuries of Western philosophy

Descartes, one of the most renowned figures of the Renaissance, describes human freedom as actions that are not predetermined even by Divine knowledge.[22] In his solution to the mind and body problem, Descartes divides the world into two: the metaphysical world of thoughts and the physical quantifiable world. According to Descartes, the physical world is deterministic but human thoughts are free.[23] He claims the superlative "perfection of man is that he acts freely" or willingly "and it is this which makes him deserve commendation or accountability."[24]

In some respect, Descartes' view on the quintessence of free will resembles the Māturīdīyah view mentioned by Nursi in *The Words*, where he explains that free will is a non-physical, non-quantifiable entity, and it can thus be attributed to humans. Dutch philosopher Baruch Spinoza, on the other hand, challenges this argument by deducing that there is no room for divine or human will in a world where everything

---

20   Rudman, D. (2002). Determinism and anti-determinism in the Book of Koheleth. *Jewish Bible Quarterly*, 30, 97-106

21   Ibid. 98

22   Descartes, R., Miller, V. R., & Miller, R. P. (1983). *Principles of philosophy*. Dordrecht, Holland: Reidel.

23   Ibid.

24   Ibid.

is necessitated by causal determinism.[25] Being an open sceptic of free will, Spinoza also rejects the claim that nonexistence of free will negates moral responsibility as he argues that the above claim is a misinterpretation of moral responsibility. For Spinoza, morality considers virtue as its own reward. Spinoza maintains that although free will is just an illusion, humans are free agents whose emotions are determined by the nature of reality.

This can be interpreted as human agents can only desire things that are already predetermined by causal necessities. Regarding causal determinism, Gottfried Wilhelm Leibniz can be considered the first Western philosopher to propose a persuasive argument with his Principle of Sufficient Reason.[26] For Leibniz "*everything can, in principle, be explained*, or that *everything that is, has a sufficient reason for being and being as it is, and not otherwise.*"[27] According to Leibniz, reason must precede everything that occurs; therefore, everything is determined by causality. He deduces that 'sufficient reason' originates from the soul. For Leibniz, the soul develops through time and the knowledge it possesses gradually becomes evident. He argues that if there was a way to reveal all the information the soul has, we could have detailed knowledge of the universe.

Leibniz's argument shows similarities to that of Plato's argument, as Leibniz also references the soul as being at the heart of knowledge but points out the soul is predictable; therefore, its development is deterministic. So, for Leibniz, the soul has a direct connection to the Divine Being. This indicates his theory is based on philosophy and theology.

That being said, contrary to theological assertions, which claim the existence of free will is necessary for moral responsibility, Leibniz argues against free will as he indicates that reality is causal, thus every occurrence has a reason for its existence.[28] Although Leibniz seems to be the originator of the argument for causal determinism, he is not accredited

---

25   Spinoza, Baruch, 1992. *The ethics and selected letters* (S. Shirley, Trans.) (2nd ed.). Indianapolis: Hackett Publishing.

26   Leibniz, G. (2016). Principle of sufficient reason. In *Stanford Encyclopedia of Philosophy*.

27   Causal determinism. (2010). In *Stanford Encyclopedia of Philosophy*. Para 5.

28   Magill, F. N. (1990). *Masterpieces of philosophy.* New York, NY: Harper Collins.

for this, simply because of the theological implications present in his arguments.

Another prominent figure of Western philosophy, David Hume, challenges Leibniz's theory by arguing that motivation behind human actions is predisposition and desire, not reason.[29] For Hume, humans are morally responsible for their actions because of their desires; therefore, they deserve reward or punishment as consequences of their behaviour.[30] Although Hume argues that humans possess the ability to reason, their reasoning is controlled by desires they cannot overcome. For Hume "reason alone can never be a motive for any action of the will"[31], as he believes reason alone cannot change the path chosen by the desire. Consequently, Hume challenges the views of all philosophers who argue for morality through reason by claiming humans are slaves to their desires and impulses. However, Hume does not repudiate the existence of free will altogether, so he is considered by many as a compatibilist.

Emmanuel Kant, considered by many as the father of modern philosophy in the West, attempts to define the quintessence of free will by claiming human free will is a faculty of desire and is determined according to the pleasures and displeasures it anticipates.[32] His argument resembles Hume's theory in some respects, but he further claims, unlike animal impulse, the human will makes its decision by determining the strongest desire. This means there is an element of reasoning in the faculty of decision making, as, according to Kant, human will is also influenced by impulse but not totally determined by it. Kant's definition of human free will as the faculty of freedom is an important contribution to the philosophical problem of free will as he claims, if human will is determined only by the natural object of desire, it would not be free.[33]

Evidently, Kant's argument on free will is despite the fact that he mentions the role of impulse it focuses chiefly on morality as he suggests

29   Ibid.

30   Reese, W. L. (1999). *Dictionary of philosophy and religion: Eastern and Western thought.* Amherst, New York: Prometheus Books.

31   Ibid. para 14.

32   Silber, J. (2012). *Kant's ethics: The good, freedom, and the will.* Boston: Walter de Gruyter.

33   Ibid.

that free will must be admitted for morality.[34] Kant argued that "free will" and "will guided by morality" are identical. For Kant, freedom is a property of will and will is an assumed feature of any rational agent.[35] Therefore, free will also acts with reason; hence it is autonomous of causes originating from the phenomenal world where the laws of classical mechanics apply. This view infers that free will has absolute freedom in the metaphysical world, thus it is uncaused or undetermined by any natural cause. This means it is not controlled by classical mechanics or laws of physics. Kant refers to this as practical freedom as the will is being determined by reason alone.[36]

The formula proposed by Kant offers a solution to determinism advocated by incompatibilism as it distinguishes the metaphysical world from the physical world where nature is governed by physical laws. To some degree, Kant's argument corresponds with the views of mainstream Islamic theology as scholars like Nursi explained that according to the Māturīdiyyah view, free will has a metaphysical existence; therefore, it does not require a physical body that is subject to causality. Consequently, Kant's argument can be considered a compatibilist perspective as it allows for free will and determinism to coexist. Furthermore, Kant's argument also establishes a balance between classical mechanics and metaphysics, meaning free will in an incorporeal form does not violate the deterministic laws of physics.

Scientific perspective on determinism and free will

Following the golden era of philosophers like Descartes, Spinoza, Leibniz, Hume and Kant, it is difficult to come across many innovative philosophical arguments that attempt to reconcile free will and determinism, although several scientific arguments were put forward for randomness and/or determinism in nature around the period leading up to contemporary times. Some of the most significant scientific theories hypothesised during this period were the Darwinian Theory of Evolution,

---

34   Kant, I. (1996). *Groundwork for the metaphysics of morals* (M. J. Gregor, Trans.). Cambridge: Cambridge University Press.

35   Yu, A. (2009). Kant's argument for free will. *Prometheus Journal.*

36   Ibid.

which supports the chance or randomness argument, and the arguments proposed by classical mechanics that evidently support universal determinism. Although some scientists argue that evolution is not a random process, they also maintain that it is not a guided process either. According to these scientists, the process of natural selection begins with genetic variation and "the genetic variation that occurs in a population because of mutation is random."[37] This indicates indeterminism at microbiological levels.

Although these scientific developments are not philosophical in nature, their theoretical implications are directly related to the argument of determinism and free action as the theory of evolution argues for indeterminism and the classical mechanics for determinism. Remarkably, both views do not support free will as the first argues for randomness in nature and the second for determinism.

The problem of free will transforms into a more perplexing topic with the development of quantum mechanics, specifically after the introduction of Werner Heisenberg's uncertainty principle. Heisenberg's principle states there is indeterminism at subatomic levels as it concludes that fundamentally there is uncertainty in the behaviour of quantum particles.[38] Basically, Heisenberg's principle argues the position and momentum of a subatomic particle cannot be measured with precision and this in turn indicates indeterminism in subatomic behaviour. Incongruously, the Heisenberg principle further complicates the work of philosophers; just like the case of determinism indicated by classical mechanics, the existence of free action is also annulled by Heisenberg's principle. The finding concludes that all phenomena in the universe, including human actions, may be the product of the random flight of subatomic particles. Therefore, it would be safe to say that the development of quantum mechanics, which is the study of the subatomic particles, has added further complexity to the debate over free will because, while the natural world displays evident signs of determinism at macro levels, it shows signs of indeterminism at subatomic levels.

---

37   Understanding Evolution. (n.d.). *Misconceptions about natural selection*. University of California Museum of Paleontology.

38   Sen, D. (2014). The uncertainty relations in quantum mechanics. *Current Science*, 107(2), 203-218

Intriguingly, both theories leave no room for free action. The reason for this is free action can only exist in a world where events do not occur through determinism or indeterminism. Therefore, theories put forward by modern physics – whether from the perspective of classical mechanics or quantum physics – do not offer any evidence supporting the existence of free will. As a result, empirical data provided by physics produces more predicaments for philosophers who try to argue for the existence of free will. This compels philosophers to include certain scientific arguments into their formulas, which aim to prove the existence of free action. Clearly, such arguments cannot be built on premises that neglect metaphysics.

As examined in the previous section, the perplexing topic was addressed by many renowned philosophers like Duns Scotus, Baruch Spinoza, Gottfried Wilhelm Leibniz, Emmanuel Kant, David Hume, René Descartes as the philosophical confusion around the existence of human free will not only originates from ontology but also from the concept of determinism established by classical mechanics. For this reason, the discourse continues all the way to modern philosophy and remains to be debated today as contemporary physics suggests we live in a deterministic universe. According to Martin Archer "the everyday world is governed by classical mechanics and that is completely deterministic"[39] That is to say, although we employ the laws of probability because of deficiency of knowledge within the discipline, theoretically, it is even possible to work out the exact number that would come up each time we roll the dice.[40] This is derived from the Newtonian Determinism, which argues the universe is a gigantic clock that was wound up at the beginning of time and has been ticking ever since in agreement to Newton's laws of motion.[41]

According to Newtonian Determinism, what time a person will take a bath in twenty years is already fixed. This means classical physics suggest there is no room for free will because everything in nature is predetermined.

---

39   Martin, M. (2013). *Use of reason in early Islamic theology* (Kindle ed.). n.p.: Amazon Digital Services Inc.

40   Ibid.

41   Kaku, M. (2011). *Why physics end the free will debate.*

The argument of determinism through classical mechanics is also supported by Albert Einstein, who stated God does not play dice with the universe. Michio Kaku, however, claims that Einstein's argument of 'God does not play dice' was valid until the establishment of quantum physics as Heisenberg's uncertainty principle, which states the position of the electron cannot be known. He argues that the electron could be in many places simultaneously. The theory suggests there is uncertainty at quantum levels; therefore, there is randomness and accordingly indeterminism in nature. Kaku claims that since there is randomness, there is always the wildcard, thus there is some form of free will.[42]

Kaku's argument, however, can be challenged since it is solely based on the movement of an electron, for everything else in the mechanical world of physics display determinism. For example, scientists have the technology to calculate the exact location of planet Mars and where it will be in six months' time or when the next lunar eclipse will occur. This suggests the motions of heavenly bodies are completely deterministic. So, in relation to the indeterministic motion of the electron, perhaps, one could argue that contemporary scientists may not have the necessary tools or knowledge to determine where an electron is at a given time, but this does not mean an electron is not at a certain location in a certain fraction of time. So, the question whether there is absolute randomness at subatomic levels remains a mystery for physicists who need to intensify their research into the area. Moreover, the assumption that the behaviour of subatomic particles is completely indeterministic does not prove the existence of free will as randomness at quantum levels does not indicate the existence of free will; the theory only alters the time of determinism suggesting that everything is predetermined at subatomic levels within a fraction of time.[43] This means that all events in the universe are decided at subatomic levels during the random flight of particles.

Furthermore, at a macro level, the current data indicates determinism in nature. This brings up the following questions:

Do humans really possess some form of free will that enables them to defy the laws of nature?

---

42   Ibid.

43   Archer, M. (2013). Why did Einstein say "God does not play dice?" *Physics World*

Do humans have freedom of action or are they mere slaves of absolute determinism (originating from classical mechanics or God, for that matter), which evidently governs natural occurrences that include human acts?

From a philosophical perspective, Carl Hoefer delineates determinism as, "the *world* is *governed by* (or is *under the sway of*) determinism if and only if, given a specified *way, things are at a time (t)*, the way things go *thereafter* is *fixed* as a matter of *natural law*".[44] He claims the "roots of the notion of determinism surely lie in a very common philosophical idea: the idea that *everything can, in principle, be explained* or that *everything that is, has a sufficient reason for being and being as it is, and not otherwise.*"[45] This concept is derived from Leibniz's Principle of Sufficient Reason.

Hoefer argues that there has been a propensity among modern philosophers "to believe in the truth of some sort of determinist doctrine."[46] George Musser also finds the notion that indeterminism reinstates free will very unconvincing. He argues: "what difference does it make if a person's conscious choices were programmed in at the *big bang* or decided on the fly by random particle events."[47] So, the real question here for contemporary philosophers and scientists is: Can the existence of free will be proven scientifically or philosophically and, if so, can free will coexist with the concept of determinism?

It is evident the empirical data provided by physicists suggests we live in a deterministic universe, as Archer argues that the macro universe is governed by classical mechanics and is completely deterministic. This scientific concept is defined by the term 'causal determinism,' which concludes that natural events are necessitated by antecedent events and circumstances together with laws of physics. In physics, the phenomenon is basically defined as cause-and-effect or, in a single word, 'causality.' According to the notion of causality, all events are bound by the principle of cause-and-effect, thus they are

44   Hoefer, C. (2016). Causal Determinism. In *Stanford Encyclopedia of Philosophy*

45   Ibid.

46   Ibid.

47   Musser, G. (2012). The quantum physics of free will. *Scientific American.*

deterministic.[48] This means the state of an event or action is determined by its prior states. So, although classical mechanics and some theologies argue for determinism, causal determinism looks at the issue only from the perspective of the laws of nature, thus explores only what can be tested through experimentation, unlike theological determinism which suggests that all events have a metaphysical origin.

Hoefer argues that the roots of causal determinism lie in Leibniz's Principle of Sufficient Reason,[49] which stipulates everything must have a reason or cause. However, Hoefer also claims that since the development of theories related to physics point to ostensibly a deterministic character in nature, philosophers of science have inclined towards investigations that focus on theories of determinism and/or indeterminism, instead of building their views on Leibniz's principle. The reason for this seems to be that classical mechanics clearly point to determinism in the macro cosmos as Pierre Simon Laplace proposed. If it was possible to know the exact location and momentum of every atom in the universe, it would be possible to calculate everything from the laws of classical mechanics.[50]

Laplace states: "all events, even those which on account of their insignificance do not seem to follow the great laws of nature, are a result of it just as necessarily as the revolutions of the sun"[51] So, according to Laplace, the present state of the universe is the effect of its anterior state and is also the cause of the one that will follow. He claims, if there was a vast intelligence that had the ability to comprehend all the forces in nature and analyse the data from the movements of the lightest atoms to the largest astronomical bodies, then there would be no uncertainty about "the future as the past would be present to its eyes."[52] The argument suggests absolute data of the past and present states of the uni-

---

48   Doyle, B. (2011). *Free will: The scandal in philosophy*. Cambridge, Mass: I-Phi Press.

49   The Principle of Sufficient Reason proposed by Leibniz is a philosophical argument stipulating that everything needs a reason, cause or ground (Leibniz, 2016).

50   Laplace, P. S. (1952). *A philosophical essay on probabilities*. New York: Dover Publications.

51   Ibid.

52   Ibid.

verse would provide information about the future universe; therefore, it would mean the universe is absolutely deterministic. Laplace's argument is based on Newtonian determinism, which concludes the future is already fixed; therefore, even if Laplace's presumed super-intelligence did not exist, the argument maintains that the classical mechanics of the universe is deterministic.

Sean Carroll, on the other hand, argues that such theory annuls free will and further claims that scientists still do not have an answer to the conundrum of free will.[53] Carroll, a research professor in the discipline of physics, further argues that the developments in quantum mechanics have only brought more perplexity to the debate on free will rather than clarifying the issue.[54] The reason for this is the Heisenberg's uncertainty principle. So, from a physics perspective, it is difficult to explain the concept of free will as the entire universe displays some form of deterministic behaviour while the quantum world suggests indeterminism.

According to Carroll, the universe can be divided into two different moments of time:

The first scenario: if it was possible to know the exact state of the entire universe at any given time, then the past and the future would be completely deterministic.

The second scenario: if it was possible to know the exact state of one part of the universe at any given time, it would then mean that region is completely deterministic.[55]

Carroll further explains that even quantum mechanics display signs of perfect determinism in Schrödinger's equation (fundamental equation of physics for describing quantum mechanical behaviour) until physicists make an observation, only to realise it is impossible to make a prediction on the outcome.[56] The Schrödinger equation confirms that the quantum system seems to be constant when it is separated from the macro world. However, it displays an indeterministic behaviour when observed by physicists. Carroll argues that this is the point where opinions differ on whether there is indeterminism, or it just appears that way.

---

53   Carroll, S. (2011). On determinism. *Discover.*
54   Ibid.
55   Ibid.
56   Ibid.

This means that scientists are not certain whether indeterminism observed at quantum levels is an illusion or real.[57]

Conversely, as pointed out before, the answer to the question of whether there is determinism or indeterminism at quantum levels do not solve the problem of free will, because both scenarios disallow the existence of free action. While the first implies that the universe was predetermined right from the beginning, as suggested by Newtonian determinism, the other suggests the future state of physical properties is decided at the random momentum of quantum particles.

Carroll rightly questions whether quantum mechanics play any role in our daily lives with an analogy of flipping a coin. He argues that the relevant probabilities are purely classical and originate from our lack of knowledge about the fine details, such as the state of the muscles, nerves, wind, and coin. He adds, if we had prior knowledge about all these details, we would know exactly what would happen to the coin. This would indicate perfect determinism.[58] In other words, we use the term 'probability' in situations where we are unable to measure or calculate the fundamental particulars of an event. This means, if it was possible to measure and calculate all the essential elements of an occurrence, there would be no room for probability as the exact result would be known to us.

On the other hand, some physicists think along the lines that all these occurrences are in some way related to quantum effects where there is evidence of indeterminism. Consequently, scientific evidence points either to determinism or indeterminism where both arguments do not offer any backing for the existence of free will; in fact, they refute its existence. Revisiting Laplace's premise, which states if there was a vast intelligence that could gather perfect information about the entire universe, then the past and future could be known, Carroll argues, even with such intelligence, the future could be predicted only in principle and not in practice.

However, these arguments do not invoke metaphysics or the supernatural in any way; they are all postulations based on philosophy and theoretical physics. The main reason for the inclusion of this statement

---

57   Ibid.

58   Ibid.

here is to clarify that the presence of a metaphysical, supernatural agent would change the entire argument as mainstream Islamic theologians point out that God is omniscient and possesses absolute knowledge about the state of the universe in the past, present and future. For Islamic theologians, unlike Laplace's hypothetical vast intelligence, not only does God know about the entire state of the universe, but He also governs the entire system from the level of quantum mechanics to the motions of celestial objects in the macro universe. This concept changes the entire equation, giving God the ability to know and govern the past, present and future states of the universe. This notion is supported by the Qur'an, which states "God's is the dominion over the heavens and the earth and all that they contain; and He has the power to will anything."[59] This indicates that space-time continuum is governed by God.

Empirical data provides some evidence that indicates the argument provided by Islamic theologians could also be considered by modern philosophy, as Carroll argues there are four possibilities to the solution of this problem: determinism coexisting with free will; determinism without free will; indeterminism coexisting with free will; and indeterminism without free will. He adds they are all possible.[60]

From a scientific perspective, it can be argued, while the universe on a large scale displays clear signs of determinism, there may be an element of indeterminism at quantum levels. Conversely, both conclusions proposed by scientific theories do not offer a plausible solution to the problem of free will, as one suggests determinism demonstrated by classical mechanics and the other indeterminism through Heisenberg's uncertainty principle.

For comparative analysis, one can conclude there is one point that Carroll makes that concurs with the Māturīdīyah methodology. He argues that using a weak sense of free will, where humans are considered rational agents capable of making choices at macro levels, would allow the existence of free will that is compatible with laws of physics. This concept is known as the 'compatibilist' view in modern philosophy and perhaps is the closest perspective to the concept of free will in mainstream Islamic theology as the argument proposed by the Māturīdītes

---

59   Qur'an 5:120

60   Carroll, S. (2011). On determinism. *Discover*.

implies free will is not a physical property; therefore, it cannot be quantified or measured by scientific methods. In simple terms, it means the quintessence of free will cannot be comprehended through scientific experimentation, yet its presence is experienced by every human throughout their daily lives. Some contemporary philosophers will support this view if they are libertarians or compatibilists; however, those who argue for incompatibilism or causal determinism may disagree, as they will question the essence and definition of free will. For this reason, a comparative study of contemporary libertarianism, compatibilism, incompatibilism and causal determinism will provide a better understanding of the concept of free will.

Contemporary philosophy on free will and determinism

Based on their experience, most humans assume they have free will yet they do not know exactly how to define the nature of this will. Hume argues that the nature of free will is the most argumentative topic of metaphysics.[61] Hume's choice of the word 'metaphysics' is interesting as it indicates free will is not a quantifiable property so it can be measured by scientific methods. Perhaps his claim is a clear indication of how difficult it is for philosophers to define the nature of free will. There are, however, contemporary academics who challenge the concept that free will can be proven through human experience. Joachim Kruger, for example, argues that the so-called free will, experienced through an act, may be one's conscious awareness that could actually be part of a causal chain.[62] In challenging Searle's argument, which claims free will can be proven as easily as by willing then raising your arm, Kruger implies that the act only proves the existence of ability – not of free will. For Kruger, the will to lift one's arm is free in a sense that the movement is not prevented by physical constrains: "but the act is not free from all antecedent conditions and events."[63]

---

61   Hume, D., & Beauchamp, T. L. (1999). *An enquiry concerning human understanding*. Oxford: Oxford University Press.

62   Kruger, J. (2018). Five arguments for free will: None of them are compelling. *Psychology Today*.

63   Ibid.

This argument can be further clarified by the fact many animals in nature also possess the ability to lift their arms, but does this really indicate free will? For example, in a scenario where three items are placed in front of a chimpanzee – cheese, doughnut and banana – it would be safe to assume the animal would choose the banana first. Does the experiment prove the chimpanzee selected the banana because it possesses free will or does it indicate an instinctual habit passed on through genetic inheritance? So, for Kruger, an ability to act does not necessarily indicate free will as it could be self-awareness that plays a role in the chain of causation. So, how do philosophers establish that human agents act through their free will or through some antecedent conditions or causes that in reality offer them only one path to follow? When a person chooses a path from the many paths that seem to be available and the selection becomes a past event, can one argue that the person had many paths to choose from but decided on this particular one or was this the only path available anyway?

The following analogy may provide some understanding about this problem: Imagine Adam is offered a position as a CEO of a large company in London, but he needs to start in a week because the position will not be available after that. However, Adam has already made arrangements for the following week to visit his seriously ill mother who lives in Canada. It seems that if he takes the job, he risks not seeing his mother alive again. Adam finally decides to visit his mother and loses the position. Can one conclude that he made this choice by using his free will or was it that certain causes necessitated the result and, given identical circumstances, the same result would have occurred?

If the latter is correct, it would mean Adam did not really have more than one path available into the future despite the assumption there were various alternatives available to him. On the other hand, the existence of free will necessitates that Adam had alternative paths to follow but he chose the one that he believed was the right course of action by using his faculty of reason. This scenario would mean his choice was not predestined; hence it did not contradict the laws of classical and quantum mechanics. It can be concluded from the analysis there are three key theoretical scenarios here:

First: Adam only had one available path into the future (determinism).

Second: He had alternative paths to choose from (freedom in human action).

Third: He had alternative paths available but the path he chose was predestined (compatibility of determinism and free will).[64]

In Western philosophy, the answer to this perplexing question depends on whether you are a libertarian, compatibilist or incompatibilist. The available literature tackles the problem of free will chiefly through these three fundamental arguments. The libertarians believe humans have free will, hence possess the ability to influence the world in numerous ways.[65] According to this view, from the many alternatives that lie before humans, they are able to reason, deliberate among them and make a choice. The libertarian view suggests it is up to the individual to choose how they would act. This means a human has the freedom to act one way or the other. According to libertarianism, embracing the idea of determinism would mean denying the concept of humans having more than one possible path available into the future and nullify human responsibility. This means it is not 'up to us' to choose from the possibilities presented. Moreover, the libertarianist view on the concept of human responsibility is adamant as the supporters of this view argue that moral responsibility necessitates free action. Basically, the argument is that a human agent cannot be held responsible for their actions in a deterministic world.

Kane, a firm supporter of libertarianism, argues that free will has a direct connection with notions such as accountability, blameworthiness and praiseworthiness for actions. Consequently, the camp of libertarianism asserts that free will could not exist in a world that is predetermined by a supernatural agent, destiny or laws of physics.[66]

In many ways, the arguments put forward by libertarianism resemble those by the school of Mu'tazila, which also claim that human agents are the originators of their own decisions and actions. This rejects determinism altogether and consequently leads to more philosophical

---

64   Fischer, J. M., Kane, R., Derk, P., & Manuel, V. (2007). *Four views on free will.* Malden, MA: Blackwell Pub.

65   Ibid.

66   Ibid.

conundrums as one of the serious philosophical problems with libertarianism is rejecting determinism altogether means embracing indeterminism, which leads to a paradox where it would be necessary to explain the existence of genuine free will in a world where events are determined by chance, as suggested by the uncertainty principle in quantum mechanics.

Consequently, to prove its argument, libertarianism must first bring evidence to the concept that free will is incompatible with determinism, and then further prove that free will can be reconciled with indeterminism and scientific data.[67] So, the challenge to libertarianism not only comes from philosophical arguments but also from empirical data as modern physics has provided evidence for determinism and indeterminism.

Some of the challenges to the total freedom argument proposed by libertarianism come from the 'Consequence Argument,' which claims:

    i. We cannot change the past;

    ii. We cannot change the laws of nature;

    iii. Our actions are necessary consequences of the past and the laws of nature;

    iv. Therefore, we cannot change the way our present actions will occur.[68]

Therefore, the four premises form an argument that free will does not play any part in human actions. On the other hand, according to the compatibilist view, the Consequence Argument does not apply to human actions for the reason that, if someone argues they can jump over a fence and has the power to do so, this would be a question of capability, which means, if the person challenged, takes on the challenge and jumps over the fence, the Consequence Argument would fail.[69] However, the compatibilist argument still fails to refute one of the premises, which is: "one cannot change the past and the laws of physics because no human being has the power to change the past or the laws of physics."[70] However,

---

67   Ibid.

68   Fischer, J. M., Kane, R., Derk, P., & Manuel, V. (2007). *Four views on free will.* Malden, MA: Blackwell Pub. p 10

69   Ibid.

70   Ibid. p 12.

Kane adds that "human beings do have the ability to jump over a fence if they wish to do so"[71] and this is an ability that cannot be denied. This means the libertarianism argument concludes there are alternative paths into the future and human agents have the freedom of choosing the path to follow. Accordingly, the libertarianism rules determinism out of free will completely by claiming "(i) open alternatives or alternative possibilities lie before us (ii) free will requires that sources or origins of our actions lie within us."[72]

Kane defines this as 'ultimate responsibility' and claims "to be ultimately responsible for an action, an agent must be responsible for anything that is a sufficient cause or motive for that action's occurring."[73] Consequently, it can be deduced from the arguments above that libertarianism clearly states it is incompatible with determinism and in several ways the philosophical perspective of libertarianism corresponds to the views of the Mu'tazila School, which also gives total freedom to human free will apart from acknowledging that free will is a power granted by God. The Mu'tazila school's argument also originates from the concept of human responsibility as they claim malevolent acts cannot originate from God and reach the conclusion that not only are human agents free in their actions, but they are also the generators of their own actions.[74]

In contrast, the compatibilists argue the notion of free will and moral responsibility is compatible with the concept of causal determinism, which suggests human behaviour is causally necessitated by events in the past and laws of physics. It is based on the notion that humans feel free and responsible for their actions most of the time as they also believe causal determinism could be real. Fischer claims it is appealing to believe that one has the freedom to choose from one path or another, yet, despite the ostensible availability of these options, there is only one available path into the future. So, Fischer argues: "paths into the future

71   Ibid.

72   Ibid. p 13.

73   Ibid. p. 14.

74   Al-Ash'arī, A. I., & McCarthy, R. J. (1953). *The theology of al-Ash'ari: The Arabic texts of al-Ash'arī's Kitāb al-Luma and Risalat Istihsan al-khawd fī'ilm al-kalam, with briefly annotated translations, and appendices containing material pertinent to the study of al-Ash'arī*. Beirut: Imprimerie Catholique. p. 69.

branch out from the present time".[75] Compatibilists claim a person who wakes up in the morning can either decide to go to work or take sick leave to enjoy the warm summer day, despite the possibility that all along there was only one path available for them. According to Fischer "a compatibilist does not need to conclude that there is only one path into the future unless physics establish this as a 100% probability." So, he believes even: "a 99.9% probability offers more than one path into the future."[76] For Fischer, the feeling of being morally responsible for our behaviour and actions is an indication we have more than one path available to us. Fischer further claims moral responsibility is an important and persuasive argument for having more than one path available into the future.

The compatibilist view of freedom is that an agent is only responsible for their actions if there was an alternative path available for them or if they could have done otherwise.[77] The compatibilist view also leaves room for the existence of causal determinism, which is the idea that every event is necessitated by prior occurrences, circumstances and laws of physics, while hoping that not all forms of causal determinism threaten freedom.[78] On the other hand, the Consequence Argument proposed by Peter van Inwagen implies that, since causal determinism argues that human actions are the consequence of the past together with the laws of nature, it leaves no room for free will.[79] For this reason, there are different views within the compatibilist camp as some claim even small changes in the past and within the laws of nature are possible so there could be freedom in action for all human agents.

Conversely, if the past is fixed and the laws of nature could not be changed at all, then the future is also fixed, and this would ultimately lead us to the conclusion of 'there is no free will.' For this reason, the compatibilist view is that free will and determinism are compatible concepts, and one can accept both without being logically inconsistent. Fischer further implies that if causal determinism, as suggested by van Inwagen,

---

75   Fischer, J. M., Kane, R., Derk, P., & Manuel, V. (2007). *Four views on free will.* 47.

76   Ibid.

77   Ibid.

78   Ibid.

79   Van Inwagen, P., & Zimmerman, D. W. (2008). *Metaphysics: The big questions.* Malden, MA: Blackwell Pub

was true then it would annul moral responsibility as it proposes that human actions are the consequence of laws of nature and the past.[80] For this reason, the compatibilist view seems to be the most accommodating contemporary view for mainstream Islamic theologians who also assert that free will and predestination can coexist.

The argument proposed by mainstream Islamic theology has one distinctive feature from the compatibilist argument, which rejects all forms of arguments based on indeterminism. The view of mainstream Islamic theology is: "since God is the originator of all phenomena in existence, there is absolute control through Divine Will"[81] and this leaves no room for randomness or indeterminism.

There is, however, another perspective in Western philosophy that argues for absolute determinism: incompatibilism. This perspective rejects human responsibility altogether based on the empirical data provided by classical mechanics, which suggests humans live in a deterministic universe. Spinoza, who could be considered a hard determinist, argues that human beings do not possess the free will which requires them to be morally responsible due to the nature of the classical mechanics of the universe. A similar view is offered by contemporary philosophers like Pereboom, who believes that humans are not free in the context required for moral responsibility. He defends this with the argument that physical theories indicate that humans are not the decisive agents of causality. Pereboom agrees with Spinoza in the claim that "human beings would not be morally responsible if determinism were to be true, but also they would not be morally responsible if indeterminism were to be true as well"[82], because in a world of indeterminism the causes of our actions would originate from states and events.

For this reason, incompatibilism is a view that claims, for an agent to be morally responsible for a decision, and that they need to have con-

---

80   Fischer, J. M., Kane, R., Derk, P., & Manuel, V. (2007). *Four views on free will.*

81   Al-Ash'arī, A. I., & McCarthy, R. J. (1953). *The theology of al-Ash'ari: The Arabic texts of al-Ash'ari's Kitāb al-Luma and Risalat Istihsan al-khawd fi'ilm al-kalam, with briefly annotated translations, and appendices containing material pertinent to the study of al-Ash'ari.* Beirut: Imprimerie Catholique.

82   Fischer, J. M., Kane, R., Derk, P., & Manuel, V. (2007). Four views on free will

trol over its production.[83] According to Pereboom, an ability to exercise such control is known as freedom of the will. However, he claims it does not mean having alternative possibilities for that particular decision as he concludes: "free will understood in this way would provide the kind of control required for moral responsibility in the basic desert sense, but it turns out that we do not have free will of this sort."[84] In philosophy, this is the condition of being deserving of something, good or bad.

The incompatibilists argue that moral responsibility can only be considered if an agent has the power to do otherwise. According to Pereboom, the best argument for incompatibilism is an action produced by deterministic process, which can be traced back to events beyond the control of an agent.[85] Incompatibilists support their claim with laws of physics as well, arguing the physical world is – generally – governed by deterministic laws; hence, if an agent was free in their actions, they would be altering the laws of nature in the instant of producing a decision. Pereboom argues that some may claim that indeterministic choices can be predicted by deterministic laws, which suggests there is no deviation from natural laws. He replies to this claim by arguing the probability of coincidences in such scenario is implausible. Clarke, on the other hand, argues that agent-causal free will can be reconciled with natural laws.[86] Pereboom disputes this claim because there are wild coincidences involved in the proposal. So, for Pereboom, the best argument against the coexistence of free will and determinism is: "the claim that an action's being produced by a deterministic process that traces back to factors beyond the control of the agent…"[87] Perhaps, Pereboom is implying, if you are not the cause of your actions, then you cannot be held responsible; thus, in a true sense, you cannot have free will.

Although incompatibilism has the support of classical mechanics, it fails to address the issue of moral responsibility and accountability, in particular with acts related to criminal offences and immoral behaviour.

---

83   Ibid. p 87

84   Ibid.

85   Ibid.

86   Clarke, R. K. (1993). *Toward a credible agent-causal account of free will*. Noûs, 27(2), 191-203.

87   Fischer, J. M., Kane, R., Derk, P., & Manuel, V. (2007). *Four views on free will*. p. 93.

The consequences of accepting such an argument as the 'whole truth' seems catastrophic for social order and harmony as no one can be held responsible for the crimes they commit because their actions are produced by a deterministic process beyond their control. In response, incompatibilists defend their argument by claiming: "moral admonition and encouragement can be applied in situations where there is a presupposition that the offender has done wrong."[88] However, Pereboom stresses: "if Incompatibilism is true, there would be no justification of punishment for a crime based on the retributivist policy."[89] Therefore, incompatibilism argues that a person who has committed a criminal offense cannot be punished with retribution. For this reason, there are insoluble problems with the concept of incompatibilism, particularly in relation to the philosophical topic of moral responsibility. Total denial of human free will, would mean no court of law on earth would have the legal right to hold anyone responsible for their actions; hence, such a deterministic view would mean chaos for social order if it was implemented by the legal system. The incompatibilist view aligns with the views of the school of Jabrīyyah in Islamic theology, again with the significant difference regarding the origin of determinism, where the Jabrīyyah attributes the origin to a Supreme Being and incompatibilists to classical mechanics.

Refutations of incompatibilism or determinism are not based on empirical data derived from classical mechanics or physics but from moral responsibility as determinism negates free will, therefore, responsibility for the consequences of human actions. Kadri Vihvelin summarises the incompatibilist view as:

If determinism is true, then no one is ever able to do otherwise. If no one is ever able to do otherwise, then no one is ever morally liable. Therefore, if determinism is true, then, no one is ever morally responsible.[90]

---

88   Waller, B. N. (1990). *Freedom without responsibility*. Philadelphia: Temple University Press. p. 130.

89   Fischer, J. M., Kane, R., Derk, P., & Manuel, V. (2007). *Four views on free will.* p. 115.

90   Vihvelin, K. (2013). *Causes, laws, and free will: Why determinism doesn't matter.* New York: Oxford University Press. p. 91.

The argument is that if human agents are unable to do otherwise, they cannot be morally accountable. Vihvelin rejects the first premise, as he calls it the 'Metaphysical Premise,' and argues: "our common-sense view of ourselves as agents with free will, who make choices and who are at least sometimes able to choose and act otherwise, is compatible with determinism."[91] While the incompatibilists argue, if determinism is true, human agents always have only one path to follow as they could not have done otherwise, compatibilists claim "there is a morally relevant sense in which even a deterministic agent could sometimes have done otherwise."[92]

Basically, the philosophical argument here is based on the concept that the actions of a free agent are unpredictable, yet classical mechanics and causal determinism indicates that all events and occurrences are predictable, at least in a theoretical sense. Consequently, this brings about the question: How can free will exist in a world where every action is predictable? According to the incompatibilist argument, coexistence of free will and determinism is a philosophical paradox as empirical data from classical mechanics and principles of causality negates free action, thus moral responsibility. It seems that tackling the issue only from the perspectives of classical mechanics and philosophy does not provide a satisfactory explanation to the problem of free will. Perhaps the equation requires a metaphysical component where free will exists as an abstract entity that is not bound by physical laws. As mentioned before, one solution to this comes from Emmanuel Kant, who argues that free will is autonomous of causes originating from the phenomenal world where the laws of classical mechanics apply, as it works on reason alone. This suggests that free will is related to metaphysics and cannot be limited by causality. Again, this is somewhat aligned with the views of mainstream Islamic theology as it also maintains that free will is a metaphysical entity, which does not have physical existence in the phenomenal world.

For the libertarians, existence of free will can simply be explained by "a capacity for rational self-determination."[93] However, Clarke also ar-

---

91   Ibid. p. 92.

92   Ibid. p. 93.

93   Clarke, R. K. (2006). *Libertarian accounts of free will.* New York: Oxford University Press.

gues that "having this capacity when one acts is not sufficient for acting with free will"[94], as free will requires that one must also have the power to exercise the capacity during the occasion. Clarke further argues: "…it must be up to one whether and how one exercises one's capacity for conscious, reflective, rational self-determination."[95] As Clarke also points out, in order to prove the libertarian argument of free will, the events leading up to an agent's act must not be causally determined. This means acts caused by predetermined factors cannot be considered free acts. For this reason, libertarians argue that events leading to an act cannot be causally determined as one can choose freely from the available paths. Clarke argues that "in acting with free will, one must actually exercise one's active power with respect to which of the open alternatives is made actual."[96]

It is important to note, for causal libertarians, human action begins with a mental action. This means a decision is made through an intention prior to an action. Clarke defines this as 'volition,' which is an agent's desire to perform an act.[97] Again, the proposed scenario requires a non-physical action that is not governed by causal determinism. This means the entire process is triggered by an abstract entity that libertarians define as the mind and theologians define as the soul-mind collaboration. Consequently, the argument will give human agents freedom to act even in the existence of causal determinism.

This view is challenged by the incompatibilists as they claim antecedent states influence the outcome of actions even if they are free actions.[98] A simple example of this is that one looks for a drink soon after one feels thirsty. Therefore, an act seemingly thought to be the result of free will is caused by an antecedent event. In connection to this view, Berofsky explains that young children do not possess the kind of freedom experienced by adults and argues that "…compatibilists must

94   Clarke, R. K. (2006). *Libertarian accounts of free will*. New York: Oxford University Press. p. 17.

95   Ibid.

96   Ibid.

97   Ibid.

98   Berofsky, B. (2012). *Nature's challenge to free will*. Oxford: Oxford University Press.

explain how freedom evolves from unfreedom."[99] Basically, the philosophical question is: How do humans attain the power to act freely as they make the transition from childhood to adulthood?

The argument here is that this is a difficult question for the libertarians. However, Berofsky concludes this is not a victory for the incompatibilists, but stresses libertarians need to explain "how indetermination enhances the freedom of an adult decision maker[100]" Berofsky has a strong case here as he states: "the supposition that a growing child's eventual freedom depends on indeterministic evolutions is fallacious"[101] as the mind of the child is shaped by adults who nurture and guide them; therefore, there are antecedent states that influence the child's decision-making faculty.

The arguments between libertarians and incompatibilists actually reinforces the compatibilist argument as they claim the world displays deterministic and indeterministic behaviour, which indicates that free will can coexist with determinism. Basically, the compatibilist attempt to reconcile libertarianism with determinism by arguing an agent is able to do other than what the incompatibilists describe as determined acts, providing the natural laws allow them to do so. The assumption is, although all events are causally necessitated by prior conditions, one should not take all these conditions into consideration when one decides if an agent is able to act one way or another.

There is another doctrine in the West that approaches the problem from a theological perspective – the Divine Universal Causality.[102] Basically, according to Divine Universal Causality, God causes all events and creaturely actions, yet this is perfectly consistent with the freedom of action defined by libertarians. This doctrine derives from Aquinas' *Summa Theologiae* and argues that "...if all that exists apart from God is caused by him, then the whole world is in God's hands; all that happens falls under his providence."[103] According to this view, free and determined

99   Ibid. p. 52.

100   Ibid.

101   Ibid.

102   Timpe, K., & Speak, D. (2016). *Free will and theism: Connections, contingencies, and concerns.* Oxford: Oxford University Press.

103   Aquinas, T., & Morris, S. (1991). *Summa Theologiae.* p. 155.

actions are caused by God. This theological argument maintains every action, including human will, can be traced back to the ultimate cause, which is God.[104]

The argument may seem to be deterministic, therefore would not allow any freedom to human agents in the libertarian sense, but according to Timpe: "at least on one account of Divine agency, there is no incompatibility between our acts being caused by God and their being free in the libertarian sense."[105] So, for Timpe not only God-caused acts are compatible with human will but also free will in this proposed premise is a required component of the Divine Universal Causality.[106] Not all libertarians will agree with this as the principles of libertarianism suggest a free agent needs to produce acts that are intentional, based on reason and uncontrolled by external causes.

This means no form of determinism could be involved in the process of decision making by a free agent. However, some libertarians argue, if "the act is determined and the agent's responsibility for the act derives from the agent's voluntary and intentional performance of some prior act that was not determined"[107], this would be compatible with libertarianism. So, in a general sense, God causing human acts is a violation of free will; therefore, it is not compatible with libertarianism unless there is a voluntary and intentional performance by humans somewhere in the process. One serious problem with the libertarian view is that the validity of its premises relies entirely on laws of physics, and if causal determinism could be proven by empirical evidence, the absolute freedom of libertarianism would collapse. Timpe & Speak argue that according to the libertarian view, human freedom depends on the percentage of impact that causal determinism has on human status as free agents.[108]

---

104 Stockhammer, M. (2013). *Thomas Aquinas dictionary*. New York, NY: Philosophical Library.

105 Timpe, K., & Speak, D. (2016). *Free will and theism: Connections, contingencies, and concerns*. Oxford: Oxford University Press. p. 216.

106 Ibid.

107 Ibid. p. 218.

108 Ibid. p. 49.

For Timpe, the status of human agents in the libertarian view is that it is hostage to theoretical physics,[109] because, if causal determinism was to be proven, the concept of undetermined freedom would be annulled.

Some libertarians challenge this view as they claim causal determinism would negate freedom in ability to perform a physical action but does not pose a philosophical liability to freedom of choice. This view could be considered as having some coherence with Divine Universal Causality as there is a requirement for the element of non-physical process in human actions. In summary, it seems the problem of determinism and free will cannot be solved through the notions of absolute determinism or total freedom, at least in a philosophical sense. Therefore, some kind of compatibilist theory is required to establish that the deterministic conclusions of classical mechanics, theoretical proposition of causal determinism and moral responsibility can coexist.

In conclusion, although the coexistence of determinism and free will is a philosophical necessity, contemporary Western philosophers have not reached agreement on a theory that incorporates this either. In Western philosophy, views that argue for the coexistence are the philosophical approach of the compatibilists and the theology of the Divine Universal Causality supporters. It is also important to point out that some of the premises of compatibilism and Divine Universal Causality continue to receive considerable criticism from the camps of incompatibilism and libertarianism.

This brief analysis of the three major views (assuming Divine Universal Causality is a theological version of compatibilism) in Western philosophy suggests that libertarianism is based on the notion that liberty is the principal objective where the existence of free will is imperative for moral responsibility; therefore, it cannot coexist with determinism. The theoretical framework of libertarianism corresponds in many ways with the Muʿtazila School of Islamic theology, as they also argue that human agents are free in their acts, hence freedom in action requires that human actions not be determined by antecedent events, causality or God. A significant dissimilarity between the two views is the Muʿta-

---

109 Ibid. p. 49.

zilites believe that the human ability to generate their own acts is given by God.

On the other hand, although the libertarian argument seems to be philosophically consistent from a human experience perspective, it fails to address the empirical data provided by the discipline of physics, specifically on a macro level where classical mechanics indicates we live in a deterministic universe. Libertarianism also fails to respond to the concept of indeterminism detected at subatomic levels, which also challenges the notion of free action as it proposes that events are decided on the random flight of subatomic particles. Moreover, libertarianism does not offer a counter-argument to theological arguments proposed by scholars of religion. Consequently, it seems the argument for absolute free will cannot be sustained, considering the experimental data provided by physics and theoretical arguments as deduced by causal determinists. Therefore, it would be safe to argue that empirical data put forward by classical mechanics and theoretical data provided by quantum physics pose a strong challenge to the views of libertarianism and the school of Mu'tazila.

Incompatibilism, on the other hand, rejects free will altogether, claiming everything in nature displays signs of absolute determinism, thus human free will is just an illusion. Generally speaking, this view argues that classical mechanics and causal determinism annul free will as they suggest human actions are the product of natural laws and antecedent events that lead to an action. Empirical data derived from the study of classical mechanics offers some form of support for the incompatibilist view as it suggests humans live in a deterministic world where all phenomena occur just as determined by the laws of physics. It can be argued, however, a claim that negates free will creates the serious philosophical problem of moral responsibility and human accountability with regard to immoral behaviour, crime and misconduct. Since moral responsibility, accountability and social justice are established concepts in all human civilisations, and are clearly identified in legal and religious rulings, their existence cannot be denied, and this generates further philosophical and ethical difficulties for the incompatibilist argument.

Even if it is a philosophical and scientific fact that one cannot change the past, and therefore the past is determined, there is no empirical evidence that proves the future is also predetermined, at least in relation to human decisions. Therefore, the argument put forward by the incompatibilists, which negates the human experience of free will, cannot be verified by experimental data.

This brief analysis of Western literature further indicates that in many aspects, the incompatibilist view is almost identical to the Jabrīyyah view with the important distinction that the Jabrīyyah attributes determinism to a Divine Being only. Both the school of Jabrīyyah and camp of incompatibilism fail to address the significant topic of moral responsibility and social liability. Mainstream Islamic theologians, on the other hand, reject both views as they believe free will is a prerequisite of moral responsibility; hence, to be held accountable for their actions, humans need to be equipped with some form of free will.

In contrast to the previously mentioned two views proposed by modern philosophers, compatibilism argues the notion of free will and moral responsibility are compatible even with the concept of causal determinism, which suggests human behaviour is causally necessitated by events in the past and the laws of physics. This means humans are morally responsible for their choices most of the time, while causal determinism could also be real. The compatibilist view is based on the theoretical approach that coexistence of determinism and free will is philosophically conceivable. Even though they acknowledge the possibility of causal determinism, compatibilists believe freedom of choice exists if there are alternative paths available to an agent. The availability of alternative paths, in turn, coerces human agents to moral responsibility.

The compatibilist argument, along with its theological twin, Divine Universal Causality, can be considered the only view in Western philosophy that attempts to reconcile the concepts of free will and determinism, and thus bears some unique similarities to the views of mainstream Islamic theologians, including some of the arguments proposed by Gülen. So, to some extent, the general compatibilist view is consistent with the views of mainstream Islamic scholarship apart from the theological assertion in which the Ash'arītes and Māturīdītes attribute causality to God only, but also acknowledge human agents possess some form of nominal will. However, the Divine Universal Causality argument is consistent in many ways with mainstream Islamic theology as it also concludes that God is the ultimate cause of causality.

Finally, and most importantly, even though the general compatibilist argument appears to have several fundamental similarities to Gülen's methodology of reconciliation, there are many idiosyncratic concepts in the arguments proposed by Gülen that distinguishes it from theories proposed by modern philosophy. One significant distinction between the Western compatibilist view and Islamic theology is noted by Gülen: the concept of predestination is directly related to omniscience, an all-knowing attribute of God[110], therefore, predestination should not be considered an instrument of absolute determinism. This means God's preordainment of human acts is based on knowledge, not an imposed or predetermined future. The following chapter focus on a reflective analysis of Gülen's methodology of reconciliation with the further objective of clarifying the distinctive concepts proposed by Gülen.

110   Gülen, F. (2011). *The essentials of the Islamic faith.* Clifton: Tughra books.

Chapter Four

GÜLEN'S PERSPECTIVE ON DESTINY
AND DIVINE WILL

Gülen's perspective focuses predominantly on the following concepts:

a. Definition of destiny
b. Concepts of *qadar* and *qaḍa*
c. Divine determinism observed in the macro universe
d. Definition of Divine knowledge and will
e. Predestination in human acts
f. Nature of free will

It is important to note that in addition to Divine revelation and tradition, Gülen also uses scientific arguments and philosophical analogies relevant to modern day understanding with an objective to explain some of the most complex topics of Islamic theology such as Divine Destiny and free will. Gülen's meticulous analysis of the topic not only stems from the principle that belief in destiny is an important part of Islamic theology, but also from its impact on the lives and actions of Muslims. In his arguments, Gülen also provides an answer to the question: Do we just submit to the predestination and Divine will or do we use our free will to make a difference in our lives?

Based on the Prophetic tradition, "do not talk about Divine Destiny because destiny is the secret of God. Do not try to explain the secret of God"[1], some scholars believed the topic of destiny is 'a slippery ground of theology' as they claimed that the essential articles of the Islamic creed may be misunderstood or misinterpreted. It can be argued that theoretical frameworks based on *'aql* (reason) alone may produce theories that comprise a divergence from the fundamental teachings of the Qur'an and Prophetic tradition. Because of this general principle, reason-based arguments are considered by some scholars as momentous risks to one's conviction in belief. The topic of destiny and free will is one of these discordant arguments that have the potential to produce theories that may contradict the creedal statements of Islam. Despite the risk, the topic of destiny has been vigorously debated within the circles of scholars of theology.

---

1   Muttaqī, -H. A. I.-H. (1895). *Kanz al-'ummāl fī sunan al-aqwāl wa-'l-af'āl*. Hyderabad, Bangladesh: Maṭbaʿat Daʾirat al-maʿārif an-niẓāmijja. 1:132

Contemporary Islamic theologians cannot be excluded from a debate that revolves around such an important problem of theology. Although *Ah al Sunna wa'l Jamāʿah* of the current times continue to base their arguments about destiny predominantly on the teachings of the Ashʿariyyah and Māturīdīyyah schools, there seems to be a need for a broader understanding of the two concepts in conjunction with the academic arguments of modern philosophy and scientific developments in recent times. For this reason, Gülen addresses the issue in several of his works with the objective of providing a modern understanding of Divine Destiny and free will.

A thorough examination of arguments indicate that Gülen builds his views primarily on the teachings of Abu Hanīfa and al-Māturīdī, with considerable influence from the teachings of Bediuzzaman Said Nursi. However, he has also formulated a modern theological approach to the concepts of destiny and free will in many aspects, such as original analogical premises that contribute to better understanding of this complex philosophical problem. He approaches the topic with in-depth theological understanding but also provides allegories that simplify an extremely complex topic. It can be argued that Gülen uses reason-based arguments more than any other contemporary Islamic theologian. He concurs with Nursi's principle, which argues that the past should be considered as destiny and the future as an invitation to exercise one's free will.[2] One may assume that this principle is the foundation of Gülen's theoretical framework regarding the reconciliation of Divine Destiny and free will.

Gülen's definition of Divine Destiny

Gülen defines Divine Destiny as God's infinite power, will and knowledge, which encompasses the past and future as if they were an infinitesimal point within God's infinite knowledge, as Islamic theology asserts God is not constrained by the different states of the space-time continuum. He explains:

Divine Destiny is God's knowledge which include the planning, programming, predetermining, preordaining of all phenomena from the quantum world to the macro universe, from atoms to galaxies and the

---

2   Nursi, S. (2012). *Mektubat* [Letters]. Istanbul: Sözler. p. 457.

future states and lifespans of all existence, including human life, and revealing what was predetermined in the physical realm through His will and power.[3]

The statement implies that all events both in the micro and macro worlds have a prior existence in the infinite knowledge of God, they are predetermined and brought into existence with precision and order through the will and power of God. Gülen further explains that "Divine Destiny is the predetermination and recording of all that has and will occur in existence, in the *Imamun Mubin* [Manifest Record]."[4] This implies that Divine Destiny encompasses both the past and the future.

In defining Divine Destiny, Gülen begins by focusing on the etymology of the term *qadar*, explaining that its meanings include 'to measure,' 'to shape' and 'to form'. He explains the term comes from the root word *qa-da-ra*, which means "he portioned it into shares and then distributed it."[5] He adds the term also carries the meaning "he determined it through his power.[6]" According to Gülen, in classical Arabic, when the term is transferred into an emphasised verb *qad-da-ra*, the meaning becomes "he decreed". Using these etymological methodologies, Gülen believes the special meaning of *qadar* is: "...the thing that God has predetermined and decreed."[7]

Accordingly, for Gülen, since everything in the universe is preordained and created by God, Divine Destiny has decreed all phenomena in the universe. This view corresponds with the views of the majority of *Ahl al Sunnah wa'l Jamāah* theologians.

Concepts of *qadar* and *qaḍa*

According to Gülen, the concept of Divine Destiny has two indispensable components; the first is defined as *qadar*, which refers to the infinite knowledge of God, and the second is *qaḍa*, which signifies the creation of this knowledge when the decreed time for the materialisation

---

3   Gülen, F. (2009). *Essentials of the Islamic faith*. NJ: Tughra Books, p. 16.

4   Ibid.

5   Ibid.

6   Ibid.

7   Ibid.

arrives; this approach is in accordance with views of al-Māturīdī. In a broader sense, Gülen explains that *qadar* is attributing the occurrence of everything to God's knowledge before they eventuate, thus affirming that God has prior knowledge of every occurrence in existence and this knowledge is recorded in *lawh al mahfūz*, the Preserved Register, with the will and permission of God.[8]

This is also in accordance with the views of Abu Hanīfa, who states "there is nothing in this world, or in the next, except through His will, knowledge, ordination, decree, and in accordance with His writing it in the Preserved Tablet."[9] Abu Hanīfa points out that God has knowledge of all occurrences before they eventuate, thus He has recorded them. Like Abu Hanīfa, Gülen also concludes that "Divine Destiny is a title of Divine Knowledge but limiting its definition to this would be an error."[10] Gülen's view on Divine Destiny also corresponds to Nursi's perspective as he too argues that Divine Destiny is a type of knowledge and Divine Determination substantiates human will as it is linked to human choice. Gülen supports Nursi's view and elaborates that the concept of destiny can be described as Divine Will and Decree through Divine Knowledge, but at the same time, includes God's *thubuti* (affirmative) attributes, such as the All-Seeing, All-Hearing and Divine Will.[11] For this reason, Gülen believes that denying destiny would also mean denying the attributes of God established by mainstream Islamic theology. This means that Divine Destiny originates from Divine Attributes.

Accordingly, many Islamic theologians conclude that whenever the attributes of God are addressed, destiny should also be included. Al-Qarī explains the term *'ilm* as things capable of being known, *ma'lumat*, and argues that God has the attribute of *'ilm*, All-Knowing; therefore, nothing as much as an atom[12] (or sub-atomic particle) from

---

8   Gülen, F. (2002). *Kitap ve sünnet perspektifinde kader* [Qur'an and sunna perspective on destiny]. Izmir, Turkey: Nil Yayınları.

9   Imam Azam, E. H. (1982). *Fıqh al Akbar.* p. 10.

10   Gülen, F. (2000). *Essentials of the Islamic faith.* Fairfax, Va: The Fountain. p. 8

11   Ibid.

12   The term atom was used here in place of the the Arabic term *dharrah* meaning the smallest thing known to humans. The Arabic term for atom is *dharatan* which comes from the same root word.

the earth and heavens could escape His knowledge. This is similar to Laplace's argument, which claims, if there was a vast intelligence that had the ability to comprehend all the forces in nature and analyse the data from the movements of the lightest atoms to the largest astronomical bodies, there would be no uncertainty about the future as the past would be present to its eyes.

For this reason, some scholars argue destiny equates to infinite knowledge of God. Gülen, however, refrains from supporting this statement as he believes it may imply exclusion of 'destiny' from the essential articles of faith and argues: "We say, as we believe in God, His angels, His books, His prophets and life after death, we also say that there is belief in destiny."[13] With this statement, Gülen affirms that destiny is directly related to Divine attributes, but the concept is also an essential article of the Islamic faith. However, for Gülen, the quintessence of the matter is, as Ahmad ibn Hanbal argued, *qadar* (predestination) emanates from *qudra* (power), an attribute of God, thus one who denies destiny also denies many attributes of God. This means the power of God requires predetermination as space-time and matter cannot come into existence without the power and determination of an All-Knowing and All-Powerful being. Therefore, the concept of predestination cannot be separated from *qudra* (power).

Gülen further argues that those who have not addressed the topic within the perspective of *Ahl al Sunnah wa'l Jamā'ah* have always deviated from the main path, as in the case of Mu'tazilite rationalism or Jabrīyyah compulsionism. According to Gülen, technically the term *qadar* (Divine Destiny) can be interpreted as all events that have been preordained and willed by God. He uses the following verse as evidence:

And with Him are the keys of the unseen; none knows them except Him. And He knows what is on the land and in the sea. Not a leaf falls but that He knows it. And no grain is there within the darknesses [sic] of the earth and no moist or dry [thing] but that it is [written] in a clear record.[14]

---

13   Gülen, F. (2000). *Essentials of the Islamic faith*. Fairfax, Va: The Fountain. p. 9.

14   Ibid. & Qur'an 6:59.

Based on this verse, it can be concluded that Divine Destiny encompasses all phenomena in existence as Divine Determinism can be observed in the macro universe.

Divine Determinism observed in the macro universe

For Gülen, Divine Determinism observed in the macro universe is absolute as he argues that "Islam does not accept the Deism's concept of God, namely, that He created the universe and left it to run itself."[15] He points out that humans are contained by space-time continuum and, for this reason, limited in drawing true conclusions about the relation between the creator and creation, while God is beyond space-time continuum and therefore, He has infinite and eternal existence.

Gülen implies that natural laws which govern the universe are the strongest evidence that all phenomena and continuous acts of destruction and survival are predetermined and unfold according to a Divine plan that has been recorded in the Preserved Tablet. He makes this point by claiming "neither the earth nor any being, or object has ever been able to remove itself from this universal tide, these continuous acts of destruction and survival."[16] He further stresses that, although these occurrences are evident in nature and indicate Divine determinism, it is puzzling how materialists continue to refer to them as natural occurrences.

Based on the verse: "...And everything is with Him in due measure..."[17] Gülen asserts the universe is governed by a deterministic plan, program, precision, measurement and balance. He supports this with another verse from the Qur'an, "And there is not a thing but that with Us are its depositories, and We do not send it down except according to a known measure."[18] So, for Gülen, scriptural evidence supports universal

15   Gülen, F. (2021). Divine decree and destiny. Retrieved January 5, 2021, from https://fGülen.com/en/fethullahGülens-works/essentials-of-the-islamic-faith/divine-decree-and-destiny.

16   Gülen, F. (2011). *Kitap ve sünnet perspektifinde kader.* Istanbul: Nil yayınları. p. 167.

17   Qur'an 13:8.

18   Qur'an 15:21.

determinism at a macro level. He supports this statement with the argument there is such a vast and comprehensive governance of destiny in the universe that no phenomenon or event can be excluded from it. He argues that the creator of the universe has preordained everything from the cracking of a seed to the arrival of spring, from the birth of a human, to the birth of stars and galaxies.

Gülen asserts, based on empirical data, scientists around the globe concur there is determinism in the macro universe and accordingly have written thousands of pages of literature on this topic.[19] So, for Gülen, the vast intelligence hypothesised by Laplace exists and He has absolute knowledge about all existence. Therefore, this supreme intelligence knows all states of matter, meaning their states in the past, present and future are readily available to Him. This indicates universal determinism, at least at a macro level.

Gülen points out that even Karl Marx speaks of determinism in his writings on revisionism. There is also an emphasis on some Islamic sociologists such as Ibn Haldun who also indicated some form of determinism in socio-political behaviour and this concept has come to be known in the Western world as Revisionism.[20] Gülen adds that followers of *Ahl al Sunnah wa'l Jamá'ah* can only accept this concept with the condition that an absolute Divine Will determines everything in existence, including human acts. So, for Gülen, there is absolute determinism at macro levels. This is also compatible with Newtonian determinism, which suggests that the past and future are fixed. In support of this view, Gülen provides an analogy where he argues that buildings are constructed according to plans drawn by architects; so how could one assume the universe with its entire systems, from sub-atomic levels to giant galaxies that function in order and harmony, originated without any plan or predestination?[21] So, for Gülen, the entire existence requires a grand architect. In addition to this, using an illustration from the discipline of botanical sciences, Gülen argues that all seeds and kernels are tiny chests

---

19   Gülen, F. (2000). *Essentials of the Islamic faith*. Fairfax, Va: The Fountain.

20   Revisionism is a Marxist philosophy based on a materialistic interpretation of history. The philosophy "was not only an explanation of what had happened in the past but an assertion of what was inevitably to come" (Bailey, 1954, p. 452).

21   Gülen, F. (2011). *The essentials of the Islamic faith*. Clifton: Tughra books.

that contain a program, which includes the future states of the plant. He points out that the destiny of a tree is already recorded in its seed.

It is evident that these arguments on universal determinism are based on classical Islamic theology; however, he also tends to support his views with evidence from renowned physicists such as James Jeans, whom he mentions as being precise in his statement: "The agent who has established the subatomic and human worlds and the rest of the universe, has without doubt designed them according to precise measurements."[22] Jeans' statement regarding the just-so measurement corresponds with a verse from the Qur'an, which points out that God creates everything with due (precise) measure.

The frequent usage of analogical illustrations based on philosophical concepts to validate the premises in Gülen's arguments is apparent throughout his works. For example, when he attempts to prove that everything in the universe is governed by predestination, he offers a philosophical allegory like the following: "The human sperm does not lie as the language of the chromosomes such as the RNA and DNA clearly testify that they are programmed to form the human body."[23] The argument infers that the biological development of the human body was already preordained in the human DNA. He considers this as determinism observed in biology and further expounds by arguing that with the discovery and advancement of computer technology, scientists have established that every living being is biologically pre-programmed from the moment it is created. This program exists throughout the entire universe, from subatomic particles to giant galaxies.

In making a point of this, Gülen emphasises this imposed determinism should be considered as 'general determinism,' which does not include human free will as it looks at preordainment from the perspective of universal determinism. He is conscious of the compulsionistic views of the school of Jabrīyyah and the camp of incompatibilism which argue for all-encompassing determinism, that includes human actions. So, in comparison to compulsionists, Gülen's view is universal rather than specific. This means that God creates whatever He wills in the micro and macro universes, excluding human intentions and desires.

---

22   Ibid. p. 11.
23   Ibid. p. 22.

Arguments put forward by classical mechanics are somewhat analogous to this as it defines 'general determinism' as 'causal determinism,' and maintains that natural events are necessitated by antecedent events and circumstances together with the laws of physics. Whether one ascribes this universal determinism to God or to the laws of physics, there is consensus on its existence as classical mechanics point to determinism in the macro universe.

Regarding this universal determinism, Gülen asserts that God is *Jabbar*, a Name of God meaning He has the ability to impose whatever He wills. This indicates that although He creates everything through causality and wisdom, these are not binding conditions for Him. The reason for this is God possesses the affirmative attribute of *qudra*, infinite power, and the opposite cannot be attributed to God. Al-Qarī expounded on this by arguing that "powerlessness is a sign of *huduth*, [which means] being originated and of *imkan* (possibility) [as opposed to having a necessary existence] for in it, is defect of being in need of something"[24], therefore, binding conditions cannot be associated to God, who is All-Powerful. Accordingly, He can do as He wishes, "One Who freely does whatever He wishes."[25] Here, the Qur'an states the decision in the creation of something belongs exclusively to God and He creates whatever and whenever He wills.

Furthermore, God determines the creation of everything in the universe: "[He] has created each thing and determined it with [precise] determination."[26] Accordingly, Divine Determination is evident in the universe as physicists like James Jeans assert there is precise geometry in the universe and such precision in measurement indicates an eternal, omniscient, omnipotent creator.

To strengthen his argument of Divine Determination in the macro universe, Gülen further argues astrophysicists have established that magnetic forces in all parts of the universe can be measured, which indicates that space with its geometric dimensions exists with precise forces that maintain its order. The findings of contemporary astrophysicists

---

24   Maghnīsāwī, A. M. (2014). *Imam Abu Hanifa's al-Fiqh al-akbar explained* (A-R. ibn Y. Mangera, Trans.). (2. ed.). London: White Thread Press. 73-74.

25   Qur'an 85:16.

26   Qur'an 25:2.

conclude the universe is governed by classical mechanics that is utterly deterministic. From an Islamic theological perspective, this deterministic feature of the universe may be interpreted as manifestations of the Manifest Record and Manifest Book[27]. For this reason, in principle, Gülen's perspective on universal determinism agrees with the views of renowned physicists like Newton and Einstein, who have also concluded the macro universe is deterministic.

Gülen further elaborates on this by construing that precise measurements in the motions of celestial bodies, the just-so design detected in the cosmos, and balance and order observed throughout the universe, is an indication of Divine Determination. For this reason, the laws of physics are fixed, not variable, and classical mechanics points to a deterministic universe. From a cosmological perspective his assessment of universal determinism concurs with the findings of modern astronomy and astrophysics.

Empirical evidence indicates that all matter is preordained, programmed with their specifics and created accordingly.[28] The argument is sustainable as the same principle is applicable throughout the cosmos, from quantum particles to stars. Gülen concludes by stating that the *Imamun Mubin* (Manifest Record) or *Lawh al Mahfūz* (the Preserved Tablet) contains the future states of matter in the universe and that "this is what we call *qadar*"[29], Divine Destiny observed in the macro universe. He further contends that the universe is the product of God's will, which creates with wisdom. However, Gülen also notes, although reason and wisdom are not binding factors for God, He does not act in an unjust or unwise manner towards His creation, as He has the attributes of All-Just and All-Wise.

In support of this argument, Gülen provides further evidence to wisdom in universal determinism by stressing the order and harmony observed in the universe is the result of determined laws. He maintains that the laws of physics are established and implemented by Divine wisdom and power. This means they are immutable and cannot be changed or modified. For example, no one has the power to alter or change the

---

27   Qur'an 6:59.

28   Gülen, F. (2011d). *The essentials of the Islamic faith*. Clifton: Tughra books. p 22.

29   Ibid.

gravitational constant as it is a law established by God and this is evidence for Divine Determinism. From a philosophical perspective, the argument seems to be valid as physical laws are discovered by scientists but cannot be designed, altered or implemented by them.

Gülen further argues that humans have no control over natural laws that govern the universe as he stresses there is no human involvement in the formation of days, months, years, seasons, sun's light emission, earth's spin on its axis and rotation around the sun. He claims all these precisely measured occurrences are the products of Divine Knowledge and Destiny that produces everything with balance, exactitude, due measure, and wisdom.[30] Therefore, the notion of fine-tuning, the delicate balance in the four fundamental forces of nature and the unchangeable precision in laws of physics, such as gravity, centrifugal and centripetal forces support the concept that the universe is governed by an All-Powerful and All-Knowing being.

Although there are counterarguments to determinism at quantum levels, Carroll claims that even quantum mechanics displays signs of determinism according to Schrödinger's equation, which describes quantum mechanical behaviour.[31] This indicates a deterministic universe at all levels. Such a universe points to preordainment, design, and purpose. For this reason, Gülen argues that the entire universe in its past, present and future states is predetermined by God. He supports his argument with the verses: "Surely in the creation of the heavens and the earth and the alternation of night and day (with their periods shortening and lengthening) there are signs (manifesting the truth) for the people of discernment '...Our Lord, You have not created this universe without meaning and purpose.'"[32]

It can be seen that the argument on the deterministic universe is based on the Qur'an and classical mechanics. However, the entire argument changes when human free will is introduced into the equation. From an Islamic theological perspective, moral responsibility requires the existence of some form of free will; therefore, Islamic theology asserts that humans possess some form of free will. The opposite cannot

30   Gülen, F. (2009). *Essentials of the Islamic faith*. NJ: Tughra Books. p. 101

31   Carroll, S. (2011). On determinism. *Discover*.

32   Qur'an 3:190.

be embraced in a reality where humans are held responsible and judged for their acts. Evidently, these Divine acts, which include preordainment and the power to create space-time and matter in specific shapes, forms, and measurement, require infinite knowledge and will.

Definition of Divine Knowledge and Will

According to Abu Hanifa, "there can be no alteration in the knowledge of God"[33]; hence, all that would occur in the future already has pre-existence in God's knowledge. **Gülen agrees with Abu Hanīfa as he also concludes that the concept of destiny includes God's infinite knowledge, the recording of everything that would come into existence in a** Preserved Register and the creation of what is known by God, when the time for its creation arrives. He also includes God's will in the equation of destiny by arguing that destiny is the knowledge that materialises through *irāda*, the Will of God.

He explains that Divine Destiny, in one sense, is almost identical to Divine knowledge and this is why the Qur'an refers to it as *Imamun Mubin*, the Manifest Record: "Everything We have written down and kept in a Manifest Record."[34] Therefore, destiny can also be defined as God's creation and design according to specific measures and precise balances.

To further elucidate the concept of Divine Knowledge and Will, two terms cited in the Qur'an: *Imamun Mubin* (Manifest Record) and *Kitābun Mubin* (Manifest Book) can be used as key concepts. The Manifest Record refers to: "Divine Knowledge and Will which encompass every phenomenon and event in the universe."[35] The element that differentiates this view from Laplace's hypothesis is that not only this vast intelligence has the ability to know the past, present and future states of all matter but it also determines and wills their motions and actions. Therefore, the concept of predestination includes Divine will and creation as *Imamun Mubin*, and *Kitābun Mubin* are inseparable actualities.

---

33   Imam Azam, E. H. (1982). *Fiqh al Akbar*. p. 10.

34   Qur'an 36:12.

35   Gülen, F. (2009). *Essentials of the Islamic faith*. NJ: Tughra Books. p. 93

Gülen states: "the Manifest Record also refers to the phenomenon that nothing can escape from the knowledge of God."[36] This perspective also supports al-Qari's view that "He [God] knows what would result [even] if the non-existent were to come into existence."[37] To shed light on the concept of the Manifest Record, Gülen uses an analogy about the human brain, elucidating that a book an author plans to write has pre-existence in the author's mind. Therefore, it exists before it is written and published. The analogy intends to explain that God is the author of the great book of the universe; hence He has prior knowledge of everything and every event that He has created and will create in the future.

The Manifest Book, on the other hand, is another name for Divine Will and God's creational and operational laws in nature. Gülen claims that the Manifest Record can be defined as theoretical destiny while the Manifest Book can be referred to as actual destiny. Therefore, he maintains that Divine Destiny has two components: destiny that exists in God's knowledge and destiny that is willed and created by God. These definitions are specific to Gülen in their modern conceptual explanations, but they have a foundation in Nursi's arguments, as he also concluded that *Kitābun Mubin* is another title for God's will and creational laws in the universe, and *Imamun Mubin* is title of Divine Knowledge.[38]

God's attribute of knowledge is directly related to destiny as this attribute manifests also as a Divine Name, *al 'Alim*, which means the All-Knowing. However, the knowledge of God is beyond human comprehension or conception, thus the human intellect can only acquire limited knowledge about His attributes by meditating on His creations and studying His acts. For this reason, Gülen concludes that God is known through His Names and attributes, not through His essence. Again, this coincides with the views of Abu Hanīfa who concluded that the essence of the attributes of God cannot be known. Gülen agrees with Abu Hanī-

---

36   Ibid.

37   Maghnīsāwī, A. M. (2014). *Imam Abu Hanīfa's al-Fiqh al-akbar explained* (A-R. ibn Y. Mangera, Trans.). (2. ed.). London: White Thread Press. p. 77.

38   Nursi, S. (2005). *The words: The reconstruction of Islamic belief and thought.* Somerset, N.J: Light. p. 486.

fa, who used the term *bila kayf,* 'essence unknown,' for all attributes of God.[39]

The argument can be further augmented with the theological principle Divine attributes can only be understood through Divine acts.

To have some comprehension about God's attributes, one needs to resort to comparisons and analogies. Theological emphasis on attributes like knowledge and will is important because formative Islamic scholars such as Ahmad ibn Hanbal also concluded that the concept of destiny is directly related to Divine attributes as it originates from attributes like *irāda* (will) and *'ilm* (omniscience). He further argued that "destiny means everything is governed by God"; however, "Divine Will is not compulsion, but an opportunity given to humans."[40]

In building a connection between the concept of destiny and the Divine attributes of knowledge and will, Gülen provides the analogy of a multitalented individual who has the skills of an architect, engineer, designer and builder, who decides to construct a unique building. Initially, the building he plans to construct exists in his mind as a concept. He then draws the plans, and the building exists as a design on a document. Finally, he constructs the building according to the plans he had conceptualised and drawn. Now, the building has material existence. The analogy expounds that the building has an existence in a number of different forms: an abstract form within the agent's mind, then a drawn form on a document as a draft and, finally, a physical existence. Gülen stresses that even if the building was destroyed completely, it would have perpetual existence in the mind of the agent and a documented archive. Likewise, God has absolute and precise knowledge of existence as a whole and its contents, without any limitations.

This argument also deduces that "if God had not created the universe, it would still have existed in His knowledge."[41] A similar concept was also put forward by Abu Hanīfa, who also stated: "there can be no amendments in the knowledge of God since all that would occur in the

---

39   Imam Azam, E. H. (1982). *Fıqh al Akbar.* p. 19.

40   Ibn Hanbal, A. Oral, R., Sarı, S., & Banna, A. (2004). *el-Müsned İmam Ahmed b. Hanbel: (el-Fethu'r-Rabbani tertibi)* [Musnad collection of Imam Ahmad ibn Hanbal]. Konya, Turkey: Ensar Yayıncılık. p. 206.

41   Gülen, F. (2009). *Essentials of the Islamic faith.* NJ: Tughra Books. p. 97.

future has pre-existence in God's knowledge."[42] This is also supported by al-Qarī who argued that an entity or phenomena that has not materialised or occurred has pre-existence in God's knowledge. The argument also deduces that the future does not exist in God's knowledge as a possibility, but as actual reality.

One can build on this premise by arguing, since God created the space-time continuum, He is not Himself restricted by space-time; therefore, the continuum exists in His infinite knowledge as a singularity or unified form. This means that the past, present, future and all other concepts of time do not exist for Him. Therefore, these slices of space-time, such as the past, present and future are only artificial categories created by God to make human life, or the lives of other conscious beings, more convenient. Since space and time, the two dimensions of creation, pre-exist in God's infinite knowledge, they were already predetermined as nothing can be omitted from His knowledge.

Gülen further elaborates on this by arguing that prior to their creation, everything in the universe had an idiosyncratic form, shape, or precise measurement in God's knowledge. Their existence in a theoretical form is then recorded in "a Preserved Tablet"[43] or, according to another verse: "...a Manifest Record."[44] In this regard, Gülen challenges Muhammad Iqbal's view, which contends that God's knowledge of the future is in the form of knowing all possibilities, as Gülen asserts that God's knowledge of the future is specific and absolute. To support his view, Gülen interprets the Qur'anic verses that mention the Manifest Record and Preserved Tablet as God's precise knowledge and the recording of this knowledge in relation to everything (creation) that existed, exists and will exist in the future. So, Gülen is adamant on the notion that God's knowledge of the future is not based on probabilities, but it is absolute and specific.

He further argues that during the creation process, whatever exists in Divine Knowledge – in their original forms with the principles and laws of creation – is brought into physical reality and given corporeal bodies within the slice of time that represents a page in the space-time

---

42   Imam Azam, E. H. (1982). *Fiqh al Akbar*. p. 11.

43   Qur'an 85:22.

44   Qur'an 36:12.

continuum. This argument is based on a verse in the Qur'an that states: "God effaces what He wills (of things and events He has created, and laws He has established), and He confirms and establishes (what He wills) ..."[45]

Accordingly, Divine Will accompanies Divine Knowledge as it is through Divine Will that every act and event is given a course or direction. This means nothing can come into existence without Divine Will. This is because the Divine Will is the cause of the order and harmony that is prevalent in the universe. Therefore, the stability and order observed in the universe is an indication that the will of one agent is in effect. The Qur'an points to this with the verse: "Had there been within the heavens and earth [other] gods besides the God, they both would have been ruined."[46] By the term 'other gods', the verse also refers to other 'doers', including accidents, chance and random events. Divine Will, on the other hand, encompasses all phenomena and events in the universe, which provides a better explanation for the order observed in the macro cosmos. For Gülen, "Divine Will gives specifics, physiognomies and a specific direction to all phenomena and event," without annulling human free will.[47] Gülen magnifies this concept by arguing that predestination is a project that exists within the Divine Knowledge in the form of a blueprint for all entities, properties and beings in the universe. He claims that knowing something and giving it corporeal existence are two different things.[48] This claim implies that knowing an event prior to its occurrence and materialising it at a predetermined time are two different things.

The premise here is that knowledge is subject to what is evident or obvious. This means that something is known according to what *is* or what it *will be*. The knowledge of God is defined by an Arabic term *muhīt*, which means All-Encompassing: "...God indeed encompasses all things in (His) Knowledge."[49] Hence, just like everything in the universe, human lives and actions also pre-exist in God's knowledge.

---

45   Qur'an 13:39

46   Qur'an 21:22

47   Gülen, F. (2009). *Essentials of the Islamic faith.* NJ: Tughra Books. p. 100.

48   Gülen, F. (2000). *Essentials of the Islamic faith.* Fairfax, Va: The Fountain.

49   Qur'an 65:12.

To illustrate Gülen's argument for predestination being a type of knowledge, an example can be taken from the discipline of astronomy where the lunar cycles are calculated by astronomers many years prior to their motions. The calculations are recorded, and the data is made available to anyone who has access to the internet. These data can be thought of as the 'destiny' of the moon; however, it does not possess the power to govern the moon's cycles. This means that data is knowledge, and it depends on what is real, obvious, and actual. This analogy is offered for the purpose of comparison and not for establishing a similarity between human and divine knowledge.

The data collected by scientists can have deficiencies and there is always a possibility of error in judgment, whereas God's knowledge is absolute and all-inclusive; therefore, it does not depend on calculations or analysis. The moon analogy demonstrates that lunar cycles do not depend on the information or data collected by astronomers; on the contrary, the accuracy of the empirical data depends on the predetermined motion of the moon.

Gülen elaborates on this by arguing that cause and effect, motive, and result, beginning and end, exist within each other and they have all been squeezed into one point of singularity in Divine Knowledge. The idea bears some resemblance to black hole mechanics, where scientists believe that time ceases to exist beyond the event horizon or, more specifically, past, present, and future coexist.[50] Analogously, for Gülen, all causes and effects, slices of space-time, exist in a form of singularity within God's infinite knowledge.[51] Thus, for God, there are no concepts like before-after, prior-subsequent or past-future. Accordingly, mainstream Muslim theologians concur on the concept that God knows all human actions prior to their occurance and creates them at the time of the action. Gülen supports this argument by expounding the view that not only does God's knowledge encompass anything and everything (including human actions), but also brings them into existence through Divine will and the power of creation. It is evident that, like his predecessors, Gülen repudiates the views of the Mu'tazila and Jabrīyyah, and the contemporary views of incompatibilism and libertarianism.

---

50   Moskowitz, C. (2011). For fully mature black holes, time stands still. Space.com.

51   Gülen, F. (2011). *The essentials of the Islamic faith.* Clifton: Tughra books.

Evidently, this perspective on determinism and free will is more aligned with compatibilism, as the concept of predestination in Islamic theology includes the notion that human life and actions are also recorded in the Preserved Tablet: "Every human being's destiny We have fastened around his neck."[52] Therefore, all human actions have pre-existence in God's knowledge and the Divine Register. So, humans perform acts that were already recorded in the Divine Register even before they come into existence. It is important to note that this concept should not be considered as compulsionism as what is recorded is knowledge: therefore, it does not enforce or impose humans to act in a certain way.

This means that having knowledge of a future event does not mean enforcing the occurrence of the event. For example, a person who has a premonition about an accident that will occur in the future cannot be held responsible for the accident when it occurs.

Predestination in human acts

Gülen maintains that everything and every event in the universe is the product of creation and God is the only creator; therefore, human acts cannot be excluded from this theological principle. So, from an Islamic perspective, all human acts, such as eating, drinking, sleeping, walking, thinking, speaking, and listening, are created by God. According to Gülen, all those who have ephemeral, transient existence would see this reality clearly.[53] There are many things that humans have no control over, even within their own lives. For example, no one decides when and where they will be born, who their parents will be or the specifics of their appearance. For this reason, the Jabrīyyah and incompatibilists often fall into the assumption there is absolute determinism or compulsion in the universe.

Although Gülen persistently emphasises that human acts also have pre-existence in God's knowledge, he also points out that one cannot be in the following frame of mind: "since my life is already predestined, I do not need to do anything," because the Qur'an also states: "And that

---

52   Qur'an 17:33.

53   Gülen, F. (2000). *Essentials of the Islamic faith.* Fairfax, Va: The Fountain.

man has only that for which he [or she] labours."[54] Although, on the surface, there seems to be some form of inconsistency between the verses that state human acts are created by God and verses that assert moral responsibility, in principle they confirm and support each other. Gülen clarifies this with an analogy where he connotes the act of placing food into the mouth does not mean nourishing the body. Humans have no cognisant control over the process of brain and muscle coordination in the mouth, the contribution of the salivary glands that prepare the food for digestion, the functions of the digestive system, the data conveyed to the stomach about the consumed food and this information on the combination of chemical substances required for digestion and transformation of the food into nourishment.[55] And this is only the beginning of the process.

The point made here is that one cannot claim, since "I have placed the food in my mouth, so I am the one who is nourishing the body."[56] For Gülen, someone who makes such a claim is in fact ascribing the acts of God to themselves. Therefore, although it is Divine Knowledge, Will and Power that acts in the process of nourishment, free will is not negated as claimed by the Jabrīyyah, who argue that human will is nothing but an illusion.[57] So, mainstream Islamic theologians believe that human agents play a minor role in the origination of their actions. Therefore, our share in determining our acts is infinitesimally insignificant. For this reason Gülen argues that "God creates the results for human acts in accordance with the laws of physics (cause and effect) which He has decreed for His creation."[58] This argument is supported with the following verse from the Qur'an, "Say, I have no power to harm or benefit myself, except by God's will."[59]

However, the Qur'an also assigns moral responsibility to humans. This moral duty is decreed by verses like: "And whoever does an atom's

54   Qur'an 53:39.

55   Gülen, F. (2007). *Questions & answers about Islam*. Istanbul: Nil Yayınları.

56   Ibid. p. 159.

57   Ibn Asakir, A.-H. (1928). *Tabyīn kadhib al-muftarī* [Disclosing the liars and slanderers]. Dimashq: Matba'at al-Tawfiq.

58   Gülen, F. (2007). *Questions & answers about Islam*. Istanbul: Nil Yayınları. p. 158.

59   Qur'an 10:49.

weight of good will see it; and whoever does an atom's weight of evil will see it."[60]

In his annotated interpretation of the Qur'an, Ali Ünal explains this verse as "in the hereafter every person will be shown all of his/her deeds, down to the smallest ones"[61] This means that no deed goes unnoticed by God. Ünal elaborates that the above verse also means "everyone will see and receive the consequences of their deeds"[62] He further argues: "this is the basic principle in God's justice in the hereafter."[63] His analysis of the verse suggests humans are morally responsible for their actions, and thus possess free will. Ünal's arguments are derivatives of Gülen's perspective that provides an answer to the question whether humans are free to choose their actions, by arguing that "being guided or being left astray relates to God and depends on His will."[64]

The argument asserts that God guides people to the right path because His divine name *al-Hadi*, the One Who Guides, requires it and He leads some people astray because His divine name *al-Mudīl*, the One Who Leads Astray, requires it. However, Gülen also points out that this does not mean God decides who will be guided and who will go astray in a compulsionistic manner. Rather, he believes that being guided or led astray depends on human intentions or inclinations. For this reason, evil cannot be attributed to God, as the verse: "Assuredly, God wrongs no one, not even so much as an atom's weight"[65] confirms this. So, human actions are the product of their intentions and choices that accord with the laws of physics, which God has decreed for His creation.

The concept of free will

Gülen's concept of free will revolves around Nursi's principle that argues: "the past should be considered as destiny and the future as invi-

---

60   Qur'an 99:7-8.

61   Ünal, A. (2015). *The Qur'an with annotated interpretation in modern English*. New Jersey: Tughra Books. p. 1190.

62   Ibid.

63   Ibid.

64   Gülen, F. (2011). *The essentials of the Islamic faith*. Clifton: Tughra books. p. 157

65   Qur'an 4:40.

tation to exercise one's free will."[66] Gülen argues that within the laws of causality, free will is an important tool in achieving great success. For Gülen free will is an ability of free action within the parameters of the divine program and causality.[67] This means humans have an ability to act within an intangible medium delimited to inclinations. This is based on al-Māturīdī's and al-Nasafī's view, which understands that God originates acts appealed by human will, but human agents become the doers through the acquisition and performance of these acts.[68]

Gülen further expounds by arguing that "We do not consider human will as an existing corporeal entity. In matters of creed this is the view of majority of Muslims and *Ahl al Sunnah wa'l Jamā'ah* scholars."[69] So, as humans, we accept the physical existence of our limbs and organs and they were all created by God, yet we do not use the same argument for our will, as human will does not have an external existence, meaning a physical substance that can empirically be tested. For that reason, it cannot be considered as a created entity, however, it may be defined as a God-given quality.

According to Gülen, things that do not have external existence are not created, yet they exist in the knowledge of God. This argument is based on al-Māturīdī's view that, since human will only have a nominal, intangible existence, it is not created. It is an ability given to humans by God. Gülen, explicates that, if human free will was created like the rest of the human limbs and organs, then its function would have been determined as well. This means, had God created our will through predetermination and compulsion, as he creates our physical bodies, we would not have been morally responsible for any of our acts. For this reason, human will is not a created entity; rather, it has an abstract existence, like hypothetical lines in geometry.

Since humans are not puppets that move upon a pull of a string by the puppet master, one can conclude that justice necessitates that those

---

66   Nursi, S. (2012). Mektubat [Letters]. Istanbul: Sözler. p. 457.

67   Gülen, F. (2019). The sorrows, heart and the tongue. Herkul.

68   Al-Nasafī, M. M., & Salāmah, K. (1990). *Tabṣirat al-adillah: Fī uṣūl al-dīn ʿalá ṭarīqat al-Imām Abī Manṣūr al-Māturīdī*. Damascus: al-Maʿhad al-ʿIlmī al-Faransī lil-Dirāsāt al-ʿArabīyah bi-Dimashq.

69   Gülen, F. (2009). *Essentials of the Islamic faith*. NJ: Tughra Books. p. 31.

who possess free will should be held accountable for the sins or crimes they commit. In a comparative analysis Gülen explains that, unlike humans, animals act on Divine inspiration (instinct) where they continuously behave in similar patterns. Humans, on the other hand, possess the ability to decide on how and where they live, what they use for clothing, what they eat and plan their future, using their cognitive faculties.

The evident difference between animal and human behaviour forms a sustainable argument for human free will. So, unlike the rest of the living species on earth, humans possess self-awareness and cognitive skills to choose from the many paths available to them. Perhaps the difference between human will and the rest of the living species on earth can be explained with the analogy of a mechanical robot that can only function as programmed as opposed to an advanced AI unit which possesses the ability to learn and make decisions on its own. Although the analogy does no justice to human complexity regarding intellectual capacity, emotional profundity, wisdom, purpose, and spirituality, it can be used for metaphorical comparison. The objective of the analogy is to establish that humans are given an abstract will that enables them to excel above the rest of the creation.

This abstract will[70] is not a substance that has a mass; rather, it is a theoretical entity like numbers. However, this nominal, abstract entity is required as a rudimentary condition for God's universal will in creating human acts.[71] Therefore, although Divine Destiny governs all phenomena in the universe, the origination of human acts is connected to human will. For this reason Gülen believes that "the existence of human will is self-evident as human conscience suffers the consequences of wrongful acts and bad behaviour"[72] and further argues, "why would human beings feel remorse and repent if they are not committing evil using their own free will?"[73] In defending the existence of free will, Gülen focuses on the

---

70   Gülen explains this with the term "zahiri vucudu olmayan," meaning an abstract entity that does not possess a physical external body.

71   Gülen, F. (2011). *Kitap ve sünnet perspektifinde kader*. Istanbul: Nil yayınları. p. 32

72   Gülen, F. (2008). *İnancın Gölgesinde* [Essentials of the Islamic faith]. Izmir, Turkey: Nil. p. 253.

73   Ibid.

human condition by stressing that humans are free in their views, words, and actions.

Furthermore, he argues that capabilities such as indecisiveness, comparison, judgment, evaluation, and preference are qualities that indicate free will. Again, he provides an analogy to strengthen his argument by stating "bees always construct their hives with hexagonal combs as they are guided by Divine inspirations. This is the reason why they do not have an ability to produce different models."[74] Humans, on the other hand, have the ability to produce different shapes, models and designs. This is clear indication that they are acting freely in their choices. So, although human free will does not have an external existence, its presence can be detected as an inclination.

Therefore, Divine Destiny is absolute, but does not negate human will; rather, it complements it. This principle is based on Nursi's argument, which concludes that free will exists so that humans cannot reject responsibility, and destiny exists so humans realise their limits and do not ascribe everything to human ability. According to Nursi, Divine Destiny prevents conceit and vanity, while free will necessitates moral responsibility.[75] Gülen supports this view with the argument that God takes human will into account when dealing with human acts; therefore, Divine Destiny is just, because it does not victimise humans as it creates what is requested or petitioned by the free will.

Gülen, however, also emphasises that the reality of free will is experienced through human emotions and argues that "no one is a victim of destiny. God does not predetermine our acts; rather, He creates whatever we will to do."[76] Consequently, as agents with the freedom to act, humans are responsible for whatever happens to them. Unlike Jahm bin Safwan, who claims that the only agent who has the power to act is God and that human will is an illusion, Gülen argues that God created humans and gifted them with certain faculties such as a capability to act freely.

For this reason, humans cannot blame destiny for misusing their God-given faculties. To support his argument, Gülen uses an analogy

---

74   Ibid. p. 255.

75   Nursi, S. (2005). *The words: The reconstruction of Islamic belief and thought*. Somerset, N.J: Light.

76   Gülen, F. (2011). *The essentials of the Islamic faith*. Clifton: Tughra books. p. 117.

of a person who experiences sunstroke because of his own laxity then blames the sun. This analogy is based on a narration from Prophet Muhammad (pbuh), who asserted that actions depend on intentions.[77] Based on this Prophetic narration, it can be argued that intentions are the soul of human actions as they determine whether a person deserves reward or punishment in the hereafter. Moreover, intention originates from free will, thus negating free will would ultimately mean negating accountability on the Day of Judgment and refusing responsibility on earth. This would mean repudiating all human obligations and moral responsibilities. Such concept would also negate the theological teachings of the mainstream Islamic scholarship.

Gülen asserts that "the Qur'an stresses individual and communal free choice and moral conduct."[78] Moreover, he argues that "although Divine Will could be regarded as, in some respect, the counterpart of Geist in Hegelian philosophy and of absolute, irresistible laws of history in other philosophies, the Qur'an never denies human free will."[79] On the contrary, the Qur'an assigns a duty for humans and promises reward for those who comply and punishment for those who disobey. Therefore, the concepts of duty, responsibility and accountability necessitate freedom of choice, or in theological terms *kasb*, an ability to acquire an action. Consequently, this requires the existence of will. For this reason, humans were created so that they could be assessed and tested in this ephemeral life with an objective to earn an eternal life. Therefore, the earth is a fertile farming ground for deeds where humans plant their seed of deeds and harvest its fruits in the Hereafter.[80]

From a justice perspective, this test can only be legalized with the existence of free will, as justice requires cognisance, being aware of responsibility and an ability to choose between right and wrong. For this reason, the Qur'an emphasises that human societies make history, thus they are not compelled by Divine Will. This means God uses human choice to bring His universal will into effect.

---

77   Nawawī, Z. Y. S. (2014). *Riyad as-salihin: The gardens of the righteous*. New Jersey: Tughra Books.

78   Gülen, F. (2011). *The essentials of the Islamic faith*. Clifton: Tughra books. p. 127.

79   Ibid.

80   Ibid.

According to Gülen, nothing could materialise unless God wills it; however, in relation to human acts, Divine Will is connected to human will with a basic condition. This basic condition is that human will acquires and Divine Will creates. There is no debate among the mainstream Islamic theologians about the existence of free will, however, the main debate is on the essence of human will as even the views of the two towering scholars of creed, al-Ashʿarī and al-Māturīdī, have some minute differences in their stance.

In mainstream theology, free will is an effort exerted by humans to make a preference on the many possible paths made available to them. This is only an ability of disposition within the limits of inclination. At this point Gülen concurs with al-Ghazālī by maintaining that, since free will is only a basic precondition for the creation of an action, one cannot look for a necessary connection between the cause and action. What this means is that although the request to act originates from human will, the origin of causality cannot be assigned to humans, for both the cause and effect are generated by God. Since God creates the cause and effect, human free will is considered as an abstract entity that has insubstantial existence.

However, Gülen also points out, it is impossible to talk about human virtues, moral responsibility or even humanity in a world where free action is utterly negated,[81] indicating that this insubstantial entity referred to as free will, can initiate the creation of significant acts which may also have devastating results. Therefore, there is no contradiction in defining the free will as having insubstantial existence and the significant results it can cause by requesting the creation of a particular act.

As briefly mentioned earlier, Gülen provides another analogy to further elucidate the relationship between the minor will of humans and absolute will of God. He explicates that humans need to consume food to sustain their bodies. However, their part in this vital process is no more than placing the food in their mouths, chewing and then swallowing. They take no further part in nourishing and sustaining the body as the entire process is done without their involvement. The analogy indicates the relative insignificance of the contribution made by the free will in human actions. In relation to this specific theological principle,

---

81   Gülen, F. (1983). Irada [Will]. *Sizinti Magazine*, 5, 57.

Gülen does not introduce any new concept; instead, he paraphrases the creedal statements established by mainstream scholars like Abu Hanīfa, al-Māturīdī and Nursi. However, by using philosophical allegories like the one mentioned above, he makes the topic more comprehensible.

According to Gülen, although human will is limited and inadequate, it carries immense significance as it is a reflection of the Divine Will. He argues that human will is a form of invitation to the prevalence of Divine Will. Through this invitation, Divine Will acts and human actions are generated. This model for free will supposes that, although humans have no power over the creation of their own actions, the intention or request to perform an action makes them the doers; therefore, it gives them moral responsibility over their acts. With this argument, Gülen also rebuts the Mu'tazila argument for theodicy, the theological problem of evil, by indicating that a sin or evil act will not materialise unless human agents request it through their free will.

For this reason, when Nursi addresses the theological concept of the problem of evil, he argues that "creation of evil is not evil, but the acquisition of evil is evil."[82] The implication is that humans intend and request the evil act through their ability of acquisition and God creates the act even if it is evil. Since the act of evil is requested by humans, they become the doers. Gülen accentuates this moral responsibility by stressing that *Ahl al Sunnah wa'l Jamā'ah* creed scholars have always preferred the middle path by rebutting the views of compulsionism and libertarianism. This means, humans have free will and through this will they invite the owner of the universal will to create their acts.

Although there is experience-based evidence for the existence of free will, defining its quintessence is a different thing. The nature of human free will can be considered as one of the most difficult problems of philosophy and theology.

In conclusion, although Gülen's definition of Divine Destiny and free will is founded on the views of formative mainstream Islamic theologians such as Imam Abu Hanīfa, Al-Māturīdī and Nursi, his analysis of the concepts is more comprehensive and include modern philosophical and scientific concepts, which support his arguments and offer an

---

82   Nursi, S. (1995). *The flashes collection*. Istanbul, Turkey: Sözler Neşriyat A.Ş.
      p. 111.

understanding for contemporary academics and scholars of theology in general. Furthermore, Gülen builds on the arguments and paradigms provided by mainstream scholars by introducing new innovative philosophical arguments, which to some extent mirror contemporary philosophy and scientific data. Gülen's perspective has some distinctive similarities to the contemporary compatibilist view with one significant difference: he constructs his methodology on the omnipotence and omniscience of a Divine Being rather than limiting it to classical mechanics, causal determinism, or philosophical premises. It has been established that Gülen's arguments are predominantly based on the views of the 'aqīda scholars of mainstream Islam, which also includes refutations of schools that hold extreme positions on the topic.

In essence, Gülen's understandings are derivatives of *naql* (revelation) and *'aql* (reasoning), which is the traditional methodology of *ahl al ray*, school of reason. Gülen also repudiates the theses of the rationalist school of Mu'tazila and the compulsionist school of Jabrīyyah by choosing the 'middle path' preferred by all mainstream Islamic scholars. He follows a methodology that aims to reconcile Divine Destiny and free will as he argues that the two concepts can coexist. The chapter further examined Gülen's views on *qadar, qaḍa, Imamun Mubin* and *Kitābun Mubin*, the main components of Divine Destiny and their relation to causality and human free will.

CHAPTER FIVE

_____

GÜLEN'S CONCEPTUALISATION ON RECONCILING
DIVINE DESTINY AND FREE WILL

"Adherence to causality is a requirement of respect to their Creator."[1]

Gülen's methodology of reconciliation consists of four premises:

- While Divine Destiny programs and governs the universe, humans have free will and ability of inclination. It can be surmised that human agents have been given the ability to act freely within the boundaries of the Divine plan, which may be considered as universal program.

- The past, present, and future have an infinitesimal existence within the infinite knowledge of God. This means, all phenomena, the states of all matter, from quantum particles to vast galaxies, and space-time continuum from the beginning to the end, have a minute existence in God's knowledge.

- God has recorded all occurrences that will take place in the future (this is the future from a human perspective). This indicates the concept of *lawh al mahfūz* (the Preserved Register) where all occurrences that eventuate in existence are pre-recorded in a Divine Register. The term 'future' in the statement "God has recorded the future" is relative to the human concept of time, as God is not bound or limited by space-time.

- Humans do not act in a certain way because God has already predetermined their acts; rather, God has recorded human destiny because He knew the choices humans would make even before they were created.

It can be argued that the reconciliation theory suggests that the future shapes the past, in the sense that Divine Destiny is written based on actual events that take place in the future and this is unique in comparison to traditional Islamic theology. Gülen's narrative of this extremely complex topic also considers the layperson; his frequent use of allegories also aims to address non-academics as well. Analysis of Gülen's strategy in exploring theological topics includes choosing the middle path where the argument is supported by academic literature and explicated with rational parables for the purpose of comprehension by a wide audience. A brief case study of Gülen's philosophy of life also indicates that his

---

1   Gülen, F. (2021). Makale Gunlugu. www.youtube.com/watch?v=p00zHX47z10

methodology of reconciliation is strengthened through the implementation of the theory in real time.

Gülen's methodology of reconciling free will and predestination

Gülen proposes a methodology that offers a theoretical framework which aims to establish an argument for the coexistence of predestination and free will. Detailed analysis of Gülen's argument indicates that he inclines towards the views of the Māturīdiyyah school of theology, although his arguments are constructed based on the teachings of Nursi who comes from an Ash'arīte tradition. However, Nursi also makes frequent usage of 'aql, reasoning, in his arguments, which aligns his theology more with the Māturīdītes. There is, however, a propensity towards libertarianism in Gülen's arguments with a condition that God has prior knowledge of all human actions and He alone is the originator of all acts, events, and phenomena in the universe, including causality. His arguments may be viewed as a refutation of unconditional libertarianism, which claims that humans have absolute will and incompatibilism, and that all phenomena in the universe, including human will and actions, are the products of absolute or causal determinism. Repudiation of both these views means that Gülen is a strong supporter of the coexistence of predestination and free will. So, what premises does Gülen use to validate his argument?

One of the principal propositions put forward by Gülen is founded on Nursi's argument that concludes 'knowledge depends on the actual, but the actual does not depend on knowledge.'[2] He expounds on Nursi's premise by arguing that all phenomena occurring from subatomic levels to galactic proportions within the space-time continuum can be considered as diminutive existence within the infinite knowledge of God. Since God is the originator of space-time, He cannot be bound or limited by His own creation; He has knowledge about all slices of space-time as, for God, they all exist simultaneously. Having knowledge of all occurrences, which include human intentions, decisions, and acts, does not indicate compulsionism as claimed by the Jabriyyah or absolute determinism, de-

---

2   Nursi, S. (2005). *The words: The reconstruction of Islamic belief and thought.* Somerset, N.J: Light.

fended by modern hard-incompatibilists, as 'knowledge depends on the actual, but the actual does not depend on knowledge.'

This argument can be elucidated with the following analogy: astronomers can calculate the exact position of planet Mars at a given time in the future. This calculation is based on knowledge and this knowledge depends on the actual occurrence. This means that changing the data will not change the position of the planet. The connection with Gülen's argument here is that Divine Destiny corresponds with infinite knowledge of God and the phenomena that eventuate in nature are the actual. Since knowledge depends on the actual, the methodology refutes the notion of compulsionism as knowledge exists as an abstract or theoretical phenomena. This means that occurrence of events does not depend on abstract knowledge as events will occur regardless of someone having knowledge of their happening. For this reason, prior knowledge of event does not annul free action because God's prior knowledge of human decisions and actions is not evidence for determinism.

According to Gülen, this means that even if God had not created the universe, all phenomena and occurrences would still have existed in His knowledge. This philosophical premise indicates that knowledge is not an enforcing factor in the occurrence of events. Gülen stresses that since God is not bound by space-time continuum: "precedence, or posteriority, sequence or division of time, and all other time-related concepts do not have any significance for Him."[3] This means having knowledge of the future state of the universe is not a concept that supports determinism, as, for God, the concept of 'future' does not exist. This is because both the future and the past are present for God. Therefore, the attribute of All-Knowing does not indicate absolute determinism.

Evidently, the philosophical and theological perplexity regarding free will originates not from God's omniscience but from His attribute of Will. In Islamic theology, nothing can occur without the Will of God.[4] For an event or action to occur, including human actions, it must be willed by God first as His will determines the specifics of the physical action and His power gives material existence to them. For this reason, the Mu'tazila assigned the creation of evil to humans. Gülen repudiates

---

3   Gülen, F. (2011d). *The essentials of the Islamic faith.* Clifton: Tughra books. p. 97.

4   Qur'an 76:30.

this by arguing that God's willing and creating does not annul human free will. This is because God wills and creates what is requested by the human will. This premise assigns moral responsibility to human agents as they become the initiators in the process of the creation of the act. This is supported with the verse: "whatever evil befalls you is from yourself."[5] The verse indicates that intention and inclination originate from human will. This argument provides a repudiation to the Mu'tazila claim by concluding that human agents initiate the process of the creation of the act with their will.

Since the entire process begins with an intention made by the free will, human agents become the doers of the act. This also means that they are responsible of its consequences. On the other hand, in Christian theology, as argued by Augustine, the origination, thus creation of evil is assigned to human agents.[6] This is quite analogous to the Mu'tazila position. In contrast, the argument is regarded as problematic in mainstream Islamic theology. The reason for this is, according to Sunni scholars, all phenomena, events, and occurrences, including human acts, are created, or originated by God. No other being has the power to originate an act. Therefore, such creedal principle requires a methodology where although God originates the act, human agents become responsible for it. Consequently, this argument concludes that "the assignation of evil to humans is not avoided" because they initiate the process of causality which results in the origination of an act.

According to Gülen, God does not will evil, but He allows it because not permitting humans to commit evil would mean the annulment of their free will. Since the Qur'an asserts humans were created for the purpose of testing so they can attain an eternal life in the hereafter, free will is a necessary component of this Divine assessment. Consequently, like the mainstream scholars before him, Gülen also believes that human acts, through a basic rule, are connected to the absolute Will of God, where the human will inclines towards an action, God wills and creates this action by giving the power, *istita'a*, to humans, which is an ability to act at the time of the action.

---

5   Qur'an 7:79.

6   Fitzgerald, A., & In Cavadini, J. C. (2009). *Augustine through the ages: An encyclopedia.*

Like al-Māturīdī, Gülen also maintains that human free will does not have a quantifiable existence but this concept does not render its existence impossible. He believes free will is like a third eye, an insight or inner force that has the ability of inclination that allows the medium for humans to make a preference from the possibilities available to them. This preference is then created by the will and power of God.[7] For Gülen, "a project or a plan has no value or use, unless you start to construct the structure according to it..."[8] The analogy implies the plan corresponds with human free will and the construction is the will and creation of the structure, which refers to the human act.

The *seed analogy* proposed by Gülen offers to explain the existence of Divine Determinism in the previous chapter also includes the significance of free will. For example, imagine a person holding the seed of an apple tree in their hand. The seed contains the entire destiny of the tree, from sapling to full grown tree that produces fruits. This means the entire life of the tree is encoded or determined in its kernel. However, this destiny will never prevail unless the person plants the seed and nurtures it. Therefore, the person has the option of destroying the seed or planting it so it can fulfil its destiny.

The analogy provides a philosophical solution to the Jabrīyyah proposition, which claims, since God predetermines and creates human actions, free will cannot exist in a real sense. It also responds to the Mut'azila claim that God does not will evil, by concluding that even though God does not command evil, He creates the evil acts which humans acquire through their free will. The association with Gülen's seed analogy is that in both cases God is the originator of the actual physical properties such as the tree and human acts, but the decision to plant the seed or to destroy it, originates from human agents. This means God creates both the good and evil acts for those who intend, request, and acquire them by using their free will. The opposite would mean the nullification of human will. Therefore, based on the arguments of mainstream theologians, Gülen constructs a methodology of reconciliation

---

7   Gülen, F. (2002). *Kitap ve sünnet perspektifinde kader* [Qur'an and sunna perspective on destiny]. Izmir, Turkey: Nil Yayınları.

8   Gülen, F. (2011). *The essentials of the Islamic faith*. Clifton: Tughra books. p. 103.

by inferring the knowledge and will of God does not nullify free will as they rest on the inclinations and choices made by humans.

To prove his proposition, Gülen argues that "God takes our free will into account when dealing with us and our acts, and then uses it to create our deeds."[9] This is in accordance with al-Nasafi's view that "God can empower human agents with an ability to act with the condition that He creates the actual act."[10] So, for Gülen, human will is inconsequential when compared to the Will of God but it is still considered the initial cause of human acts. Consequently, Gülen's argument is based on the compatibility of Divine Destiny and free will where, although human will, *irāda al juz'īyya*, is negligible in comparison to the absolute will of God, *irāda al kullīyah*, it still plays a major part in the causation of human acts. This is also compatible with the Qur'an which states: "you do not will unless God wills…"[11]

Gülen further argues that – excluding human agents who possess free will, and therefore are liable for their acts – Divine Destiny is the dominant factor in the universe. Although the first premise of this argument agrees with the libertarian view, which claim humans are free in their actions, the second premise concurs with incompatibilism, which argues for determinism. Perhaps Gülen's theoretical framework of reconciliation can be explained with an analogy of a video game, where the game is constrained by the parameters encoded by the programmer, but the player still has limited control over the characters. The player can fail or achieve the tasks available in the game but cannot breach the boundaries of the programmed software. This is what Gülen suggests when he argues that "human will is included in destiny."[12] So, for Gülen, humans are neither dry leaves blowing in the wind of destiny, as argued by the Jabrīyyah, nor completely independent of it, as claimed by the Mut'azilites.

---

9   Ibid. p. 104.

10   Al-Nasafi, M. I.-M. (1993). *Tebsiratü'l edille fi usûli'd-dîn*. Ankara: Diyanet İşleri Başkanlığı Yayınları. p. 175.

11   Qur'an 81:29.

12   Gülen, F. (2000). *Essentials of the Islamic faith*. Fairfax, Va: The Fountain. p. 106

Causality and Divine Destiny

The principle here is that cause and effect cannot be seperated in defence of predestination. This means Divine determinism takes cause and effect into account, thus one cannot claim 'I have committed this evil because I was destined to do it.' In Islamic theology, predestination is not analysed based on the concept of *effect* alone. This means God's knowledge includes the cause and the effect; therefore, the destiny of a human agent is recorded accordingly. For example, Abu Hanīfa argues that the destiny of a given individual is not written as 'he will be a disbeliever' but it is written as 'he will be a disbeliever through his own choice and free will.'[13] This argument is important because, if one builds an argument on predestination, solely based on the *effect*, it will result in compulsionism or absolute determinism; however, the inclusion of *causality* reconciles predestination with free will.

The attempt of reconciliation is evident in Gülen's philosophy as he asserts that "[*tawakkul*] reliance means total confidence in God", as reliance is "...doing all that is necessary to obtain a desired result" while *taslim* (surrendering) means "waiting for the Eternally-Powerful One to bring about His will."[14] Therefore, submitting to the will and preordainment of God means abiding by the principles of causality then embracing the *datum* that God is the final decision-maker and creator of the results. For Gülen, humans are created within the laws of causality; therefore, they need elements such as air, water, sun, earth, sustenance, natural laws, etc. Rejection of adherence to causality and natural phenomena would mean the denial of natural laws, which were also established by God. This perspective implies that what science refers to as 'natural laws' are in fact laws governed by God, thus they should be observed by Muslims, just as the rest of the obligatory acts of the Islamic faith established by the Qur'an and Sunna.

For this reason, Gülen believes that surrendering to destiny and the will of God also incorporates compliance to *asbab*, causes or laws

---

13   Imam Azam, E. H. (1982). *Fıqh al Akbar*. p. 12.

14   Gülen, F. (2004). *Key concepts in the practice of Sufism*. New Jersey: Light Inc. p. 67.

of causality.[15] The important notion here is being in a state of constant awareness that God is the cause of all causation. So, unlike al-Ghazalī, who argues that the connection between cause and effect is not necessary, Gülen asserts that necessity of the connection is a reality with the condition that God is the cause of all causes, *musabbib al asbab*. Semantically, there is a difference between the views of al-Ghazalī and Gülen here, as the former argues there is no real connection between what physics refers to as cause and effect; instead, there is only one cause and that is what God causes to happen.[16] Gülen however, acknowledges the effects of causes with the condition that God is the real cause. Gülen's view is different to that of Ghazali's and Ibn Rushd's, as it proposes a middle path between the views of al-Ghazali who discards the necessity of the connection between cause and effect and Ibn Rushd who inclines towards causal determinism. Casual determinism concludes that human actions are generated due to antecedent events of causality and therefore, causality is the main factor in the generation of human acts.

Gülen, on the other hand, stresses that believers surrender to the Predestination and Will of God with their life philosophies and embrace whatever comes their way; however, they also use their free will to its limits in fulfilling the necessary exertion required by causality. This means they consider the past as unchangeable – therefore, predestined – but the future as many paths available for human will to choose from. For this reason, the future is evaluated as a world of possibilities where human exertion is coupled with submission to Divine Will. God's knowledge of the future does not annul the existence of these paths.

For example, a person that has a medical condition seeks refuge in God with absolute reliance, yet at the same time benefits from the science of medicine by seeking medical attention. Putting this theory into practice, Gülen received the vaccination for coronavirus at the age of 82 and stated afterwards, "adherence to causes is a requirement of respect to their Creator."[17] The implication here is that balance between preordainment, free will and causality needs to be established and implemented in

---

15   Gülen, F. (1993). Tevekkul, Teslim, Tevzih ve Sika. *Kalbin Zumrut Tepeleri*.

16   Moad, E. O. (2005). Al-Ghazali's occasionalism and the natures of creatures. *International Journal for Philosophy of Religion*, 58(2), 95-101.

17   Gülen. F. (2021). Makale Gunlugu. youtube.com/watch?v=p00zHX47z10

daily lives and this means adherence to causality. According to Gülen, this can be done by embracing the fact that all events are predestined, willed, and created by God, but, since this process does not annul free will, one should also make the required effort allowed by free will, science, and God-given abilities to make a difference. This perspective also implies causes are a reality and should be considered in discussions that focus on predestination. So, for Gülen, submitting to the Destiny of God means: "doing what is necessary to obtain a certain result without attributing any creative effects to them…"[18] This means that reliance on God includes loyalty to *asbab*, causality.

Al-Ghazalī, however, believes accepting the effects of causes in occurrences and events would violate Divine Omnipotence. Gülen, on the other hand, proposes a different solution by arguing that causes are real and that the universe functions with the laws of physics. This is referred to as *sunnatullah* in Islamic theology. This supports the notion that destiny and free will coexist. Therefore, Gülen's argument embraces the practicality of causation without violating God's Omnipotence, while al-Ghazalī's intention to protect Divine Omnipotence seemingly negates one of the fundamental principles of physics – the necessary connection between cause and effect.

As mentioned before, the difference in the two views, however, can be considered semantic as al-Ghazalī also construes that God must be the intermediary link between all events.[19] Gülen supports the same concept with the exception that he indicates that the connections between causes and effects are necessary in natural occurrences. This means Gülen encourages people to adhere to causation with the conviction that God is the definitive causer. This concept protects the members of mainstream Islam from the views of determinism, compulsionism and incompatibilism, philosophies that negate human free will altogether with the assumption that any effort made by humans to change their fate would be

18   Gülen, F. (2004). *Key concepts in the practice of Sufism*. New Jersey: Light Inc. p. 69.

19   Garber, C. P. (2017). Al-Ghazalī on causation, omnipotence and human freedom. Quaerens Deum: *The Liberty Undergraduate Journal for Philosophy of Religion*, 2(1), art. 4, p. 3.

futile as God or natural causes determine how things would eventuate and will cause them to occur as they were predetermined.

Gülen argues that the role of causality plays out in all acts that require a physical cause, and this also needs to be created by God. So, for Gülen, adherence to causality is mandatory as human ability to perform actions has the potential to earn an everlasting life in paradise. This is the point where Gülen's perspective differs from al-Ghazali's, as Gülen uses the concept of *tenasüb-ü illiyet*, a term derived from the Ottoman language, which means congruity of causality.[20] He then goes on to say that this is what we call causation or causality in physics. For Gülen, causality, human free will and the absolute will of God are interconnected and human acts originate from the collaboration of these three essentials. Therefore, human agents are responsible for playing their parts in the process by observing the laws of physics and leaving the result to God.

This view is aligned with a Prophetic narration that mentions a man who came to the masjid in Medina and asked Prophet Muhammad whether he should secure his camel by tying it up or rely on God to protect his camel. Prophet Muhammad replied: "Secure your camel and then submit to the will of God."[21] Based on this Prophetic advice, Gülen argues that establishing a balance between predestination and free will means taking all necessary precautions and measures by complying with the laws of causality and then placing one's full trust in God's will. Consequently, Gülen infers that submitting to the Will of God is the last step in a process that involves using one's free will and ability, exploring all options available and taking all necessary measures compatible with the laws of physics.

This means that for Gülen, practical implementation of a theory which maintains that predestination coexists with free will, is the amalgamation of free will, acquisition, free action, supplication, submission, reliance, and patience. The implementation of this theory is evident throughout Gülen's life as his biography suggests. While he displayed total reliance on God during the most difficult and testing times, he was not dissuaded from his activities.

---

20   Gülen, F. (2019). *The sorrows, heart and the tongue.* Herkul. Retrieved from herkul.org/bamteli/bamteli-huzun-gonul-ve-dil/

21   Tirmidhi, *Sifat al Qiyama*, p. 60.

As mentioned above, Gülen's methodology of reconciliation incorporates causality into the equation, which concludes Divine Destiny and Divine Knowledge are identical and from the perspective of God's omniscience, the past, present and future are unified in His infinite knowledge. This premise deduces that having unconstrained knowledge about space-time where the past and future are also present, repudiates the argument which claims that predestination negates free will. Consequently, prior knowledge about human actions does not lead to compulsionism because knowledge is contingent on the actual. This means God's prior knowledge of all human acts does not necessitate the nullification of free will.

For example, if an individual chooses to drive through a red light and as a result has an accident, this was already known by God prior to its occurrence. When the time for the incident recorded in the relevant person's destiny arrives, God wills and creates the event. But the responsibility belongs to the individual who wilfuly drove through a red light. If, for argument's sake, God did not create the incident to prevent the accident, the individual's free will would be negated as the decision to drive through a red light was made freely and willingly by the individual, not by God. Therefore, God cannot be held responsible for knowing and creating the incident.

Gülen applies a basic rule to refute compulsionism by arguing that "we do not do something because God recorded it; [on the contrary] God knew beforehand what we would do and recorded it."[22] I would argue that 'knowing beforehand' in this context is a figure of speech as the concepts of 'before' or 'after' do not apply to God. This means that the concept of 'waiting for future events to occur' cannot be associated with God, as the past, present and future are instantaneously available to Him. Therefore, He knows what occurs within the space-time continuum, which includes all slices of space-time and all states of the universe. This argument is quite original as it repudiates determinism through the notion that God has recorded all human acts that have already occurred from His perspective. This means that God has registered the future as it happened, because He is not bound by the space-time continuum.

---

22   Gülen, F. (2011d). *The essentials of the Islamic faith.* Clifton: Tughra books. p. 108.

The concept can be further explicated with an analogy where time is represented by a river flowing in one direction. The source of the river indicates the beginning of time and the point at which it flows into the sea indicates the end of time. All parts of this flowing body of water would be present to an agent who could observe the entire river from its source to its end. Perhaps this is what Gülen is referring to when he states that "all existence [space-time] is like a minute particle in God's infinite knowledge."[23]

Although most mainstream theologians concur on the understanding that God has prior knowledge of all future events, they have not critically analysed the implications of the theological principle which concludes that God is not bound by space-time. This is important as the philosophical premise that 'God has prior knowledge of future events' is not enough to explain the concept of God as not being contingent on space-time, meaning not being restricted or limited by time. The premise also means not being bound by the future as well. This profound premise needs to be analysed from the perspective that, for God, the past, present and future coexist; therefore, He (God) does not predict the future, but creates and observes it as it happens. This allows for the existence of free will and therefore moral responsibility.

For this reason, Gülen emphasises the significance of free will by arguing it is a prerequisite for moral responsibility as he stresses that "this world is an arena for testing, a place where we [humans] seek to acquire the state for the other life [the eternal abode]."[24] Gülen concludes that "Destiny's decrees and verdicts are based on its consideration of our free will."[25]

God's prior knowledge of human actions

Gülen's methodology of reconciliation of human will and God's will may contribute to solving the problem of free will to a certain degree; however, the perplexity surrounding the concept of human ac-

---

23   Gülen, F. (2008). *İnancın Gölgesinde* [Essentials of the Islamic faith]. Izmir, Turkey: Nil. p. 226.

24   Gülen, F. (2000). *Essentials of the Islamic faith*. Fairfax, Va: The Fountain. p. 112

25   Ibid. 117.

tions having pre-existence in God's knowledge also requires a theological solution. The question is 'since God's knowledge cannot be altered
then how could humans be free in their actions and have more than
one path to choose from?' This is an important philosophical problem
as well, because having precise knowledge of human actions prior to
their occurrence seems to indicate absolute determinism. Responding
to this problem, Gülen stresses that human acts are not bound by what
is known; rather, what is known is bound by human acts. In simple
terms, what this means is God does not predestine human acts in a
fatalistic fashion; on the contrary, human acts are predestined in based
on human decisions. To shed some light on this argument, one can
think of an architect who designs the plans of a house and then, within
the linear flow of space-time, constructs the house according to these
plans. In comparison with God's knowledge and will, the above scenario needs to be altered such that the linear flow of time is removed.
This means that the architect has concurrent knowledge of all stages of
the constructing from the beginning to the final product. Therefore,
from the architect's perspective, the house is already built somewhere
in the future slice of space-time continuum that is already present to
his eyes. In this scenario, the architect draws the plans according to the
finished product.

This analogy implies that time has no relevance to God as it does
not have a necessary existence, thus it is a contingent product of creation. Theoretical physics provide some support to this argument. The
Big Bang theory holds that the equations related to the beginning of the
universe describe singularity at T=0 (time equals zero). The implication
is that there was a point during the creation of the universe where time
had a beginning and originated with the creation of space and matter.
Many philosophers believe that an actual infinite cannot exist, meaning
a set of things that regress infinitely, therefore, just as space – which began to exist – time also had a beginning. This leads us to the conclusion
that time itself was created. Accordingly, a Supreme Being who holds the
ability to create time, cannot be bound by it.

This corresponds to Gülen's argument, which understands that
all matter and space-time existing as an infinitesimal knowledge within
God's infinite knowledge. Gülen's argument also emphasises the all-encompassing knowledge of God includes human thoughts, imagination,

intentions, decisions, actions and, consequently, the origination of those actions. Ali Ünal further expounds on this by arguing that God gives external, visible, and material existence to human intentions, choices, and actions.[26] He further argues that the earlier schools of the Jabrīyyah and Mut'azila were confused about the act of creation of human actions, assuming there were two kinds of destiny, one for the cause and the other for the effect.[27] In contrast, mainstream scholars argue that destiny encompasses both cause and effect.

Gülen also favours the middle path in the predestination–free will debate with the inclusion of causality in the equation. He concludes the verse: "For whoever wills among you to take a right course"[28] indicates freedom of choice and moral responsibility for human agents, while the verse immediately following it: "You cannot will unless God wills"[29] indicates that everything in the universe, including human actions, occurs through the will of God. According to Gülen, while the verse, "He creates you and your actions", indicates some form of determinism, another verse, "And that there is not for man except that [good] for which he strives"[30] emphasises the significance of free will.

Gülen maintains that while most philosophers study the concept of determinism by conceptualising events from the past and present, the Qur'an's perspective is based on unchanging principles. He stresses that, according to the Qur'an, individuals and societies have freedom of choice; therefore, they are responsible for their moral conduct. This means the Qur'an never negates human capability to act freely as the consensus among Islamic scholars is that this life is a period of testing for humans; it is a transient journey where they are given the opportunity to earn eternal life. Such testing requires accountability and the existence of some freedom.

Ünal, who is inspired by Gülen's works, confirms this by arguing that human responsibility towards God is voluntary, yet the rest of the

26   Ünal, A. (2015). *The Qur'an with annotated interpretation in modern English*. New Jersey: Tughra Books

27   Ibid.

28   Qur'an 81:27-28.

29   Qur'an 81:29.

30   Qur'an 53:39.

creation on earth carries out specific duties assigned to them without being aware of the duty. This means biological organisms other than humans are pre-programmed to undertake certain duties in the absence of free will. For example, a honeybee does not have an option regarding its duty, which is to produce honey. The absence of the alternative paths indicates absence of free will; therefore, this cancels out moral responsibility in the animal kingdom. In contrast, human responsibility towards God is voluntary, which indicates the existence of alternative paths and free action.[31]

This theological concept is important in Islamic law as well, because free action is a prerequisite for legal accountability. There is an incident at the time of ʿUmar ibn al Khattab, the second Khalifa of Muslims which explicates this principle. A man who had committed theft was brought before ʿUmar. The perpetrator claimed it was the will of God that caused him to commit the crime. This angered ʿUmar, who gave the man a punitive penalty. ʿUmar concluded that the man committed an additional crime by accusing God of the crime he had committed using his own free will.[32] Al-Māturīdī clarifies this by arguing that the knowledge and will of God do not force a human to act in a certain way.[33] Gülen also supports this view by inferring humans are not victims of God's Destiny. He adds that *will* is an element of the mechanism of conscience; therefore, God has built the human future upon human will.[34]

According to Gülen, human emotions, such as a guilty conscience, remorse, and repentance, also indicates the existence of free will. If human actions were decided by predestination, humans would not experience the feeling of penitence after committing a wrongful act. So, for Gülen, human qualities such as reasoning, judgment, hes-

---

31 Ünal, A. (2015). *The Qur'an with annotated interpretation in modern English*. New Jersey: Tughra Books

32 Desûkî, A. F. (1982). *El-Kaza ve'l-Kader fi'l-İslam* [Destiny and preordainment in Islam], Alexandria: Darü'd-dâve. n.p.

33 Al-Māturīdī, M. M., & Topaloğlu, B. (2005). *Kitâbü't-Tevhîd tercümesi* [Translation of Kitāb al Tawḥīd]. Ankara: İSAM, Türkiye Diyanet Vakfı İslam Araştırmaları Merkezi.

34 Gülen, F. (2014). Willpower and being tested with it. *Fountain Magazine*. Issue 97

itation, planning, and decision-making are arguments for free will. In the context of Islamic theology, the transformation of these human emotions and qualities into actions is considered as evidence for the existence of free will.

Gülen specifically mentions that these human emotions and qualities necessitate the existence of free will and free action. Consequently, the theological methodology of reconciling God's prior knowledge of all events and human free will is as follows:

a. Human decisions and actions are known by God prior to their materialisation. Omniscience, Will and predestination of God regarding human actions are defined as Divine Destiny in mainstream Islamic theology.

b. Humans do not act in a certain way because it was predestined for them; on the contrary, their actions were predestined according to the way they would choose to act. With a simple analogy, it can be argued that if an individual decides to take a day off from work the next day, this information existed in God's knowledge long before the person made the decision; therefore, the destiny of this individual would have already been written as he will not turn up for work the next day.

The important point in the entire argument is the theological principle that nothing could occur without the will of God. This means the given person's decision can only materialise through the will of God. Therefore, the will and creation of God regarding human actions are linked to human will with a basic condition that humans will and decide on the act and God wills and generates the act. For this reason, Gülen believes that submission to predestination means observing the principles of causality by using one's free will to its limits for making choices in life. Consequently, Gülen asserts that the coexistence of destiny and free will should not be limited to a theological theory; rather, it should be implemented in a practical sense as well.[35] According to this notion, the real-life implementation of the theory of coexistence would further strengthen Gülen's argument.

---

35   Gülen, F. (1993). Tevekkul, Teslim, Tevzih ve Sika. *Kalbin Zumrut Tepeleri*.

Gülen's principle of *aktif sabır* (active patience)

A brief analysis of Gülen's application of the theory that proposes the coexistence of predestination and free will is an important element that may strengthen the validity of the proposed premises. An investigation into Gülen's life indicates his perspective on Divine destiny and free will is not limited to a theory as there is sufficient evidence of practical application throughout his life. A scrupulous study of Gülen's literature, seminars, sermons, and lifestyle demonstrates that establishing a balance between causality, free action and submission to God's will has been one of the main principles of his life philosophy. The spiritual concepts of *tawakkul* (reliance) and *taslim* (surrender) have been pivotal doctrines of Gülen's philosophy throughout his life. Gülen's philosophy regarding the role of Divine destiny and free will in human life can be better understood through a brief look into his life. A limited study of events from his life can be used as evidence for his practical application of theory.

Gülen is a contemporary scholar who was persecuted most of his life in Turkey for his religious, educational and dialogue activities. He faced several charges in relation to the formation of the Hizmet Movement. Following the failed coup attempt in Turkey on 15 August 2016, the government accused the followers of the Hizmet Movement of taking part in the attempt to overthrow the government. Five days after the failed coup attempt, the president of Turkey announced a state of emergency and thousands of people, including military officers, judges, journalists, police officers, academics, teachers, clergy, and businesspersons from the Hizmet Movement were arrested. Gülen, who was in self-exile in Pennsylvania at the time, advised his students using a verse from the Qur'an: "And We will surely test you with something of fear and hunger and a loss of wealth and lives and fruits but give good tidings to the patient."[36] The Turkish government then requested Gülen be extradited from the United States to face charges; however, the US legal system announced that Turkey had not provided any evidence of his involvement in the coup attempt.[37]

---

36   Qur'an 2:155.

37   DeYoung, K. (2016, August 19). Turkish evidence for Gülen extradition pre-dates coup attempt. *The Washington Post.*

While the purge continued in Turkey, Gülen persevered in his focus on the concept of '*aktif sabır*' (active patience), a term he had coined, indicating the importance of appreciating the coexistence of Divine Destiny and free will (Gülen, 2017).[38] A*ktif sabır* is another original concept proposed by Gülen, as I have not come across this concept in the literature of formative or classical theologians. In summary, active patience is showing consistency on the path of serving God but also accepting what Divine Destiny has predetermined for you. Gülen's model of active patience rejects the notion of unconditional submission to predestination through indolence and lethargy as it proposes that submission and patience should be supported with action, effort, application, and motion.

The methodology of Gülen's implementation consists of actively taking all the necessary precautions, *tawakkul* (relying on God) and *sabr* (patience in waiting for God's decision). I would say the concept implies that humans are responsible for acting in the manner required from their humanity by embracing the principle that the final decision belongs to God.

Therefore, Gülen's theological stance on establishing a balance between determinism and free will is concentrated on accepting what God has predetermined for you, not through lassitude and indolence but through active patience. For Gülen, free will plays an important role in shaping human destiny. The argument that 'free will shapes destiny' finds supports from another Prophetic tradition where a disbeliever approached Prophet Muhammad (pbuh) with the aim of refuting the creedal article of belief in destiny. The man, who had a piece of bread in his hand, asked the Prophet if it was in his destiny to eat the piece of bread. Prophet Muhammad replied, "It will be your destiny, if you eat it."[39] Accordingly, for Gülen, the concept of coexistence requires exertion from the human capability to act and recognition that ultimately all occurrences are the products of Divine Will and Destiny. Gülen believes that even if an individual or team had accomplished great things

---

38   Gülen, F. (2017). We will show patience with active patience. Bamteli.

39   Cited in Oral, O. (2007). *Kaza ve Kadere Inanıyorum* [I believe in preordainment and destiny]. Izmir: Caglayan Matbasi. p. 53

in life, they should refrain from claiming that the achievement is theirs, as God gave them success based on their intention and efforts.

The analysis of available data suggests that Gülen attempts to achieve balance between the concepts of predestination and free will in a practical sense as well. Evidence at hand shows that majority of people who have been inspired by his teachings follow Gülen's philosophy. The activities of the Gülen Movement are beyond the scope of this book; however, I would argue that a brief analysis of his implementation of theory into practice was relevant to this topic.

In conclusion, Gülen's methodology and theoretical framework are established on formative, classical and modern mainstream Islamic theology, yet they also include innovative concepts relevant to contemporary theology, philosophy, and empirical data, such as the theory of the space-time continuum. Gülen's argument for the existence of free will is based on two key premises. The first is the theological notion of 'life is a test,' which necessitates the existence of free will because human agents can only be held morally responsible for their actions if they have the freedom to choose their actions. The concept that 'moral responsibility requires freedom in action' is universally accepted by almost all scholars, academics, scientists and thinking minds. The second premise is based on human experience as Gülen argues that although it may not be established through empirical data, all humans feel and experience the existence of free will. Therefore, the argument for the existence of free will is self-evident as every person is aware of their intellectual and physical capabilities to choose, decide, acquire, and perform an act. Since it is evident the concepts of compulsionism and absolute freedom in action cannot occupy the same space, there was a need for an argument that reconciles the two concepts or, at the very least, provides evidence that predestination and free will can indeed coexist. Arguments provided by Gülen satisfy the philosophical criteria of validity of premises and the Islamic theological criteria that require all theological arguments to be based on text and tradition.

Gülen's principle of *aktif sabır* (active patience) allows the theory of coexistence to be put into practice as it attemps to establish a connection between the concepts of Divine Destiny, Will and Power, human will, acquisition, adherence to causality and reliance on God. Additionally, to some extent, Gülen's perspective on the coexistence of destiny and free will also finds support from Western philosophy and science as the universal determinism of classical mechanics corresponds with his perspective on Divine Destiny.

CHAPTER SIX

ANALYSIS OF EVIDENCE FOR COEXISTENCE

The previous chapters examined the historical development of the concepts in Islamic and Western perspectives and analysed the different arguments on the coexistence of destiny and free will, then focused on Fethullah Gülen's perspective, critically analysing the theoretical frameworks and methodologies of reconciling the concepts of predestination and free will. The examination concluded that Gülen provides some original arguments, which aim to satisfy the Muslim audience at scholastic, academic and perhaps layperson levels. It is evident that his arguments are mainly based on the views of scholars like Abu Hanīfa, al-Māturīdī and Nursi. However, some contemporary philosophers may not show specific interest in Gülen's arguments as most of his premises are limited to arguments founded on religious texts, theological concepts, and tradition. Conversely, some of his arguments that challenge contemporary views such as libertarianism and incompatibilism could be introduced into mainstream academic literature as philosophical arguments.

Comparative analysis of Classical Islamic theologians and Gülen's works show that Islamic theology contain some important philosophical elements that may provide significant contributions to modern philosophy as well. The fact that these arguments are limited to a specific worldview may be considered a weakness by mainstream philosophers; however, it is essential to note that scholars like Gülen are not a philosopher in an academic sense – they are Islamic scholars and theologians. It would be more accurate to evaluate Muslim scholars' views and theoretical frameworks from an Islamic theological perspective: but limiting their methodologies to premises that can only be applicable in Islamic teachings would be an inaccurate assumption as some of the philosophical insinuations in their arguments can be considered noteworthy contributions to contemporary philosophy. Although Muslim theologians' theoretical frameworks are based on Islamic theology, they also propose a methodology that includes sustainable philosophical premises that intend to build a valid argument. Let us look at some of the fundamental premises proposed by Gülen:

a. Based on the Nursi argument, he argues that destiny is a type of knowledge, and knowledge depends on the actual, but the actual does not depend on knowledge.

b. Gülen refers to *'aql* (reason) and modern sciences to explain some of the most difficult concepts of Islamic theology. This is an important methodology of *Usul al Dīn* (Islamic theology).

c. He proposes the theological principle that space-time continuum with all its slices in the past, present, and future has an infinitesimal existence in God's knowledge.

d. Gülen includes the *tenasüb-ü illiyet* (necessary connection between cause and effect) concept to support the coexistence of predestination and free will.

e. Again, based on the Nursi argument, Gülen supports the principle that the past should be considered as predestined and the future as many paths available for free will.

f. He interprets the notion of *tawakkul* (reliance on God) with the term *aktif sabır* (active patience), a theological principle which aims to establish a balance between free will and predestination.

From a theological perspective, some of these arguments can be considered as significant contributions to contemporary philosophy. Let us briefly anlayse some key arguments.

Using *'aql* (reason) and modern sciences to explain some of the most difficult concepts of Islamic theology

The frequent usage of reason-based arguments and references to scientists and empirical data is evident in Gülen's works. It can be argued that he favours this methodology to provide a better understanding for a contemporary audience as some of the theological concepts put forward during the formative and classical period can be difficult to comprehend by the average layperson. Moreover, our understanding about determinism have changed with the advancement of science and current theories on quantum physics, classical mechanics, space-time continuum and black hole mechanics.

While classical mechanics indicates determinism in the universe at macro levels, there is also an indication of possible indeterminism at quantum levels. Such findings reignite the free will debate not just in the disciplines of theology and philosophy but also in theorical physics. Consequently, any future arguments that attempt to reconcile determinism with free will need to include theoretical physics into the equation.

Islamic theology would support this as most Muslim theologians and philosophers of the classical era have used theoretical physics in their arguments. One example is the kalam cosmological argument for temporal regress proposed by people like al-Kindi and al-Ghazali. The argument concludes that an actual infinite cannot exist therefore, the universe (space-time) had to have a beginning. This argument incorporates causality and impossibility of an actual infinite into its premises, construing that the chain of cause and effect requires a beginning. This beginning is not limited to space but also to time. Therefore, since time itself was created, the creator cannot be bound by His creation. Consequently, such ability indicates an infinite knowledge.

In modern physics, the only world that seems to contradict the notion of universal determinism is the quantum world. In 1927, Werner Heisenberg caused significant confusion in the study of quantum physics by introducing the *Uncertainty Principle* which stated that the position and velocity of a particle cannot be known at the same instant.[1] The discovery suggested that the quantum world was indeed an enigmatic place where particles seemed to behave in an unpredictable way. However, fundamental principles of philosophy and human reason cannot embrace an idea which suggests that the quantum world is governed by absolute randomness. There are several arguments which support this. One is the fact that particles seem to behave as we assume the way they should when observed and measured, like a particle. But when we are not observing, they seem to behave a like wave, and this suggests that a particle for example like an electron has a mind of its own. This is called wave-particle duality. However, the key term here is the 'observer effect' as when particles are observed and measured, the quantum world becomes deterministic. Scientists do not know what causes the observer effect. It is quite perplexing that although human consciousness and quantum physics are not related in anyway, one seems to be manipulating the behaviour of the other. In simple terms, human observations seem to force particles like photons and electrons to behave in a determined manner. Since it would be absurd to assume that particles know when they are being watched and therefore change their behaviour in-

---

1   Robertson, Howard Percy. "The uncertainty principle." *Physical Review* 34, no. 1 (1929): 163.

stantaneously, it is safe to assume that something else is causing them to behave both as a wave and particle. This in turn indicates a universal determinism yet to be discovered.

Divine knowledge that encompasses all slices of the space-time continuum

Divine knowledge includes detailed information about all events and occurrences in the existence as a whole and this in turn requires infinite omniscience. This knowledge encompasses all matter and space-time in the past, present and future. Moreover, the all-encompassing information about existence has an infinitesimal reality within God's infinite knowledge. One may suggest that the argument can be used as a steppingstone for further research as the concept of space-time in contemporary physics is relevant to this theological premise proposed by Gülen and some scholars before him.

David Mermin, for example, argued that "space-time is an abstract four-dimensional mathematical continuum."[2] This is based on Herman Minkowski's concept of space-time, where he maintains that the absolute motion of space-time cannot be detected because the observers would not only have different times but also different places in space. The sequential duration of time depends on the observer, a concept known as time dilation where time changes according to the observer. Petkov supports this by arguing that time dilation cannot exist in a three-dimensional world; therefore, as Minkowski discovered, space-time is four dimensional.[3]

This means space-time cannot be separated and need to be mentioned together. Evidently, this also indicates that space-time was created simultaneously, which would indicate that the agent who caused the existence of space-time would have absolute knowledge about its minutiae. Therefore, all slices of space-time in the past, present and future would be readily available to this super-intelligent agent.

---

2   Mermin, N. D. (2009). What's Bad About This Habit? *Physics Today* 2009, p. 8

3   Minkowski, H. (2012). *Space and time: Minkowski's papers on relativity* (F. Lewerto & V. Petkov, Trans.) (free ed.). Montreal: Minkowski Institute Press. p. 34

There are, however, some string theorists who would love to brush the singularity concept that existed prior to *Big Bang* under the carpet, argue that an infinitely empty space may have existed before the *Big Bang*. There was some type of radiation fluctuating around this empty space and after a while it became so dense that it caused the *Big Bang*. The existence of this exotic radiation maybe a possibility, however, an infinitely empty space that has no beginning in time will not hold in philosophy. The argument *"after awhile"* has no significance in a timeless emptiness as it signifies a finite period which has a beginning point in time. Another problem with the argument is why did the Big Bang occur 13.8 billion years ago within a timeless space? Conversely, it is quite difficult to imagine an empty space that has no beginning in time as if time did not have a beginning, we should have never arrived at the present. Basically, this philosophical argument means that if we travelled to the past, no matter how far we go back, we would never reach a beginning. The next question would be: how did we arrive at the present then?

For this reason, current model which suggest that the universe (space-time) had a beginning is the best theoretical model that can be sustained by philosophy as well. If this theoretical model of space-time is analysed from Gülen's perspective, it would mean, to have an all-encompassing knowledge of the absolute motion of space-time, the observer would have to be unbound by space-time continuum. In simple terms, the observer should not be restricted or limited by the four-dimensional space-time. Since the concept of God's transcendence in Islamic theology parallels this description, an observer with such attributes would have absolute knowledge of space-time in all its states in the past, present and future.

To a certain extent, the view in theoretical physics regarding 'what would happen to an observer who falls into a black hole' may support this perspective, as Charles Liu argues that if an astronaut falls into a black hole at the size of a galaxy and survives, they will be able to see everything that has fallen into the super massive black hole in the past and everything that will fall into it in the future.[4] Theoretical physics conclude, in this scenario, that the past, present and future would instantaneously be available to the observer. Consequently, the astronaut

---

4   Liu, C. (2011). What would happen if I fall into a black hole? Physics4Me

would be in a world where time would have no significance as its dilation would be in extraordinary proportions. From a theoretical perspective, if this were conceivable even for a physical being, it would be difficult to envisage any limitations of knowledge possessed by a Supreme Being who is not bound by space-time. Black hole mechanics indicate that the moment a person passes through the Event Horizon (a boundary that is considered as the entrance to a black hole), defined as point of no return where space-time as we know it, ceases to exist. Assuming the person survives, they will have the opportunity to observe the past, present and future at the same instance. This is exactly what is indicated by Divine Omniscience.

As argued by Gülen, if all the information about the space-time continuum, from the beginning to the end has an infinitesimal existence within God's knowledge, one cannot challenge the argument that an agent who is not limited by space-time will possess the ability to observe space-time in all its slices in the past, present and future. Minkowski's argument supports this as he maintains that "...space by itself, and time by itself, are doomed to fade away into mere shadows, and only a kind of union of the two will preserve an independent reality."[5] This means that space-time is not only four-dimensional, but it is also in a state of continuum because it can be divided into incalculable slices without any bounds in size or measured intervals. According to this view, space-time does not develop; it simply exists. It is like a linear object where you can cut a slice out of it to examine what space-time looks like at that instant. This examination will evidently provide data about the minute particulars and expansion of the universe.

Remarkably, the theory concurs with the argument that for God, the past, present and future exist concomitantly. Having such encompassing knowledge about the space-time continuum would also indicate preordainment; however, this would not annul free will because prior knowledge of events depends on the actual events, but the actual events do not depend on information. Regarding human choices, one may argue that they are part of human destiny as destiny is written according to one's choices. This is a view that suggests the future affects the past where

---

5   Jammer, M., & Einstein, A. (2012). *Concepts of space: The history of theories of space in physics* (3rd ed.). n.p.: Dover Publications. p. 339.

the past has recorded the events as they happenned in the future. What this means is, for God, the past and the future occurs simultaneously, and therefore, He can record the future events, in the past or the present for that matter.

This view also finds some support in quantum physics where an experiment conducted in 2015 suggests the future may affect the past in the quantum world as well.

Introducing the notion of *tenasüb-ü illiyet* (necessary connection between cause and effect) to support the coexistence of predestination and free will

Gülen proposes an argument that prefers a middle path position between the Ibn Rushd and al-Ghazalī arguments by accentuating that the link between cause and effect is necessary, however, this connection is also generated by God, who is the cause of all causes. With this argument Gülen asserts that Muslims need to comply with the laws of causality on the condition that they affirm that these causes also originate from God. This principle supports the concept of *tawakkul* (reliance on God's will and destiny), by asserting that free will requires observing the laws of causality. This means, prior to reliance on God's will and destiny, humans need to take all precautions by using their free will and what is permitted by the laws of causality. A simple analogy would be that a person who is preparing to go on a long journey through the desert needs to make sure they have enough supplies of rations and water, their vehicle is mechanically sound and perhaps a satellite phone for emergencies. Taking all necessary measures to prevent a catastrophe while relying on God's will and destiny can be considered as putting the theory of coexistence into practice. In conclusion, submitting to destiny means using one's free will, making the right moves, including causality into the equation, and relying on God's will.

Theological principle which suggests the past should be considered as predestined and the future as many paths available for free will

This principle is also based on Nursi's argument, and it suggests that since from the human perspective the past cannot be altered, it should be considered as predestined, while the future, not having occurred yet, should be considered as many possibilities that can be selected using free will. This principle is based on the notion that although God knows what will happen in the future, humans do not. Since, humans are trapped within a particular slice of space-time, for them, the past is past, and the future has not arrived yet. Being in a situation where the future is unknown gives humans an opportunity to develop the future. Such development can only be realised through free will, advancement in knowledge, effort, exertion, and application. God's knowledge of the future is not an obstacle for development as His knowledge encompasses human decisions, knowledge, ventures, and advancement. Since, predestination is not compulsion, the principle of considering the past as destiny and the future as many possibilities for the free will is a form of reconciliation.

The principle of *aktif sabır* (active patience) which aims to establish a balance between free will and predestination

Active Patience implies that true reliance on God's Destiny and will, can only be achieved through action and patience. Active patience is defined as making all the necessary effort to solve the issue at hand while relying on God's decision by submitting to His will after what was predestined occurs. Therefore, the argument rejects fatalism by arguing that submission and reliance can be shown through active patience. The concept of active patience can be considered as an antonym of giving up with the assumption that one has no control of their life. It encourages people to make that extra effort to achieve the envisioned goal. It is impossible for compulsionists or fatalists to achieve great things as they have unconditionally surrendered to a destiny which in their minds has already decided their fate. The concept of active patience saves people from indolence and idleness as it encourages them to be proactive even in most difficult times during which all hope seems to be lost.

Final word

The analysis and examination of the formative, classical and contemporary literature available in Islamic theology indicates that it is possible to formulate a sustainable theory that supports the coexistence of destiny and free will. The comparative analysis of different theologies shows that there are some distinctive similarities and dissimilarities between Islamic theology and Western philosophy.

It is evident that Gülen's argument for the coexistence of destiny and free will is firmly rooted in mainstream Islamic theology; however, to some degree it also corresponds with the compatibilist camp of Western philosophy. We could further argue that Gülen's understanding of determinism on a macro cosmological level agrees with the findings of classical mechanics and standard physics as most physicists assert that we live in a deterministic universe. On the other hand, Gülen's perspective also provides a contemporary understanding of Divine Destiny and free will specifically for Muslim scholars, academics and laypersons who continue to debate on the topic. His theoretical framework and methodology of reconciliation is a revised version of the mainstream theology but also includes theories from contemporary sciences and philosophy supported by easy-to-comprehend analogies.

The study of historical development of the discourse on destiny and free will in Islamic theology indicates that the development of key arguments can be delineated into three major periods that consists of the formative, classical and modern. We examined the development of the theological discourse on destiny and free will in these periods and then analysed the arguments in chronological order with the objective to explore the changes in views and formations of opposing schools in Islamic theology.

This research project concluded that during the formative period, three major views emerged in Islamic theology and throughout the classical era, these opposing schools continued to attempt to verify and validate their own theological arguments. The study found that mainstream theology, which argued for the coexistence of destiny and free will, initiated their arguments as a reaction to some theological schools which segregated from mainstream theology to argue either for absolute free will where humans possess the ability to generate their own actions or for compulsionism that rejects any form of free action.

It is established that throughout the past twelve centuries, the views of mainstream theologians continued to thrive and became the dominant methodology and framework for Muslim scholars. This gradually led to collapse of the Mu'tazila and Jabrīyyah schools, even though there are some modern rationalists attempting to revive the Mu'tazila perspective in contemporary times.

I included a brief analysis and examination on the concepts of libertarianism, incompatibilism and compatibilism, which to some degree corresponds with the Mu'tazila, Jabrīyyah and mainstream Islamic schools of theology. The study of Western literature included examination of the historical development in discourse, again in chronological order with the objective to compare the views of Western scholars with Islamic theologians. The study also found that while the school of Mu'tazila may have been influenced by Aristotelian philosophy, Western theologians such as Thomas Aquinas were influenced by the views of al-Ghazalī. The conclusion of the comparative analysis suggested that within Western theology, the argument for Divine Universal Causality, which can be considered as compatibilism, offers the position most closely aligned with that of the mainstream Islamic theology. The modern Divine Universal Causality view argues that God causes all events directly, including the actions of all creatures, while humans are free in their choices. This is analogous to the mainstream Sunni view, which argues that, although human agents are free in their choices and acquisition, their acts originate from God.

The main objective of this book project was to focus on Islamic theology and Gülen's definitions of Divine Destiny, predeterminism observed in the macro universe, Divine Knowledge, Will and Power, and free will. Accordingly, we examined Gülen's methodology in using 'aql (reasoning) to interpret naql (text and tradition) with the inclusion of modern science and philosophy to construct arguments for Divine Destiny and free will. Gülen's perspectives on Divine Destiny, determinism in the macro universe, causality, materialisation of phenomena, and also omniscience and omnipotence of God, the involvement of human will in actions were examined separately with an objective to establish the grounds for his argument on coexistence.

The study found that while Gülen based his arguments on the popular positions of mainstream Islamic theologians, he also contributed to their methodologies and theoretical frameworks by providing arguments from contemporary science and philosophy. Gülen further develops the argument for coexistence by providing several philosophical analogies and original arguments such as the principle that concludes: Divine Destiny takes causality and human will into account. Gülen achieves this by preferring a middle path between the views of al-Ghazalī and Ibn Rushd. Furthermore, he includes concepts such as *aktif sabır* (active patience), a principle that establishes reliance on God's Destiny through patience, but at the same time exerts the necessary effort to make a change. The study concluded that Gülen's emphasis on *tenasüb-ü illiyet* (coherence in the connection between cause and effect) as constituting an important part of Divine Destiny is a significant contribution to the argument for coexistence.

Another important contribution made by Islamic theologians and Gülen is the argument that Divine Knowledge encompasses all slices of space-time, which maintains that, for God, the past, present and future coexist; therefore, this infinite omniscience does not annul human will. As also argued by Nursi, knowledge depends on the actual, but the actual does not depend on knowledge. It can be argued that from the perspective of general philosophy and principles of *Usul al Dīn* (Islamic theology), the theological and philosophical premises put forward by Gülen for the coexistence of destiny and free will are valid.

Consequently, it seems that further research is required in this field as the philosophical or theological notions that indicate the coexistence of destiny and free will may find substantiated support in contemporary physics. Exploring the principles of standard physics, quantum mechanics and concepts of space-time may provide more detailed understanding of how predestination could coexist with free will in a universe where evidential traits of determinism and indeterminism can be detected. This may also assist contemporary Islamic theologians and philosophers to develop their arguments further. As a final point, this study concluded that Gülen's methodology of reconciliation may be used as a stepping-stone for further research into this extremely complex topic of theology and philosophy.

It is important to note that the concept of the coexistence of destiny and free will is a complex one. This study offers a comprehensive understanding for contemporary academics and clergy; however, it also concludes that a team of experts which include theologians, philosophers and physicists working together, may produce better results.

BIBLIOGRAPHY

Abd al-Jabbar, Khuḍayri, M. M., Madkūr, I., & Ḥusayn, T. (1965). *Al-Mughnī fī abwāb al-tawḥīd wa-al-'adl: Al-Juz'* 5 [Summa on the matters of divine unity and justice]. Cairo: al-Dār al-Miṣrīyah lil-Ta'līf wa-al-Tarjamah.

Abduh, M. (1986). *Tevhid Risalesi: Risaletü't - tevhid* [The book of divine unity]. Ankara: Fecr Yayınları.

Abduh, M., & Imārah, M. (1972). *Al-A'māl al-kāmilah* [the perfect deed]. Beirut: n.p.

Abduh, M., Masa'ad, I., & Cragg, K. (2004). *The theology of unity: Risālat al-tauḥīd.* London: Allen and Unwin.

Abdulbaqi, M. F. (n.d.). *Jabr* [Title translation]. Location: Al Mu'jam.

Abdulhamid, I. (1995). Ebü'l-Hasen Alî b. *İsmâîl* b. Ebî Bişr *İshâk* b. Salim el-Eş'arî el-Basrî. In Abdulhamid I. (Ed.) *Islam Ansiklopedisi* (v. 11, p. 445). Ankara: Turkiye Diyanet Vakfi.

Abū Hanafi, & Oʻz, M. (1981). *İmâm-ı A'zamın beş eseri: El-Âlim ve'l-müte'allim, el-fikh el-ebsât, el-fikh el-ekber, Risâletü Ebi Hanîfe, el-Vasiyye* [The five books of Imam Azam]. Istanbul: Kalem Yayıncılık.

Abū Zahra, M. (2011). *İslâm'da itikadi, siyasi ve fıkhi mezhepler tarihi* [History of political and creedal sects in Islam]. Istanbul: Çelik.

Abu Zayd. (1998). *Al-'Itijāh al-'Aqli* [The rational trend of the exegisis]. Beirut: Al-Markaz aṯ-Ṯaqāfi al-'Arabi

Abū, Zahra. M., Fığlalı, E. R., & Eskicioğlu, O. (1970). *İslam'da siyasi ve itikadi mezhepler tarihi* [History of political and creedal sects in Islam]. Istanbul: Yağmur Yayınevi.

Ackermann, R. (1982). An alternative free will defense. *Religious Studies, 18*(3), 365-72.

Adamson, P. (2003). Al-Kindi and Mu'tazila: Divine attributes, creation and freedom. *Arabic Sciences and Philosophy, 13*(1), 45-77.

Advocates of Silenced Turkey. (2018). *At least 3 victims drowned while trying to cross Meriç/ Evros River.* Retrieved from https://silencedturkey.org/at-least-3-victims-drowned-while-trying-to-cross-meric-evros-river

Ahval News. (2019). *NBA takes Enes Kanter's assassination fears seriously.* Retrieved from https://ahvalnews.com/enes-kanter/nba-takes-enes-kanters-assassination-fears-seriously-commissioner

Aktan, H. (2014). *Bir âlim portresi: M. Fethullah Gülen Hocaefendi* [A portrait of a scholar: M. Fethullah Gülen Hocaefendi]. Istanbul: Yayınları.

Alamiri, Z. (2021). Some critical reflections on Al Jahiz's notions of tab and tiba (innate dispositions). *Australian Journal of Islamic Studies, 6*(1), 32-46.

Al-Ash'arī, A. I., & McCarthy, R. J. (1953). *The theology of al-Ash'ari: The Arabic texts of al-Ash'arī's Kitāb al-Luma and Risalat Istihsan al-khawd fi'ilm al-kalam, with briefly annotated translations, and appendices containing material pertinent to the study of al-Ash'arī.* Beirut: Imprimerie Catholique.

Al-Ash'ari, A. I. (1928). *Kitāb maqālāt al-Islāmiyyīn* [The doctrines of Muslims]. Istanbul: n.p.

Al-Ash'arī, A. I. (2005). *İlk dönem İslam mezhepleri: Makalatü'l-İslamiyyin ve ihtilafü'l-musallin* [Islamic sects of the formative period]. Istanbul: Kabalcı Yayınevi.

Al-Ash'arī, A. I., & Klein, W. C. (1940). *al-Ibānah 'an uṣūl ad-diyānah: the elucidation of Islām's foundation.* New Haven: American Oriental Society.

Al-Ash'ari, A. I., & Ritter, H. (1929). *Kitāb maqālāt al-Islāmiyyīn wa-iḳtilāf al-muṣallīn.* Istanbul: Maṭba'at al-dawla.

Al-Baġdādī, A. (1973 & 2001). *Tarikh Baghdad.* Beirut: Dar Al Gharb Al Islaami.

Al-Baġdādī, A. -Q. T., Raṣ'anī, A. -R. R. A., & Hitti, P. K. (1924). *Muḵṭaṣar Kitāb al-Farq bayn al-firaq* [Differences between sects]. Cairo: Maktabat al-Ṭaqāfa al-Dīniyya.

Al-Baġdādī, A.-Q. I.-T. (1928). *Kitāb uṣūl ad-dīn* [The book of systematic theology]. Istanbul: Matbạ'at ad-Daula.

Albayrak, I. (2011). *Mastering knowledge in modern times: Fethullah Gülen as an Islamic scholar.* New York, NY: Blue Dome Press.

Al-Ghazālī, M. & Kamali, S. A. (1963). *Al-Ghazalī's Tahafut al-falasifah (incoherence of the philosophers).* Lahore: Pakistan Philosophical Congress.

Al-Ghazalī, M. (1993). *Tahafut al-Falasifa* [The incoherence of the philosophers] (J. Jihami, Ed.). Beirut: Dar Fikr al-Lubnani,

Al-Ghazālī, M. (2014). *Ihya' Ulumuddin* [The revival of the religious sciences]. Kuala Lumpur: Pustaka Al Shafa.

Al-Hajjaj, M. (2008). *Müslim b. el-Haccac, es-Sahih* [Authentic collection of Muslim b. al-Hajjaj]. Beirut: Daru'n-Nevadir.

Al-Jurjānī, A. M., & Abū A. M. A. (2017). *al-Ṭạ'rīfāt* [Definitions of Islamic terminologies]. Location: Publisher.

Almaany. (n.d.). *Translation and meaning of* جرب *in Almaany English Arabic dictionary.* Retrieved from https://www.almaany.com/en/dict/ar-en/%D8%AC%D8%A8%D8%B1%D8%A7/

Al-Maḥallī, J.-D. M. A., & al-Suyūṭī, J. (2007). *Tafsir al-Jalalayn* [Exegesis of the two Jalaluddins] (F. Hamza, Trans.). Amman: Royal Aal al-Bayt Institute for Islamic Thought.

Al-Maḥallī, J.-D. M. A., Suyūṭī, J., & Mu'assasat Āl al-Bayt lil-Fikr al-Islāmī. (2008). *Tafsir al-Jalalayn* [Exegesis of the two Jalaluddins] (F. Hamza, Trans.). Louisville, Ky: Fons Vitae.

Al-Māturīdī, E. M. (2005). *Te'vilatü'l - Kur'an* [Interpretation of the Qur'an]. Istanbul: Mizan Yayınevi.

Al-Māturīdī, M. M., & Kholeif, F. (1982). *Kitāb al-tawḥīd* [Book of unity]. Beirut: Dār al Mašriq.

Al-Māturīdī, M. M., & Topaloğlu, B. (2005). *Kitābü't-Tevhîd tercümesi* [Translation of Kitāb al Tawḥīd]. Ankara: İSAM, Türkiye Diyanet Vakfı İslam Araştırmaları Merkezi.

Al-Māturīdī, M. M., Topaloğlu, B., & Aruçi, M. (2003). *Kitāb al-Tawḥīd* [Book of unity]. Ankara: Waqf Diyānat Turkiyā, Markaz al-Buḥūth al-Islāmīyah.

Al-Murtada, A.-M. L. A. Y., & Arnold, T. W. (1902). *Al-Mutazilah: Being an extract from Kitābu'l Milal wa -n Nihal.* Leipzig, Germany: Harrassowitz.

Al-Nasafî, M. I.-M. (1993). *Tebsiratü'l edille fî usûli'd-dîn.* Ankara: Diyanet İşleri Başkanlığı Yayınları.

Al-Nasafî, M. M. (1987). *Kitâbu't-Temhîd li-Kavâidi't-Tevhîd.* Cairo: n.p.

Al-Nasafî, M. M. (2003) *Tebsiratu'l-Edille.* Ankara: Hüseyin Atay-Şaban 'AliDüzgün.

Al-Nasafî, M. M., & Aḥmad, J. A. H. (1986). *Kitāb al-Tamhīd li-qawā'id al-tawḥīd.* al-Azhar Cairo: Dār al-Ṭibạ'ah al-Muḥammadīyah.

Al-Nasafî, M. M., & Salāmah, K. (1990). *Taḅṣirat al-adillah: Fī uṣūl al-dīn 'alá ṭarīqat al-Imām Abī Manṣūr al-Māturīdī.* Damascus: al-Mạ'had al-'Ilmī al-Faransī lil-Dirāsāt al-'Arabīyah bi-Dimashq.

Alper, H. (2013). *Māturīdi's criticism of Mu'tazila: Is God obliged to create the best?* n.p.: Kelam Arastirmalari.

Al-Qurtubī. (n.d.). *Al-Jamiu al-Ahkam al-Qur'an* [Complete exegesis of the Qur'anic rulings]. Retrieved from https://www.altafsir.com/

Al-Rahim, A. H. (2006). Islam and Liberty. *Journal of Democracy, 17*(1), 166-169.

Al-Razī, F. (1981). *Mafatih al-Ghayb*. Beirut: Dar al-Fikr.

Al-Razī, F. (n.d). *Al Tafsir* [The exegesis]. Retrieved from https://www.altafsir.com/

Al-Shahrastānī, M. (1975). *Al-Milal Wa'n Nihal*. Beirut: n.p.

Al-Shahrastānī, M. A. K., O'z, M., & Dalkılıç, M. (2008). *El Milel ve-l Nihal: Dinler, mezhepler ve felsefi sistemler tarihi* [History of religions, sects and philosophical systems]. Istanbul: Litera Yayıncılık.

Al-Tabarani, S. (n.d.). *Mujham*. V. 10. Baghdad.

Al-Tahāwī, A. J. A. M. (1971). *Sharh al-'Aqīdah al-Tahāwīyyah* [Commentary on the creed of al-Tahāwīyyah]. Beirut: al-Maktab al-Islami.

Al-Tahāwī, A. J. A. M. (2011). *Al-Aqīdah al-Tahāwīyyah* [The creed of al-Tahāwīyyah] (M. F. Hoosen, Trans.) n.p: Dar al-Hikmah.

Ansari, S. (2020). The use of historical information in conducting content criticism on hadith. *Australian Journal of Islamic Studies, 5*(3), 30-49. Retrieved form https://ajis.com.au/index.php/ajis/article/view/301.

Aqidah. (2003). In J. L. Esposito (Ed.), *The Oxford Dictionary of Islam*. Retrieved from http://www.oxfordislamicstudies.com/article/opr/t125/e176.

Aquinas, T., & Morris, S. (1991). *Summa Theologiae*. n.p.: n.p.

Archer, M. (2013). *Why did Einstein say "God does not play dice?"* Physics World. Retrieved on September 23, 2014, from http://physicsworld.com/cws/article/multimedia/2013/mar/04/why-did-einstein-say-god-doesnt-play-dice

Armağan, M. (2017). *Kozadan kelebeğe* [Cocoon to Butterfly]. Harbiye, Istanbul: Gazeteciler ve Yazarlar Vakfı Yayınları.

Arslan, A. A. (1980). İslam İnançları ve Felsefesi [Islamic beliefs and philosophy]. Istanbul: Çağrı Yayınları.

Arslan, R. (2017). *Kilicdaroglu: 15 July is a controlled coup*. BBC. Retrieved from https://www.bbc.com/turkce/haberler-turkiye-39478777

Aslan, A. (2019). *An alternative view of the 28 February coup*. Politics Today. Retrieved from https://thenewturkey.org/an-alternative-view-of-the-28-february-coup

Atmanspacher, H., & Bishop, R. (2002). *Between chance and choice: Interdisciplinary perspectives on determinism*. Exeter: Imprint Academic.

At-Ṭabari, (n.d.). *Al-Jamiul Bayan* [Collection of statements on interpretation of the verses of the Qur'an]. Retrieved from https://www.altafsir.com/

Augustine,., Boulding, M., Rotelle, J. E., & Augustinian Heritage Institute. (1997). *The works of Saint Augustine: A translation for the 21st century*. Brooklyn, N.Y: New City Press.

Ay, H. (2016). *Erdogan: We decided on 3 months of state of emergency*. Takvim. Retrieved from https://www.takvim.com.tr/guncel/2016/07/20/cumhurbaskani-erdogan-konusuyor-1469055709

Bailey, S. (1954). The revision of Marxism. *The Review of Politics, 16*(4), 452-462. Retrieved February 10, 2021, from http://www.jstor.org/stable/1405129

Bāqillānī, M. I.-T., & MacCarthy, R. J. (1957). *Kitāb at-tamhīd* [The book of prefix]. Beyrouth: Librairie orientale.

Barton, G., Weller, P., & Yilmaz, I. (2013). *The Muslim world and politics in transition: Creative contributions of the Gülen movement*. London: Bloomsbury.

BBC. (2016). *Zaman Gazatesine Kayyum Atandi* [Trustee appointment to Zaman newspaper]. Retrieved from https://www.bbc.com/turkce/haberler/2016/03/160229_zaman_gazetesi_kayyum

Belnap, N. (2012). Newtonian determinism to branching space-times indeterminism in two moves. *Synthese, 188*(1), 5-21.

Benjamin, A. S., & Hackstaff, L. H. (Trans.). (1964). *Saint Augustine: On free choice of the will*. Indianapolis: Bobbs-Merrill.

Berofsky, B. (2012). *Nature's challenge to free will*. Oxford: Oxford University Press.

Bhat, A. R. (2006). Free will and determinism. *Journal of Islamic Philosophy, 2*(1), 7-24.

Boaz, D. (2007). *A note on labels: Why libertarian?* Cato Institute. Retrieved from https://web.archive.org/.web/20120716203439/.www.libertarianism.org/. ex-3.html

Bobzien, S. (1998). *Determinism and freedom in stoic philosophy*. Oxford: Clarendon Press.

Canan, I. (n.d.). *Kutüb-i Sitte Muhtasar ve Tercümesi* [Kutub al Sittah and translation]. n.p.: n.p..

Carroll, B. J. (2007). *A dialogue of civilizations: Gülen's Islamic ideals and humanistic discourse*. Somerset, N.J: Light, Inc.

Carroll, S. (2011). *On determinism*. Discover. Retrieved from http://blogs.discover magazine.com/cosmicvariance/2011/12/05/on-determinism/#.VCzyx-GeSx8E

Causal determinism. (2010). In *Stanford Encyclopedia of Philosophy*. Retrieved from http://plato.stanford.edu/archives/spr2010/entries/determinism-causal

Aref Chaker. (January 01, 2016). The Life of Abu Mansur Al-Maturidi and the Socio-Political and Theological Context of Central Asia in the Tenth Century. *Australian Journal of Islamic Studies, 1,* 1, 39-64.

Chaker, A. (2021). A critical appraisal of Al-Māturīdī's contributions to theological exegesis in his book Ta'wilat Ahlu Sunnnah: A study of the verses related to some of the attributes of God. Master's thesis, Charles Sturt University. Retrieved from https://researchoutput.csu.edu.au/en/publications/a-critical-appraisal-of-Al-Māturīdī's-contributions-to-theological-3.

Choy,K.(1994).A case for Augustine's free will defense. Retrieved from http://www.chinese theology.com/Reformation/AUGUSTINEOnFREEWILLDEFENSE.htm

Clarke, R. K. (1993). Toward a credible agent-causal account of free will. *Noûs, 27*(2), 191-203.

Clarke, R. K. (2006). *Libertarian accounts of free will*. New York: Oxford University Press.

Conway, T. D. (2014). *Cross-cultural dialogue on the virtues: The contribution of Fethullah Gülen*. n.p.: Springer International Publishing.

Dalrymple, G. B. (2001). The age of the Earth in the twentieth century: A problem (mostly) solved. *Special Publications, Geological Society of London, 190*(1), 205–221.

Daly, J. J. (1958). *The metaphysical foundations of free will as a transcendental aspect of the act of existence in the philosophy of St. Thomas Aquinas*. Washington: Catholic University of America Press.

Darwin, C. (2008). *On the origin of species* (D. Quammen, Ed.). New York: Sterling.

De Cillis, M. (2014). *Free will and predestination in Islamic thought: Theoretical compromises in the works of Avicenna, Ghāzālī and Ibn 'Arabī*. Abingdon, Oxon: Routledge.

Denis, L. (2012). Kant and Hume on morality. In *Stanford Encyclopedia of Philosophy*. Location: Publisher.

Descartes, R. (1984). *The philosophical writings of Descartes* (J. Cottingham, R.

Stoothoff, & D. Murdoch, Trans.). Cambridge: Cambridge University Press.

Descartes, R., Miller, V. R., & Miller, R. P. (1983). *Principles of philosophy*. Dordrecht, Holland: Reidel.

Desûkî, A. F. (1982). *El-Kaza ve'l-Kader fi'l-İslam, Darü'd-dâve* [Destiny and preordainment in Islam]. Alexandria: n.p.

Devellioğlu, F. (1993). *Osmanlıca-Türkçe ansiklopedik lûgat: Eski ve yeni harflerle* [Ottoman-Turkish encyclopedia dictionary]. Ankara: Aydın Kitabevi.

DeYoung, K. (2016, August 19). Turkish evidence for Gülen extradition pre-dates coup attempt. *Washington Post*. Retrieved from https://www.washingtonpost.com/world/national-security/turkish-evidence-for-Gülen-extradition-pre-dates-coup-attempt/2016/08/19/390cb0ec-6656-11e6-be4e-23fc4d4d12b4_story.html?noredirect=on&utm_term=.7d7875a3fd58

Double, R. (1991). *The non-reality of free will*. New York: Oxford University Press.

Doyle, B. (2011). *Free will: The scandal in philosophy*. Cambridge, Mass: I-Phi Press.

Duignan, B., & Bird, O. A. (2021). Immanuel Kant. In *Encyclopedia Britannica*. https://www.britannica.com/biography/Immanuel-Kant

Duns, S. J., & Vos, A. (2003). *Duns Scotus on divine love: Texts and commentary on goodness and freedom, God and humans*. Aldershot, England: Ashgate.

Ebaugh, H. R. F. (2010). *The Gülen movement: A sociological analysis of a civic movement rooted in moderate Islam*. Dordrecht, Netherlands: Springer.

Ehli Sunnet Buyukleri. (2020). Abdulaziz Dehlevi. In *Islam Alimleri Ansiklopedisi*. Retrieved from http://www.ehlisunnetbuyukleri.com/Islam-Alimleri-Ansiklopedisi/Detay/ABDULAZIZ-DEHLEVI/3857

Einstein, A. (1926). *The Born-Einstein letters*. Newyork: Walker and Company.

Einstein, A. (2010). *Relativity: The special and the general theory; a popular exposition*. Mansfield Centre, CT: Martino Publishing.

Ekinci, M. (2011). Risale-i Nur Külliyatında İtikadî Mezheplerin Değerlendirilmesi [The analysis of creedal sects in Risale-i Nur collection]. *Harran Üniversitesi İlahiyat Fakültesi Dergisi, 26*(26), 23-29.

Ekstrom, L. W. (2000). *Free will: A philosophical study*. Boulder, Colo: Westview Press.

Ekstrom, L. W. (2019). *Free will: A philosophical study*. Boulder, Colo: Routledge.

Epictetus. (1990). *Letter*. Raleigh, N.C: Alex Catalogue.

Epicurus. (2004). *Letter to Menoeceus* (R. D. Hicks, Trans.). Adelaide: The University of Adelaide Library.

Erce, H. Z. (1968). *İslâmda kaza ve kader* [Destiny and decree in Islam]. Istanbul: Yaylacık Matbaası.

Esposito, J. L., & Yilmaz, I. (2010). *Islam and peacebuilding: Gülen movement initiatives*. New York: Blue Dome.

Faḥr-ad-Dîn, -R. M. I.-U., & Saqqā, A. H. (1987). *al- Maṭālib al-ʻālīya min al-ʻilm al-ilāhī: Wa-huwa al-muṣammā fī lisān al-Yūnānīyin "bāṭulūǧiya"*. Beirut: Dār al-Kitāb al-ʻArabī.

Fakhry, M. (1983). *A history of Islamic philosophy*. New York: Columbia University Press.

Falkenburg, B., & Weinert, F. (2009). Indeterminism and determinism in quantum mechanics. In D. Greenberger, K. Hentschel & Friedel Weinert (Ed.), *Compendium of Quantum Physics* (pp. 307-311). Berlin: Springer.

Fischer, J. M., Kane, R., Derk, P., & Manuel, V. (2007). *Four views on free will*. Malden, MA: Blackwell Pub.

Fitzgerald, A., & In Cavadini, J. C. (2009). *Augustine through the ages: An encyclopedia*.

Foley, R. (1978). Compatibilism. *Mind*, 87(347), 421-428.

Frank, R. M., & Gutas, D. (2011). *Early Islamic theology: The Mu'tazilites and al-Ash'arī*. Aldershot: Ashgate Variorum.

Frede, M., & Long, A. A. (2011). *A free will: Origins of the notion in ancient thought*. Berkeley: University of California Press.

Garber, C. P. (2017). Al-Ghazalī on causation, omnipotence and human freedom. *Quaerens Deum: The Liberty Undergraduate Journal for Philosophy of Religion*, 2(1), art. 4.

Gardet, L. (1999). Al-Jubbā'ī. In *Encyclopedia of Islam*. Leiden, The Netherlands: Brill. Retrieved from http://www.muslimphilosophy.com/ei2/Jubai.htm

Gazette DuvaR. (2019). *511 thousand people were arrested following 15 July*. Retrieved from https://www.gazeteduvar.com.tr/gundem/2019/03/10/15-tem-muz-sonrasi-511-bin-kisi-gozaltina-alindi/

Giddy, P. (2016). Human agency and weakness of will: A neo-Thomist discussion. *South African Journal of Philosophy*, 35(2), 197-209. doi: 10.1080/02580136.2016.1167346

Glasse, C. (2001). In *The New Encyclopedia of Islam Altamira*. Lanham MD: Rowman & Littlefield. p. 443.

Gölcük, S., & Toprak, S. (1998). *Kelam* [Islamic Theology]. Konya, Turkey: Tekin Kitabevi.

Gosson, M. (2001). *The principles of Newtonian and quantum mechanics: The need for Planck's constant, h*. London: Imperial College Press.

Gülen Movement. (2018). *What is the Gülen movement?* Retrieved from http://www.Gülenmovement.com/Gülen-movement/what-is-the-Gülen-movement

Gülen, F. (1977, March). *What are Kulli Irada and Juz'-i Irāda?* Sermon at Bornova Mosque, Izmir, Turkey.

Gülen, F. (1983). Irada [Will]. *Sizinti Magazine*, 5, 57.

Gülen, F. (1993). *Tevekkul, Teslim, Tevzih ve Sika*. Kalbin Zumrut Tepeleri. Retrieved from https://fGülen.com/tr/fethullah-Gülenin-butun-eserleri/53-Kalbin-Zumrut-Tepeleri/1034-Fethullah-Gülen-Tevekkul-Teslim-Tefviz-ve-Sika

Gülen, F. (1995b). *Kader* [Destiny]. Izmir, Turkey: Nil Yayınları.

Gülen, F. (1997). *Prizma* [Prism]. Izmir, Turkey: Nil Yayınlari.

Gülen, F. (1999). Destiny and man's free will. *Fountain Magazine*, Jan-Mar.

Gülen, F. (2000). *Essentials of the Islamic faith*. Fairfax, Va: The Fountain.

Gülen, F. (2002). *Kitap ve sünnet perspektifinde kader* [Qur'an and sunna perspective on destiny]. Izmir, Turkey: Nil Yayınları.

Gülen, F. (2004). *Key concepts in the practice of Sufism*. New Jersey: Light Inc.

Gülen, F. (2005). *Çağ ve Nesil* [Century and generation]. Izmir, Turkey: Çağlayan.

Gülen, F. (2007a). *Questions & answers about Islam*. Istanbul: Nil Yayınları.

Gülen, F. (2007b). The middle path in destiny-free will association. Retrieved from https://fGülen.com/tr/fethullah-Gülenin-butun-eserleri/iman/fethul-lah-Gülen-inancin-golgesinde/576-Fethullah-Gülen-Kader-Irade-Mu-nasebetinde-Orta-Yol

Gülen, F. (2008). *İnancın Gölgesinde* [Essentials of the Islamic faith]. Izmir, Turkey: Nil.

Gülen, F. (2009). *Essentials of the Islamic faith*. NJ: Tughra Books.

Gülen, F. (2010). *Veils and guidance*. Herkul Retrieved from http://www.herkul.org/bamteli/perdeler-ve-hidayet/

Gülen, F. (2011a). *Asrın getirdiği tereddütler* [Doubts brought by the century]. Clifton: Tughra books.

Gülen, F. (2011c). *Kitap ve sünnet perspektifinde kader.* Istanbul: Nil yayınları.

Gülen, F. (2011d). *The essentials of the Islamic faith.* Clifton: Tughra books.

Gülen, F. (2012). *Gülen's response to Erdogan's invitation.* Retrieved from https://www.haber3.com/guncel/erdoganin-hasret-bitsin-cagrisina-fethullah-Gülen-cok-duygulu-cevap-haberi-1338921

Gülen, F. (2014). *Test and consistency in truth.* Herkul. Retrieved from http://www.herkul.org/bamteli/imtihan-ve-hakta-sebat/

Gülen, F. (2014). *Willpower and being tested with it.* Fountain Magazine. Retrieved from https://fountainmagazine.com/2014/issue-97-january-february-2014/willpower-and-being-january-2014

Gülen, F. (2015). *It is our turn.* Herkul. Retrieved from http://www.herkul.org/bamteli/bamteli-sira-bizde/

Gülen, F. (2016a). *Prizma Serisi 1-9* [Prism series]. Clifton: Blue Dome Inc.

Gülen, F. (2016b). *Who was behind the coup?* Herkul. Retrieved from http://www.herkul.org/bamteli/darbeyi-kim-kime-nicin-yapti/

Gülen, F. (2016c). *You are as valuable as your patience.* Retrieved from http://www.herkul.org/bamteli/bamteli-sabrin-kadarsin/

Gülen, F. (2016d). *We will show patience with active patience.* Retrieved from http://www.herkul.org/bamteli/bamteli-aktif-sabirla-sabredecegiz/

Gülen, F. (2018, December 30). *Mirac.* Heart Strings. Retrieved from http://www.herkul.org/tag/mirac/

Gülen, F. (2019). *The sorrows, heart and the tongue.* Herkul. Retrieved from http://www.herkul.org/bamteli/bamteli-huzun-gonul-ve-dil/

Gülen, F. (2019). *The Taste of Faith, love for Humanity and Hope.* Herkul. Retrieved from http://www.herkul.org/bamteli/bamteli-imanin-tadi-insana-sevgi-ve-umit/

Gülen, F. (2020). *Fethullah Gülen in short.* Retrieved from https://fgulen.com/en/fethullah-Gülens-life/about-fethullah-Gülen/fethullah-Gülen-in-short.

Gülen, F. (2020). *Tevekkul* [Reliance]. Herkul. Retrieved on March 23, 2020, from http://www.herkul.org/tag/tevekkul/

Gülen, F. (2021). *Divine decree and destiny.* Retrieved January 5, 2021, from https://fGülen.com/en/fethullahGülens-works/essentials-of-the-islamic-faith/divine-decree-and-destiny.

Gülen, F. (2021). *Fethullah Gülen in short.* Retrieved on 6 March 2021 from https://fgulen.com/en/fethullah-gulens-life-en/fethullah-gulen-in-short-en

Gülen, F., & Crooks, L. (2006). *The essentials of the Islamic faith.* Somerset, NJ: The Light/Nil.

Gülen, F., & Erdoğan, L. (1995a). *Fethullah Gülen Hocaefendi: "küçük dünyam"* [My small world]. Istanbul: AD Yayıncılık.

Gülen, F., & Ünal, A. (2011b). *Key concepts in the practice of Sufism: Emerald hills of the heart.* Clifton, New Jersey: Tughra Books.

Gülen's website. (2015). *Fethullah Gülen in short.* Retrieved January 17, 2015, from http://fGülen.com/en/fethullah-Gülens-life/about-fethullah-Gülen/fethullah-Gülen-in-short

Gündoğar, H. (2011). *Kelam Araştırmaları* [Research on Islamic theology]. Şırnak Üniversitesi 9:1, p. 204.

Hamilton, E., & Huntington, C. (1999). *The collected dialogues of Plato.* Princeton, NJ: Princeton University Press.

Hamsici, M. (2014). *10 Soruda: 17-25 Aralık Operasyonlari* [17-25 December operations in 10 questions]. BBC. Retrieved from https://www.bbc.com/turkce/

haberler/2014/12/141212_17_25_aralik_operasyonu_neler_oldu_10_soru-da

Harrington, J. C. (2011). *Wrestling with free speech, religious freedom, and democracy in Turkey: The political trials and times of Fethullah Gülen*. Lanham, Md: University Press of America.

Hecker, J. K., & Al-Asadābādī, A. -J. A. (1975). *Reason and responsibility: An explanatory translation of Kitāb al-tawlīd from al-Mughnī fī abwāb al-tawhid wa-l-ʿadl by Qadī ʿAbd al-Jabbār al-Hamadhānī, with introduction and notes*. Berkeley.

Hendrick, J. D. (2013). *Gülen: The ambiguous politics of market Islam in Turkey and the world*. New York: New York University Press.

Hizmetten. (2021). *Hoca Efendi Corona Aşısı Oldu* [Hoca Efendi received the corona virus vaccination]. Retrieved from https://hizmetten.com/hocaefendi-korona-asisi-oldu/

Hoefer, C. (2016). Causal Determinism. In *Stanford Encyclopedia of Philosophy*. Retrieved from https://plato.stanford.edu/entries/determinism-causal/

Hourani, G. (1976). Islamic and non-Islamic origins of Muʿtazilite ethical rationalism. *International Journal of Middle East Studies*, 7(1), 59-87. Retrieved February 3, 2021, from http://www.jstor.org/stable/162550

Hume, D., & Beauchamp, T. L. (1999). *An enquiry concerning human understanding*. Oxford: Oxford University Press.

Hume's Moral Philosophy. (2018). In *Stanford Encyclopedia of Philosophy*. Retrieved from http://plato.stanford.edu/entries/hume-moral/#pw

Iammarino, D. (2013). *Religion and reality: An exploration of contemporary metaphysical systems, theologies, and religious pluralism*.

Ibn Abi'l-Hadid. (n.d.). *Sharhu Nahji'l-Balaga*. [Commentary on Nahji'l-Balaga] Beirut: Daru'l-İhyâi't-Turâsi'l-Arabî.

Ibn al-Murtaḍā, -M. -D. A. I.-Y., & Arnold, T. W. (1902). *al-Muʿtazilah: Being an extract from the Kitābu-l milal wa-n niḥal*. Leipzig: Harrassowitz.

Ibn Asakir, A.-H. (1928). *Tabyīn kadhib al-muftarī* [Disclosing the liars and slanderers]. Dimashq: Matbaʿat al-Tawfiq.

Ibn Ashur, M. T. (n.d.). *At-Tahrîr Wa't-Tanwîr* [Title translation]. Tunisia: Daru Sahnun Li'n-Nashr Wa't-Tawzi.

Ibn Furak, & Gimarat, D. (1987). *Mujarrad maqālāt al-Shaykh Abī al-Ḥasan al-Ashʿarī: Min imlāʾ al-Shaykh al-Imām Abī Bakr Muḥammad ibn al-Ḥasan ibn Fūrak (t. 406/1015)*. Beirut: n.p.

İbn Hacer. (n.d.). *el-İsabe fi temyizi'z-sahabe. V. II.* Mısır: Mektebetü't-Diraseti'l-İslami. p. 242.

Ibn Hanbal, A. Oral, R., Sarı, S., & Banna, A. (2004). *el-Müsned İmam Ahmed b. Hanbel: (el-Fethu'r-Rabbani tertibi)* [Musnad collection of Imam Ahmad ibn Hanbal]. Konya, Turkey: Ensar Yayıncılık.

Ibn Kathir, I. U. (2000). *Tafsir ibn Kathir* [Exgesis of Ibn Kathir] (abridged). Riyadh: Darussalam.

Ibn Manzur. (1968). *Lisanü'l-Arab* [Language of the Arab]. Beirut: Daru Sadr.

Ibn Murtada, A. Y., & Diwald-Wilzer, S. (1961). *Kitāb ṭabaqāt al-Muʿtazilah* [Biography of Muʿtazila scholars]. Beirut: Muʾassasah al-Rayyan.

Ibn Rushd, & Kasim, M. (1964). *Manajihu'l Adilla fi Aqaidi'l Milla* [The Exposition of the Methods of Proof Concerning the Beliefs of the Community]. Cairo: n.p.

Imam Azam, E. H. (1982). *Fıqh al Akbar*.

Imam, Nawawī, & Kader, H. (2013). *Riyazü's-salihin: Tam metin ve açıklam'Ali* [Riyazu's salihin: full text with commentary]. Istanbul: Ensar Neşriyat.

Imran, M., & Taib, M. (2000). The problem of predeterminism and its impact on Muslim thought. *The Fount Journal, 2*. Retrieved from https://dialogosphere.wordpress.com/2016/11/01/the-problem-of-pre-determinism-and-its-impact-on-muslim-thought/

Incetas, Y. (2018). Politics, education, and a global movement: Gülen-inspired educators and their views on education in politically turbulent times. *Journal of Educational Issues, 4*(1), 191-211. doi: 10.5296/jei.v4i1.13172

Inertia. (2020). In *Encyclopaedia Britannica*. Retrieved from https://www.britannica.com/science/inertia

Information Philosopher. (n.d.). *Chrysippus*. Retrieved from http://www.information philosopher.com/solutions/philosophers/chrysippus/

Iqbal, S. M. (1971). *The reconstruction of religious thought in Islam*. Lahore: Sh. Muhammad Ashraf.

Iqbal, S. M. (2017). *The reconstruction of religious thought in Islam*. Lahore: Sang-e-Meel Publication.

Isfarayini, A. -M. T. M., Kawthari, M. Z.-H., & Ḥusayni, I. -A. (1940). *al-Tabṣīr fī al-dīn wa-tamyīz al-firqah al-nājiyah 'an al- firaq al-hālikī*. Cairo: Maṭbaʻat al-Anwār.

Işık, K. (1967). *Mutezile'nin doğuşu ve kelâmi görüşleri* [The birth of Muʻtazila and its theological views]. Ankara: Ankara Üniversitesi Basımevi.

Jabrīyyah. (2003). In J. L. Esposito (Ed.), *The Oxford Dictionary of Islam*. Retrieved from http://www.oxfordislamicstudies.com/article/opr/t125/e1149

Jackson, S. A. (2009). Maturidism and Black Theodicy. In S. A. Jackson, *Islam and the problem of black suffering* (pp. 47-74). Oxford: Oxford Scholarship Online.

Jammer, M., & Einstein, A. (2012). *Concepts of space: The history of theories of space in physics* (3rd ed.). n.p.: Dover Publications.

Jarullah, Z. H. (1974). *Al-Muʻtazila, al-Maktabat'ul Ahliye*. Beirut: Publisher.

Journalists and Writers Foundation. (1999). *Gülen meets with Christian and Jewish leaders to advocate dialogue tolerance*. Retrieved from http://jwf.org/Gülen-meets-with-christian-and-jewish-leaders-to-advocate-dialogue-tolerance/1999/

Journalists and Writers Foundation. (2010). *Understanding Fethullah Gülen*. Istanbul, Turkey: Journalist and Writers Foundation.

Kader. (2018). In *Etimoloji Türkçe*. Retrieved from https://www.etimolojiturkce.com/kelime/kader

Kaku, M. (2011). *Why physics end the free will debate*. Retrieved on September 23, 2014, from http://bigthink.com/videos/why-physics-ends-the-free-will-debate

Kamal, M. (2003). Muʻtazilah: the rise of Islamic rationalism. *Australian Rationalist, 62*(Autumn), 27-34.

Kane, R. (1996). *The significance of free will*. New York: Oxford University Press.

Kant, I. (1996). *Groundwork for the metaphysics of morals* (M. J. Gregor, Trans.). Cambridge: Cambridge University Press.

Karadeniz, T., & Gumrukcu, T. (2017). EU says needs concrete evidence from Turkey to deem Gülen network as terrorists. *Reuters*. Retrieved from https://www.reuters.com/article/us-eu-turkey-security/eu-says-needs-concrete-evidence-from-turkey-to-deem-Gülen-network-as-terrorist-idUSKBN-1DU0DX

Kazancı, A. L. (1966). *İslâmda irade, kaza, ve kader: Akaid dersleri* [Will, preordainment and destiny is Islam: creed classes]. Istanbul: A. Said Matbaası; Umumî tevzi.

Kılıçer, M. E. (1994). *Ehl-i Re'y*. TDV Islam Ansiklopedisi. Retrieved from https://islamansiklopedisi.org.tr/ehl-i-rey

Kırkıncı, M. (2010). *Cebriye* [The school of Jabrīyyah]. Mehmed Kırkıncı Hocaefendi. Retrieved on December 29, 2014, from http://www.mehmedKırkıncı.com/index.php?s=article&aid=358

Knight, K. (2017). *The Summa Theologiæ of St. Thomas Aquinas* (2nd ed.). Retrieved from http://www.newadvent.org/summa/

Kreeft, P. (1988). *Fundamentals of the faith: Essays in Christian apologetics*. San Francisco: Ignatius Press.

Kruger, J. (2018). *Five arguments for free will: None of them are compelling*. Psychology Today. Retrieved from https://www.psychologytoday.com/us/blog/one-among-many/201803/five-arguments-free-will

Lanius, D. (2019). *Strategic indeterminacy in the law*. Oxford: Oxford University Press.

Laplace, P. S. (1952). *A philosophical essay on probabilities*. New York: Dover Publications.

Leibniz, G. (2016). Principle of sufficient reason. In *Stanford Encyclopedia of Philosophy*. Retrieved from https://plato.stanford.edu/entries/sufficient-reason/

Lindley, D. (2007). *Uncertainty: Einstein, Heisenberg, Bohr, and the struggle for the soul of science*. New York: Doubleday.

Liu, C. (2011). *What would happen if I fall into a black hole?* Physics4Me. Retrieved from https://physicsforme.com/2011/06/24/top-3-questions-people-ask-an-astrophysicist-and-answers/#more-1044

Long, B., & Feng, F. (2015). Augustine's theory of free will. *Studies in Literature and Language, 11*(5), 41-44. doi: 10.3968/7800

Maghnīsāwī, A. M. (2007). *Imam Abu Hanifa's al-Fiqh al-akbar explained* (A-R. ibn Y. Mangera, Trans.). London: White Thread Press.

Maghnīsāwī, A. M. (2014). *Imam Abu Hanifa's al-Fiqh al-akbar explained* (A-R. ibn Y. Mangera, Trans.). (2. ed.). London: White Thread Press.

Magill, F. N. (1990). *Masterpieces of philosophy*. New York, NY: Harper Collins.

Mamas, M. (2004) *Free will vs. predestination*. The Center for Rational Spirituality. Retrieved from http://www.rationalspirituality.org/articles/free_will_vs_predestination.html

Maqrīzī, & Wiet, G. (1911). *Kitāb al-Mawā'iz wa-'l-I'tibār fī dikr al-hitat wa-l-ātār*: Cairo: Impr. de l'Inst. Français d'Archéologie Orientale.

Markham, I. S., & Birinci, P. S. (2011). *An introduction to Said Nursi: Life, thought and writings*. Farnham, Surrey: Ashgate.

Marmura, M. E. (1964). Book review: Islamic philosophy and theology by W. Montgomery Watt. *Philosophy East and West, 13*(4), 368-369.

Martin, M. (2013). *Use of reason in early Islamic theology* (Kindle ed.). n.p.: Amazon Digital Services Inc.

Maruf, M. (2003). *Iqbal's philosophy of religion: A study in the cognitive value of religious experience*. Lahore: Iqbal Academy Pakistan.

McCarthy, R. (1953). *The theology of al-Ashari: The Arabic text of al-Asharis Kitāb al-luma and Risalat istihsan al-khawd fi ilm al-kalam*. Beirut: Imprimerie Catholique.

Mercan, F. (2019). *Allah yolunda bir omur*. Süreyya Yayınları.

Mermin, N. D. (2009). *What's Bad About This Habit?* Physics Today 2009, p. 8.

Mert, M. (2008). *Kelam tarihinin problemleri* [Problems of the history of Islamic theology]. Ankara: Ankara Okulu Yayınları.

Minkowski, H. (2012). *Space and time: Minkowski's papers on relativity* (F. Lewerto & V. Petkov, Trans.) (free ed.). Montreal: Minkowski Institute Press.

Moad, E. O. (2005). Al-Ghazalī's occasionalism and the natures of creatures. *International Journal for Philosophy of Religion, 58*(2), 95-101.

Moad. E. O. (2008). A significant difference between al-Ghazalī and Hume on causation. *Journal of Islamic Philosophy, 3,* 22-39.

Moskowitz, C. (2011). For fully mature black holes, time stands still. Space.com. Retrieved on month day, 2020, from https://www.space.com/10702-black-hole-kerr-state-spacetime.html#:~:text=An%20illustration%20of%20a%20 supermassive,the%20center%20of%20a%20galaxy.&text=The%20end%20 of%20a%20black,from%20reaching%20this%20end%20state

Munk, S. & Joel, I. (1930). *Daldldt al-Hd'irin.* Jerusalem, ed. 1. p. 71

Muslim. (n.d.). *Sahih Muslim* (A. H. Siddiqui, Trans.), Book 46. Retrieved from https://sunnah.com/muslim/46

Musser, G. (2012). The quantum physics of free will. *Scientific American.* Retrieved from http://www.scientificamerican.com/article/quantum-physics-free-will/

Muttaqī, -H. A. I.-H. (1895). *Kanz al-'ummāl fī sunan al-aqwāl wa-'l-afʿāl.* Hyderabad, Bangladesh: Maṭbaʿat Daʾirat al-maʿārif an-nizāmijja.

Naik, Z. (2013). *Man is given a free will.* Dr Zakir Naik: Question and Answer. Retrieved from https://zakirnaikqa.wordpress.com/tag/man-is-given-a-free-will/

Najm al-Dīn ʿUmar al-Nasafi. (n.d.). *Madarik al-Tanzil, Haqaiqi al-Ta'wil.* Retrieved from https://www.altafsir.com/Tafasir.asp?tMadhNo=2&tTafsirNo=17&t-SoraNo=39&tAyahNo=70&tDisplay=yes&Page=3&Size=1&LanguageId=1

Nasr, S. H. (1975). The religious sciences. In R. N. Frye (Ed.), *The Cambridge History of Iran* (pp. 464-480). Cambridge: Cambridge University Press.

Nawawī, Z. Y. S. (2014). *Riyad as-salihin: The gardens of the righteous.* New Jersey: Tughra Books.

Nursi, S. (1988). *Mesnevi Nuriye.* Istanbul: Sözler Yayınevi.

Nursi, S. (1992). *The words* (V. Şükran, Trans.). Istanbul, Turkey: Sözler Neşriyat.

Nursi, S. (1993). *The words* (V. Şükran, Trans.). Istanbul, Turkey: Sözler Publications.

Nursi, S. (1994). *The letters.* London: Truestar.

Nursi, S. (1995). *The flashes collection.* Istanbul, Turkey: Sözler Neşriyat A.Ş.

Nursi, S. (1997). *The words.* Izmir, Turkey: Kaynak Publishing.

Nursi, S. (2004). *Şuâlar* [Rays]. Istanbul: Sözler Neşriyat.

Nursi, S. (2005). *The words: The reconstruction of Islamic belief and thought.* Somerset, N.J: Light.

Nursî, S. (2007). *Risale-i Nur külliyatı'ndan* [From the Risale-i Bur collection]. Istanbul: Saldamar Yayınları.

Nursi, S. (2009). *Kastamonu lâhikası* [Kastomonu notes]. Istanbul: Sözler.

Nursi, S. (2012). *Mektubat* [Letters]. Istanbul: Sözler.

O'Daly, G. (1989). *Predestination and freedom in Augustine's ethics.* Cambridge: Cambridge University Press.

Odenwald, S. (2018). *Special and general relativity questions and answers.* Stanford University. Retrieved from https://einstein.stanford.edu/content/relativity/q411.html

Oral, O. (2007). *Kaza ve Kadere Inanıyorum* [I believe in preordainment and destiny]. Izmir: Caglayan Matbasi.

Ozakpınar, Y. (2002). *İnsan Düşüncesinin Boyutları* [Dimension of human thought]. Istanbul: Ötüken Yay.

Pahl, J. (2019). *Fethullah Gulen: A Life of Hizmet*. NJ: Blue Dome Press.

Pereboom, D. (1997). *Free will*. Indianapolis, IN: Hackett Pub. Co.

Pessagno, J. M. (1984a). Irāda, Ikhtiyār, Qudra, Kasb: The view of Abū Manṣur al-Māturīdī. *Journal of the American Oriental Society, 104*(1), 177-191.

Pessagno, J. M. (1984b). The uses of evil in Māturīdīan thought. *Studia Islamica*, 60, 59-82.

Pezdevi, Y. (1989). *Ehl-i Sünnet Akaidi* [Creed of ahl al Sunna] (Ş. Gölcük, Trans.). Istanbul: Kayıhan Publishing.

Physics Stack Exchange. (2018). Did space-time exist before the big bang? Retrieved from https://physics.stackexchange.com/questions/5150/did-spacetime-start-with-the-big-bang

Pusey, E. B. (Trans.). (1949). *The confessions of Saint Augustine*. New York: Modern Library.

Qadī, A. (2013). *Sharhu'l Usuli'l Hamsa* (I. Çelebi. Trans. Istanbul: Pasifik Ofset

Qadī, ʿAbd, -J. A.-A. (1960). *al-Mughnī fī abwāb al-tawḥīd wa-al-ʿadl*. Al-Qāhirah: Wizārat al-Thaqāfah wa-al-Irshād al-Qawmī, al-Idārah al-ʿĀmmah lil-Thaqāfah.

Qalqašandī, A.-A. A. (1938). *Kitāb Ṣubḥ al-a̕šā: Ǧuz'*. Cairo: Dār al-Kutub al-Miṣrīya.

Qurṭubī, M. A. (2007). *Tafsir Al Qurthubi* [Qurtubi exegesis]. Jakarta: Pustaka Azzam.

Qushayri, A. (2015). *Laṭā'if al-Isharat bi-Tafsīr al-Qur'ān*. Bayrūt : Dār al-Kutub al-ʿIlmīyah. Retrieved from https://www.altafsir.com/

Reese, W. L. (1999). *Dictionary of philosophy and religion: Eastern and Western thought*. Amherst, New York: Prometheus Books.

Remes, P. (2008). *Neoplatonism*. n.p.: Acumen publishing.

Reuters. (2017, March 19). German spy chief does not believe Gülen is behind the coup attempt. Retrieved from https://www.reuters.com/article/us-turkey-security-germany-idUSKBN16P0LQ

Robinson, N. (1998). *Ashʿarī and Muʿtazila*. Muslim Philosophy. Retrieved on 22 June, 2019, from http://www.muslimphilosophy.com/ip/rep/H052

Rubin, B. M. (2003). *Revolutionaries and reformers: Contemporary Islamist movements in the Middle East*. Albany, NY: State University of New York Press.

Rudman, D. (2002). Determinism and anti-determinism in the Book of Koheleth. *Jewish Bible Quarterly, 30*, 97-106.

Rudolph, U. (2015). *Al-Māturīdī and the development of Sunnī theology in Samarqand*. Leiden: Brill.

Russell, R. P. (Trans.). (2004). *The Fathers of the Church: St Augustine the teacher, the free choice of the will, grace and free will*. Washington, D.C: Catholic University of America Press.

Ryan, H. (2007). *Zeno of Citium*. n.p.: n.p.

Şabuni, A. M., & Topaloğlu, B. (1979). *Māturīdiyye akaidi: Al-Bidāyah fī uṣūl al-dīn* [The creed of Maturidi]. Ankara: Diyanet İşleri Başkanlığı.

Şaritoprak, Z. (2005-2007). *An Islamic Approach to Peace and Nonviolence*. Oxford, UK: Blackwell Publishing. The Muslim World (Hatford).

Şaritoprak, Z. (2007). Gülen and his global contribution to peacebuilding. p. 636.

Retrieved from https://www.Gülenconference.org.uk/userfiles/file/Proceedings/Prcd%20-%20Saritoprak,%20Z.pdf

Saritoprak, Z. (2018). *Islamic spirituality: Theology and practice for the modern world.*

Schwarz, M. (1972). *Acquisition (Kasb) in Early Kalam, Islamic Philosophy and The Classical Tradition.* Oxford: n.p.

Searle, J. (2013). *Our shared condition – consciousness.* TED talk. https://www.ted.com/talks/john_searle_our_shared_condition_consciousness...

Sen, D. (2014). The uncertainty relations in quantum mechanics. *Current Science, 107*(2), 203-218.

Sevindi, N., & Abu-Rabi', I. M. (2008). *Contemporary Islamic conversations: M. Fethullah Gülen on Turkey, Islam, and the West.* Albany, NY: State University of New York Press.

Sezgin, F., Amāwī, M., Ehrig-Eggert, C., & Neubauer, E. (2000). *The teachings of the Mu'tazila: Texts and studies.* Frankfurt am Main: Institute for the History of Arabic-Islamic Science, Johann Wolfgang Goethe University.

Shanab, R. E. A. (1974). Ghazalī and Aquinas on causation. *The Monist, 58*(1), 140-150.

Sharif, M. M. (1963). *A history of Muslim philosophy: With short accounts of other disciplines and the modern renaissance in Muslim lands.* Wiesbaden: Harrassowitz.

Sharples, R. W. (Trans.) (1983). *Alexander of Aphrodisias on fate: Text, translation, and commentary.* London: Duckworth.

Sharples, R. W. (Trans.). (1994). *Alexander of Aphrodisias: Quaestiones 2.16-3.15.* London: Duckworth.

Sherman, H. (1981). Marx and determinism. *Journal of Economic Issues, 15*(1), 61-71.

Silber, J. (2012). *Kant's ethics: The good, freedom, and the will.* Boston: Walter de Gruyter.

Sinanoğlu, A. (2006). *Fate comprehension of Mu'tazila, the first partisan of freedom school in Islam.* n.p.: KSÜ İlahiyat Fakültesi Dergisi.

Slick M. (2017) *What is libertarian free will and is it biblical?* Christian Apologetics & Research Ministry. Retrieved on November 4, 2014, from http://carm.org/what-is-free-will

Sozcu. (2015). *What happened in the December 17 corruption operation?* Retrieved from https://www.sozcu.com.tr/2015/gunun-icinden/17-aralik-yolsuzluk-operasyonuda-neler-olmustu-1010713/

Spinoza, Baruch, 1992. *The ethics and selected letters* (S. Shirley, Trans.) (2nd ed.). Indianapolis: Hackett Publishing.

Stockhammer, M. (2013). *Thomas Aquinas dictionary.* New York, NY: Philosophical Library.

Stockholm Center for Freedom. (2018). *Purge.* Retrieved from https://stockholmcf.org/?s=purge

Sullivan, D. J. (Ed.) (1955). *The Summa theologica of Saint Thomas Aquinas,* vol. 20. Chicago: Encyclopaedia Britannica.

Sülün, M. (2021). *Zemahşerî (ö. 1144) El-Keşşâf 'an hakâ'ikı Gavâmidı't-tenzîl ve 'uyûni'l-ekāvîl fî vucûhi't-te'vîl.* Istanbul: Türkiye Yazma Eserler Kurumu Başkanlığı.

Ṭabarī, & Yaghma'ī, Ḥ. (1961). *Tarjumah-'i tafsir-i Tabari* [Translation of Tabari exegesis]. Ṭehrān: Chāpkhānah-i Dawlatī-i Īrān.

Taftāzānī, M. U., Uludağ, S., & Nasafī, U. M. (1980). *Kelâm ilmi ve İslâm akâidi: Şer-*

hu'l-Akâid [Islamic theology and creed: commentary on creed]. Istanbul: Dergâh Yayınları.

Tan, D., Weber., S., Siddiqi, I., Mølmer, K., & Murch, K. (2015). Prediction and retrodiction for a continuously monitored superconducting qubit. *Physical Review Letters, 114*(9). doi: 10.1103/PhysRevLett.114.090403

Tarihi, G. (2012). Erdoğan: Bu hasret artık bitsin [Erdogan: This longing is over now]. Sabah. Retrieved from https://www.sabah.com.tr/gundem/2012/06/15/erdogan-bu-hasret-artik-bitsin

Taylor, A. (2013, December 19). The political future of turkey may be decided on this quiet road in rural Pennsylvania. *Business Insider*. Retrieved from https://www.businessinsider.com.au/fethullah-gulens-pennsylvania-home-2013-12?r=US&IR=T

Taylor, L. (1984). *Born to crime: The genetic causes of criminal behavior*. Westport, Conn: Greenwood Press.

TDV. (2020a). *Takdir*. Islam Ansiklopedisi. Retrieved from https://islamansiklopedisi.org.tr/takdir

TDV. (2020b). *Tedbir*. Islam Ansiklopedisi. Retrieved from https://islamansiklopedisi.org.tr/tedbir

The Physical World. (2014). *The restless universe: The clockwork universe*. Retrieved on October 23, 2014, from http://physicalworld.org/restless_universe/html/ru_2_14.html

Thilly, F. (1957). *A history of philosophy*. New York: Holt.

Thomas, ., & Shapcote, L. (2017). *Summa Theologiae: Tertia Pars. 60-90.*

TimeTurk. (2016). *Will military schools be closed?* Retrieved from https://www.time turk.com/askeri-okullar-kapatilacak-mi/haber-216688

Timpe, K. (2008). *Free will: Sourcehood and its alternatives*. London: Continuum.

Timpe, K., & Speak, D. (2016). *Free will and theism: Connections, contingencies, and concerns*. Oxford: Oxford University Press.

Tirmidhi, Sifat al Qiyama, p. 60

Tittensor, D. (2014). *The house of service: The Gülen movement and Islam's third way*. Location: Publisher.

Translation of Chapter Wal'asr. (1963). *Tafsir surah Wal'ashri*. Bandung, Indonesia: Almạ'arif.

Ünal, A. (1993). Man and religion. *Fountain Magazine, 3*. Retrieved from https://fountainmagazine.com/1993/issue-3-july-september-1993/man-and-religion

Ünal, A. (2013). *The Qur'ān with annotated interpretation in modern English*. Retrieved from https://www.academia.edu/7004875/The-Qur'an-with-annotated-interpretation-in-modern-english-ali-Ünal.

Ünal, A. (2015). *The Qur'an with annotated interpretation in modern English*. New Jersey: Tughra Books.

Understanding Evolution. (n.d.). *Misconceptions about natural selection*. University of California Museum of Paleontology. Retrieved from https://evolution.berkeley.edu/evolibrary/article/evo_32

Valkenberg, P. (2016). *Renewing Islam by service. A christian view of Fethullah Gülen and the Hizmet movement*. Baltimore: Catholic University of America.

Van Inwagen, P., & Zimmerman, D. W. (2008). *Metaphysics: The big questions*. Malden, MA: Blackwell Pub.

Vihvelin, K. (2013). *Causes, laws, and free will: Why determinism doesn't matter*. New York: Oxford University Press.

Wagner, W. H. (2013). *Beginnings and endings: Fethullah Gülen's vision for today's world.* Location: Publisher.

Waller, B. N. (1990). *Freedom without responsibility.* Philadelphia: Temple University Press.

Watt, W. M. (1943). The origin of the Islamic doctrine of acquisition. *Journal of the Royal Asiatic Society, 75*(3-4), 234-247.

Watt, W. M. (1948). *Free will and predestination in early Islam.* London: Luzac.

Watt, W. M. (1962). *Islamic philosophy and theology.* Edinburgh: University Press.

Watt, W. M. (2009). *The formative period of Islamic thought.* Oxford: Oneworld.

Waxman, R. (2016). *Five philosophers on free will: Plato, Leibnitz, Hobbes, Hume, and Hegel.* Retrieved from https://www.academia.edu/28486811/Five_Philosophers_on_Free_Will_Plato_Hobbes_Hume_Leibniz_and_Hegel

Wehr, H. (1976). *A dictionary of modern written Arabic* (J. M. Cowan, Ed.) (3rd ed). New York: Spoken Language Service, Inc.

Winter, T. J. (2008). *The Cambridge Companion to Classical Islamic Theology.* Cambridge: Cambridge University Press, p. 4-5.

World Heritage Encyclopedia. (2006). *Jahm bin Safwan.* Retrieved from http://self.gutenberg.org/articles/Jahm_bin_Safwa

Yavuz, H. M., & Esposito, J. L. (2003). *Turkish Islam and the secular state: The global impact of Fethullah Gülen's Nur movement.* Syracuse, N.Y: Syracuse University Press.

Yavuz, Y. S. (1995). *Ebü'l-Hasan el-Eş'arî* (ö. 324/935-36) *tarafından kurulan kelâm mektebi* [The school of theology establish by Ebu'l Hasan al-Ash'arī]. In *Islam Ansiklopedisi.* Ankara: Türkiye Diyanet Vakfı.

Yazıcıoğlu, M. S. (1992). *Mâtürîdî ve Nesefî'ye göre insan hürriyeti kavramı* [Human freedom according to Maturīdī and Nasafî]. Istanbul: Millî Eğitim Bakanlığı.

Yu, A. (2009). Kant's argument for free will. *Prometheus Journal.* Retrieved from http://prometheus-journal.com/2009/02/25/morality-rationality-and-freedom-kant%E2%80%99s-argument-for-free-will/

Yücel, S., & Albayrak, I. (2015). *The art of coexistence: Pioneering role of Fethullah Gülen and the Hizmet movement.*

Yücel, S. (2018). *A life in tears: Understanding Fethullah Gülen and his call to service.*

Yücel, S. (2011). *Spiritual Role Models in Fethullah Gulen's Educational Philosophy,* TAWARIKH: International Journal for Historical Studies, 3(1) 2011: 65-76.

Zhussipbek, G., & Moldashev, K. (2019). Rawlsian liberalism and rationalistic Māturīdī Islam in Central Asia. In A. Frigerio & R Isaacs (Ed.), *Theorizing Central Asian politics: The state, ideology and power* (pp. 95-118). Cham, Switzerland: Springer International Publishing.

INDEX